Welcome to

THE

EVERYTHING

PROFILES SERIES ®

Welcome to the EVERYTHING® Profiles line of books—an extension of the bestselling EVERYTHING® series!

These authoritative books help you learn everything you ever wanted to know about the lives, social context, and surrounding historical events of fascinating people who made or influenced history. While reading this EVERYTHING® book you will discover 3 useful boxes, in additional to numerous quotes:

Fact: Definitions and additional information
Question: Questions and answers for deeper insights
They Said: Memorable quotes made by others about this person

Whether you are learning about a figure for the first time or are just brushing up on your knowledge, EVERYTHING® Profiles help you on your journey toward a greater understanding of the individuals who have shaped and enriched our lives, culture, and history.

Visit the entire Everything® series at *www.everything.com*

The
EVERYTHING®
Guide to Edgar Allan Poe

Dear Reader,

Edgar Allan Poe was the father of the modern detective story, one of the pioneers of science fiction, and the first true American literary critic. In *The Everything® Guide to Edgar Allan Poe*, find out how he did in school, whether his classmates liked him, what happened at West Point, what led to his marriage proposal to his (yes, thirteen-year-old) cousin, how he felt about those Boston writers, women in general, cats, God, abolition— and Congress. Sample the firsts, bests, favorites, lasts, and onlys among his work. Read about his romances, his enemies, his lasting influence, and his own myth-making. Learn all about the man who was Edgar Allan Poe.

Shelley Costa Bloomfield

THE

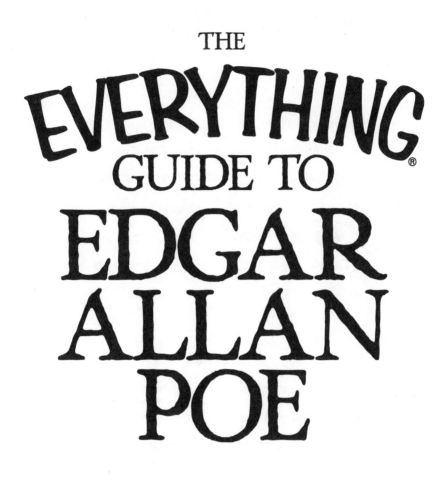

EVERYTHING®
GUIDE TO
EDGAR
ALLAN
POE

The EVERYTHING Series

Editorial

Innovation Director	Paula Munier
Editorial Director	Laura M. Daly
Executive Editor, Series Books	Brielle K. Matson
Associate Copy Chief	Sheila Zwiebel
Acquisitions Editor	Lisa Laing
Development Editor	Elizabeth Kassab
Production Editor	Casey Ebert

Production

Director of Manufacturing	Susan Beale
Production Project Manager	Michelle Roy Kelly
Prepress	Matt LeBlanc
	Erick DaCosta
Interior Layout	Heather Barrett
	Brewster Brownville
	Colleen Cunningham
	Jennifer Oliveira
Cover Design	Erin Alexander
	Stephanie Chrusz
	Frank Rivera

Visit the entire Everything® Series at *www.everything.com*

THE

EVERYTHING®
GUIDE TO
EDGAR ALLAN POE

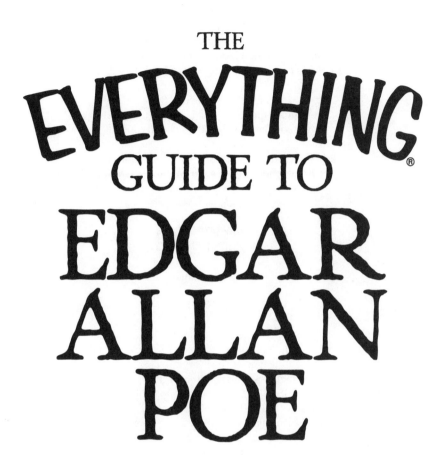

The life, times, and work of
a tormented genius

Shelley Costa Bloomfield, Ph.D.

Foreword by Jeffrey A. Savoye,
Edgar Allan Poe Society of Baltimore

A adamsmedia

Avon, Massachusetts

For Edgar, who mattered

An Everything® Series Book.
Everything® and everything.com® are registered
trademarks of F+W Publications, Inc.

Published by Adams Media, an F+W Publications Company
57 Littlefield Street, Avon, MA 02322 U.S.A.

www.adamsmedia.com

ISBN-10: 1-59869-527-4
ISBN-13: 978-1-59869-527-4

Printed in Canada.

J I H G F E D C B A

Bloomfield, Shelley Costa.
The everything guide to Edgar Allan Poe / Shelley Costa Bloomfield.
p. cm. – (The everything series)
Includes bibliographical references.
ISBN-13: 978-1-59869-527-4 (pbk.)
ISBN-10: 1-59869-527-4 (pbk.)
1. Poe, Edgar Allan, 1809-1849. 2. Authors, American–
19th century–Biography. I. Title.
PS2631.B57 2007
818'.309–dc22
2007018979

This publication is designed to provide accurate and authoritative information with regard to the subject matter covered. It is sold with the understanding that the publisher is not engaged in rendering legal, accounting, or other professional advice. If legal advice or other expert assistance is required, the services of a competent professional person should be sought.

—From a *Declaration of Principles* jointly adopted by a Committee of the American Bar Association and a Committee of Publishers and Associations

Many of the designations used by manufacturers and sellers to distinguish their products are claimed as trademarks. Where those designations appear in this book and Adams Media was aware of a trademark claim, the designations have been printed with initial capital letters.

This book is available at quantity discounts for bulk purchases.
For information, please call 1-800-289-0963.

Contents

Top Ten on the Poe Parade

1. Although born in Boston, Edgar Allan Poe was raised in Richmond, Virginia, and was a consummate Southern gentleman in the antebellum South.

2. Out of an early love for the military—and to get out of his foster father's house—Poe enlisted in the U.S. Army, without parental consent, and served for two years.

3. Devastated by the death of his foster mother—and as a swipe at his foster father—Poe got himself expelled from West Point.

4. At twenty-seven, he married his cousin, Virginia Clemm, who was thirteen at the time. Due to family objections, it was a secret ceremony.

5. Poe is considered the first professional American writer. His determination to make a living solely from his written work doomed him and his dependents to a life of poverty.

6. With a droll, deadpan sense of humor, Poe wrote several hoaxes so convincing that one ended up being reprinted as "fact" in the Congressional Record.

7. Poe was both the father of the modern detective story and an early author of science fiction. Crime detection was just another puzzle for him—and he was an expert cryptographer.

8. His death in Baltimore in 1849 remains mysterious to this day. When he was discovered, unconscious, he appeared to be wearing someone else's clothing.

9. A bad judge of character, Poe entrusted his literary legacy to a man who despised him. This enemy was almost single-handedly responsible for the public perception of Poe as a drug addict and madman.

10. After midnight on every January nineteenth since 1949, a mysterious figure has placed flowers on Poe's grave to commemorate the anniversary of the writer's birth.

Acknowledgments

Thanks to Michael, Jess, Bec, and Lize, for showing an interest; to Marnie, for asking the questions; and to RBS, for teaching me how, all those years ago.

Foreword

Edgar Allan Poe is an intriguing cipher, an enigma, a puzzle with no key. He might be a character from one of his own tales, or a merry prankster gently mocking readers who fall under his spell.

Poe yearned for fame—and he achieved it, but he never managed to find the money he thought would be his just reward. He wanted to be a poet, but fate forced him to find other means to support his little family. Working as an editor for various magazines helped to pay his rent and put food on the table but left him with little time to follow his own muse. His collected works fill a scant seventeen volumes and are far outweighed by the words which have been written about him. His literary reputation now rests on a handful of evocative poems and powerful tales of mystery and horror.

Judging by the well-worn pages of most standard collections, Poe's world seems populated by madmen and frail angelic women, all doomed to an unhappy end by obsession, the whims of fate, or dark and half-forgotten knowledge. Who is this man who could dream of a melancholy raven, a demonic cat, and a razor-wielding orangutan? Is Poe the defiant optimist of "Israfel" or the dystopian cynic of "The Conqueror Worm"? Is he a singer of truth or a charlatan—a genius or Emerson's "jingle-man"?

Poe has been studied and analyzed, his works deconstructed and psychoanalyzed. He has been glorified as the prophet of *Eureka*, and vilified as an immoral drunkard. Even during his lifetime, Poe was a misunderstood object of curiosity. Some myths about him grew from his own tendency to weave a tale to cover an unhappy past, and others were added by people who did not know him or had felt the sting of his critical pen. Rufus Wilmot Griswold, a secret enemy with a long savored grudge, became Poe's first biographer. He sought to destroy Poe's reputation with innuendo and accusations, suppressing Poe's virtues and exaggerating Poe's flaws, even forging letters to bolster his own claims and to isolate Poe's friends.

Ironically, Griswold created a mythic figure which captured the imagination of a generation and created much trouble for future scholars but brought Poe's writings to a wider audience than he had ever enjoyed while he was alive.

Poe's works are still read, and Poe is remembered, but the man is lost to the legend.

For over 150 years, readers have sought the fountain from which sprang Roderick and Madeline Usher, Montresor and Fortunato, Annabel Lee and Lenore. Some have claimed that Poe mined his own life, while others have traced influences from various writers and even newspapers of his own day. The quest for a definitive answer puts one in the place of Legrand, bitten by the gold bug, or the nameless knight of "Eldorado." When a treasure proves to be so elusive, it is probably good that there is so much pleasure to be found in the search.

Jeffrey A. Savoye,
The Edgar Allan Poe Society of Baltimore

Introduction

MADMAN, PERVERT, ADDICT.

That's been Edgar Allan Poe's reputation for nearly two hundred years. For young American readers, when the English teacher gets to the place in the two-pound anthology where Poe begins, everyone (including the teacher!) is ready to leave behind the poems, stories, and essays that come at you like tranquilizer darts. By the time you're done with Puritan sermons and ranting political speeches and book chapters titled "Natural Sense of Propriety Inherent in the Female Bosom," you are positively crying out for a madman, pervert, addict.

Coming back from the dead, coming back from the presumed dead, swarming rats, buried treasure, slasher apes, deafening hearts—truly, what's not to like? He gives us "the shivers." Casting Poe the author as one of his characters adds to the fright, adds to the mystique, adds to the drama. What mixture of personal losses, shortcomings, and brilliance drove him to create such classics of American literature as "The Tell-Tale Heart" and "The Raven"? Was his own life a bigger horror than anything he could write?

These words that hover around Poe dictate how we think of him: poverty, tragedy, alcoholism, drug use, mental illness—in short, the American nightmare. But if Poe was in fact a madman, pervert, addict, when did he find time to write enough stories and poetry to fill the ten books published during his brief lifetime? Writing in the mid-nineteenth century was an amusing hobby, a diverting luxury for the upper classes. Poe was the first American determined to live his life as a professional writer. He succeeded, although it all but doomed him and his dependents to a life of relentless poverty.

Chapter 1

The Fall of the House of Poe

Edgar Poe was born into a new nation and a family of actors. National—and personal—identity were shifting things in 1809. Possibilities abounded. In time, Edgar would harness the drama that inspired his parents and the lore surrounding his ancestors to become one of the greats in American literature. But there was much for him to overcome. The early loss of both mother and father thrust Edgar into a foster family that irrevocably shaped the course of his life.

Nothing Short of Complete Justice

The Boston of 1809, when Edgar Poe was born, was a vibrant city with a population of 30,000 (including upwards of 1,000 slaves) and a history of European settlement dating back nearly two hundred years. Called the Cradle of Liberty for its central role in the Revolutionary War—site of the Boston Tea Party, the Boston Massacre, and the first battles in neighboring Lexington and Concord—Boston was entering the nineteenth century as a wealthy international port. Fish, tobacco, salt, and rum were the chief exports in this bustling seaport, and the citizens were incensed at the Embargo Act—Congress's attempt to maintain neutrality in the conflict between England and France by forbidding trade with foreign powers.

fact

Because it was just a two-minute walk to the theater district, what was called Carver Street when Poe was born housed many actors. It was a charming, narrow street with gaslights. Now it's called Charles Street South, and it houses the Massachusetts Transportation Building.

Just two weeks after Poe's birth, the Boston *Gazette* commented, "The spirit of New England is slow in rising; but when once inflamed by oppression, it will never be repressed by anything short of complete justice." It is a quintessential New England point of view (although you can hear its echoes in Confederate rhetoric a generation later), and in it there is both a reminder of Boston's recent Revolutionary War history and a portent of things to come. What would become the abolitionist movement, with its far-reaching national and humanitarian consequences half a century hence, was simmering but not yet boiling. With its unique infrastructure, coastal location, and population—descendants of people who always grappled with ideas—Boston was poised for its role in the new century.

Poe was born in Bay Village, a neighborhood no bigger than a quarter of a square mile, a place of trim, red brick row houses. If

Beacon Hill was home to the Brahmins, the First Families of Boston, Bay Village was home to the bohemians. In housing artists, artisans, and shopkeepers, the development of this section of the city reflected Boston's economic vitality—and the emergence of the middle class. The first house was built in Bay Village around the same time the Arnolds arrived from England.

> "The United States' motto, E pluribus unum, may possibly have a sly allusion to Pythagoras' definition of beauty—the reduction of many into one."—Poe, equally sly, in 1845

Life upon the Wicked Stage

Henry and Elizabeth Arnold were a London theater couple who performed at Covent Garden Theatre Royal and other theater towns in England. They were itinerant stage performers and had to scramble for a livelihood. Their only child, Elizabeth ("Eliza") was born in 1787 and joined her parents on stage when she was very young. The stage was her work, her play, her education, her life—a single, powerful influence on the development of the child who would become the mother of Edgar Allan Poe. The theater, for all its hardships, was all she knew. When life suddenly became more difficult with the death of her father in 1793, she and her mother continued to support themselves as performers for three more years, until the widow decided the American stage might offer more opportunities for them.

So they set out for Boston, bringing along Charles Tubbs, another English actor who became Eliza's stepfather, and arrived in January of 1796. Three months after she arrived, Eliza debuted at the Federal Street Theater, singing a favorite called "The Market Lass" in a clear, sweet voice.

The audience loved it, and the family thought their American career was launched. But life on the American stage looked a lot like life on the English stage, and the transatlantic move didn't improve either the fortunes or talents of Eliza Arnold's little family. At the end of the eighteenth century, American drama was little more than a plodding derivation of popular European stage fare. Theater as a seductive, established institution for players, playwrights, and audiences was still half a century away. So the Tubbs couple traveled with Eliza from town to town along the Eastern seaboard, wending their way south, until finally they found some stability when they joined the Charleston Comedians troupe in 1798. But in 1798, Elizabeth Arnold Tubbs died of yellow fever. Eliza soon left the care of her stepfather, who had become manager of the troupe, and set out on her own as an actress.

> "The fact is, the drama is not now supported for the sole reason that it *does not deserve support.* We must burn or bury the old models — We need *Art* . . . that is to say, in place of absurd conventionalities, we demand *principles* of dramatic composition founded in *Nature,* and in common sense.
> —Poe on theater in America

It was a knockabout life for a teenager, especially one whose striking dark looks were as much a matter of comment as her work on the stage. At the age of fifteen, Eliza Arnold married another young actor, C.D. Hopkins, and they played the Virginia theater circuit. In three years he, too, died of yellow fever. Eliza Arnold Hopkins was an eighteen-year-old widow with no children and no family—but a sizeable repertoire—when she met a Richmond law student named David Poe, Jr.

Promoting "General" Poe

The law student named David Poe, Jr. was the oldest son in a large Baltimore family of seven children. By the time he was born in 1784, the Poes were third generation Americans who had established themselves in the New World as merchants, patriots, and landowners.

Poe's great-grandparents, John Poe and his wife Jane McBride Poe, emigrated from Ireland to America (with their son, David) and were living in Lancaster County, Pennsylvania by 1750. David, who was Edgar's grandfather, was the oldest of ten children, and only one of three to have children of his own. By 1755, John and Jane Poe had moved their family to Baltimore.

Edgar's paternal grandfather, David Poe, Sr. was a patriot, in fact, a zealot in the cause of the colonies' independence from England. It was a passion the Baltimore wheelwright and dry goods merchant backed with the dizzying amount of $40,000—a fortune in those days.

question

How much was David Poe's gift in today's dollars?
To give you a sense of just how extravagantly David Poe, Sr. put his money where his mouth was, in today's dollars, his gift of $40,000 to the cause of American independence is roughly equivalent to $475,000.

David Poe, Sr. was instrumental in pushing the Tories—British sympathizers—out of Baltimore. His chief function in the nascent American army was that of quartermaster, providing patriot soldiers with military supplies. Even his wife, Elizabeth, mother of ten children, contributed to the cause by sewing uniforms. It was life lived in service to a glorious cause. For his work as quartermaster, Poe Sr. received the honorary title of "General." And "General" he would remain to his ambitious young grandson, Edgar, whose vast romantic imagination discovered an interest in the military.

The Short, Scrappy Life of David Poe, Jr.

David Poe, Jr. took his life in a different direction than the one his family had charted for him. While studying law in Baltimore, David Jr. joined an all-male amateur theatrical group called the Thespian Club, and what began as a hobby soon became the reason he abandoned his law studies. He saw a performance by a young actress named Eliza Arnold Hopkins and fell in love, both with her and the delectable possibility of life as an actor. In a nation newly committed to the pursuit of happiness, David Poe, Jr. began promoting himself as an actor and singer.

The rest of the Poe family was not pleased.

---

fact

A rumor started floating among the West Point cadets that Poe's other grandfather—not the one Edgar later referred to as the "intimate" friend of Lafayette—was Benedict Arnold. It was Eliza Poe's maiden name, Arnold, that led to the rumor, and Edgar, who liked the cachet of military hero grandsires—apparently even traitorous ones—didn't set the record straight.

No pictures of David Poe, Jr. survive, but a review of his professional debut pronounced his appearance "much in his favor." One reviewer sniped that Poe was well suited to any role requiring a backwoodsman—which, of course is not what you want to hear if you're picturing yourself as Hamlet—although his performance was timid. David Poe pursued acting with a kind of deluded passion but received nothing but enthusiastic disdain for his efforts, wounding his pride. By the time David and Eliza married in 1806, she had a decade head start in the theater over her vain young husband, and it was she who received all the praise. The couple had two sons—William Henry Leonard Poe was born at the end of January 1807, followed by Edgar (named for the legitimate son in King Lear, in which Eliza and David were appearing at the time) two years later, on January 19.

Was David Poe jealous of his wife's success? Was he a reluctant father? Was he broken by the financial hardship the Poes could never quite outrun? In three years, David fathered two sons, garnered many bad reviews, developed a severe drinking problem, and earned a reputation for scrappiness. The marriage became stormy, and sometime during Edgar's infancy his father disappeared. The father of Edgar's sister, Rosalie, who was born more than a year after David Poe deserted his family, remains a mystery.

Run, Eliza, Run

One of the most damaging events in the life of Edgar Allan Poe was the death of his mother a month before his third birthday. In the fifteen years since she arrived in Boston with her actress mother, Eliza Hopkins Poe had mastered seventy roles, played three hundred performances, toured the eastern seaboard, been widowed once, abandoned once, and given birth to three children. She was a remarkably dedicated actress who had no support system either to ease her financial hardship or participate in the upbringing of her little family.

Everything fell to Eliza.

Eliza's Exit

At twenty-four, Eliza wound up back in Richmond, broke and ailing, with three children all under the age of five. An ad in the Richmond *Enquirer* of November 29, 1811, brought Eliza's plight to the attention of the Richmond community.

question

What did the ad say?

"To the Humane Heart," ran the headline, "On this night, Mrs. Poe, lingering on the bed of disease and surrounded by her children, asks your assistance; and asks it perhaps for the last time. The generosity of a Richmond Audience can need no other appeal."

Some civic-minded women affected by the ad visited the penniless Eliza Poe, sheltered at the home of a Scotch milliner. One was Frances Allan, the wife of a Richmond tobacco merchant. Eliza's distress, though, went beyond anyone's ability to help, and by early December 1811, she was dying, either of pneumonia or tuberculosis.

At her bedside, in a home not their own, were her son, Edgar, and her daughter, Rosalie. (Henry, the oldest, was already staying with his paternal grandparents in Baltimore.)

The Allan Family Enters

Eliza Hopkins Arnold Poe was buried at Old St. John's Church. Due to the vocal displeasure of some of the church members at having anyone so scandalous as an actress buried in their sacred ground, her grave was in a spot as far from the actual church as possible. It remained unmarked until 1927.

Eliza's children were scattered to various foster homes. Poe went to live with Frances Allan and her husband, John. All the destitute Eliza left Poe was a treasured watercolor of Boston Harbor, which she hoped would remind him of his birthplace.

To Add to the Drama

Although there are discrepancies in the record, the vanished David Poe, Jr. died—elsewhere—within days of his abandoned wife, probably of yellow fever. And not even three weeks after Eliza's death, the Richmond Theater, where she had performed, burned to the ground. Scenery caught fire during a crowded performance and because there weren't enough exits, sixty-eight people died in the fire (some, trampled to death), including the governor of Virginia. It was as if the daily theater life in Poe's family background was cut off, signaling changes a child so young couldn't possibly understand.

But even though the stage as a Poe family way of survival disappeared from Poe's life, the love for dramatizing human stories that drew his parents to the theater in the first place was part of the boy's deepest nature, and it found a different form of expression as he grew. Is it any wonder that a bright and sensitive little boy who watches his beautiful, talented mother die—and watches her burial—returns to the theme of the premature burial of a beautiful woman in his own creative work, over and over again? Or that the tone is always one of horror?

Chapter 2

The Old Foster Folks at Home

The well-to-do Allan family of Richmond, Virginia, provided the orphaned Poe with the love of a foster mother and the indifference of a foster father, who funded unique educational opportunities for the boy in both Britain and America. But with Poe's adolescence came his first forays into the realm of romance, a growing definition of his artistic ambitions, a recognition of his Poe ancestors—and an inevitable struggle with John Allan.

Richmond in 1811

The Richmond where Edgar Allan Poe was raised by his foster parents was emerging as a small city to be reckoned with. After all, it earned its stripes during the Revolutionary period, and it was positioned better than Charlottesville, seat of the landed aristocracy. Richmond seemed to be the Virginian town best able to take advantage of mercantile opportunities the new United States was interested in undertaking.

"It is a thousand pities that the puny witticisms of a few professional objectors should have power to prevent . . . the adoption of a name for our country. . . . There should be no hesitation about 'Appalachia.' In the first place, it is distinctive. 'America' is not, and can never be made so. . . . South America is 'America,' and will insist upon remaining so. . . . I yet hope to find 'Appalachia' assumed." — Poe on his nation's name

By 1800, Richmond had become the state capital—with a capitol building—and it had recovered from its burning twenty years before at the hands of Benedict Arnold. Richmond, Virginia, had divided itself into Congressional districts, established a bank, a public library, stagecoach lines, and steamboat service up and down the James River. Virginia was the birthplace of some of the finest minds and spirits behind the American Revolution, the closest things to an aristocracy the country would know.

But the Richmond of 1800 also saw the first glimmer of national catastrophe still half a century down the road. A slave uprising—depending on the report, involving anywhere from 1,000–4,000 slaves—was quelled just outside Richmond.

Overlooking the new century that spread out before it, Virginia was discovering in itself the makings of a true commonwealth, what with the rise of a merchant class and opportunities for the general advancement of all its people—its free people, that is. Its free, white people. The Virginia of Poe's youth was developing its Southern identity. So, in fact, was he.

Make Mine a Bitters—With an Oliver Twist

If you asked John Allan, a social climbing, hardworking Richmond merchant, how he felt about his childless marriage up to the end of 1811, he would either say it suited him just fine, thank you—or he might say he really hadn't noticed the absence of any offspring. Richmond was a city on the rise, what with its growing tobacco, flour, and coal industries, where an already wealthy aristocracy sought the services of capable merchants.

John Allan was a canny Scotsman who built a successful business brokering goods and services with his partner, Charles Ellis. But the success Allan wanted was more than financial. He wanted standing in the community as well, which meant conspicuous churchgoing, philanthropy, and participation in civic affairs. Himself an orphaned immigrant, Allan valued self-reliance and hard work—practically the embodiment of Benjamin Franklin's all-American ideal, Poor Richard.

fact
In response to a foster father who performed his duty but without any deep affection for the boy—or, at least, any he could express—many years later the child taken in the day after Christmas in 1811 only ever signed his name Edgar A. Poe, Edgar Poe, or E.A. Poe.

On the day after Christmas, when his compassionate wife, Frances, brought home one of the Poe orphans—in fact, the last one to find a foster home—Allan may have seen the event as an opportunity for performing a long-term civic duty, or maybe as an experiment in shaping one example of the nation's youth, or merely as a hobby for his childless wife. But nowhere is there a record of his looking upon the arrival of two-year-old Edgar Poe as a chance to be a loving father. He himself had no role model. Besides, he was a busy man. John Allan had the child baptized, but although he added his own family name to the child's, he never formally adopted Poe.

In 1811, the Allans were living over a store at the corner of Main and Thirteenth Streets. The two-year-old Edgar Poe was beginning a new life as a foundling. The soft, loving Frances Allan had seen to that. But what would be the psychological effects of John Allan's lifelong refusal to see the boy as anything other than a permanent foster child?

The Household Pet

The boy who came into the Allan home that December day was appealing, with his black curls and gray eyes. Because of Poe, Frances Allan discovered instant motherhood, and she wasn't alone. Her unmarried sister, Nancy Valentine, was living with them at the time, and so the child who couldn't understand where his own mother had gone suddenly found himself at the center of the combined universe of two strange, doting women. He was their pet, and they overdressed and spoiled him. Frances and Nancy were a double dose of attention, indelibly shaping the boy's tendency to turn to women for love and approval. John Allan was always either absent or distant.

John Allan was caught in a forked stick. His cool duty to do right by the boy—with a little prodding from his wife—led him to take Edgar with them on pricey vacations and to enroll the boy in good schools. On the other hand, although Allan may have viewed this as just another attempt to fulfill his duty to the boy, he tried to offset his wife and sister-in-law's coddling by weighing in severely. To the orphan, though, the Allans were always Ma and Pa, and his desire to be treated fully as a son and heir was a source of conflict and sorrow in his life.

Still, the duty-bound John Allan sent the boy off to school at age five.

Edgar was off again at age six to a school for boys run by a schoolmaster. Although Edgar's formal education had begun, it wasn't until 1815 that he had his first real adventure, when John Allan moved his family to London in order to expand his business overseas. For five years, the little Richmonder became an American abroad—or, maybe the way he saw it, a British schoolboy.

fact

In terms of child welfare in the United States of the early 1800s, foster care increasingly became the goal, with Massachusetts in the vanguard. Children elsewhere were rescued from poorhouses and often shipped via "orphan trains" to the Midwest, where they were taken into farming families to work for room and board.

Not Quite Dotheboys Hall

In the first six years of his formal education, Edgar attended five schools. One of the significant influences in his life was the tension between his need for home as a safe, settled place, and frequent relocations as a lifestyle. The itinerant lifestyle became a trait of his, either out of necessity, when he moved to search for work as a writer, or as a delicious matter of choice as a free man in a new nation full of opportunities. Edgar's early experiences—the utter change in his family circumstances when his mother died, two different schools in two years, then living in a foreign country for what would become five crucial years—may have made him resilient. They may also have persuaded the boy, on some level, that the world is full of unsettling surprises and grim possibilities, a psychic state repeatedly seen in his macabre tales. These experiences may have made him insecure.

The figure of "the American abroad" wouldn't become popularized, or explored by such great writers as Mark Twain, Henry James, and Edith Wharton, until a generation after Poe set foot on British soil at the age of six. And that social critic Charles Dickens wouldn't address the problems of child welfare (in "proper British" homes, schools, and orphanages) until twenty-five years later. When Dickens wrote *Nicholas Nickleby,* the location for his exposé was the fictional Dotheboys—do the boys—Hall.

But in 1812, there was Edgar, the pampered American boy, making a dazzling round of visits to Allan's Scottish relatives in Ayrshire and then boarding in a Scottish school, while Frances and John Allan went on without him to London. Soon Edgar joined them, staying for a year at a boarding school in Chelsea where he studied spelling, geography, and Church of England catechism—"high church," similar to the Allans' Episcopalianism back home. Reports home said Poe was happy and well.

fact

During Charles Dickens's tour of America in 1842, he expressed a desire to meet the man who had correctly guessed the ending of his serialized novel, *Barnaby Rudge*—Edgar Allan Poe. The meeting went well, and the two exchanged letters. Dickens hoped to find a British publisher for Poe's *Tales of the Grotesque and Arabesque,* and Poe hoped Dickens would submit a piece to *Graham's Magazine,* where he was then working. Both hopes died.

The bills for Poe's education during these years in Great Britain were sent to John Allan, on behalf of "Master Allan," and it's clear that these childhood school years were the closest the boy ever came to being considered Allan's son. Finally, Poe enrolled at Manor House School a few miles outside of London, where he first showed a real aptitude for languages. Under the headmaster, Reverend Bransby, who was a classics scholar, Master Allan excelled at Greek and Latin. It was here that it first became apparent that the boy had something that would later earn him some respect by his peers— real athletic ability.

On the Dark Side of Russell Square

The years in England from 1815–1820 were the most settled in Poe's life up to that point. Home was an apartment in London's Russell Square, where Frances tried to adjust to a move she hadn't wanted. The Manor House School for Poe accounted for most of the time he spent among British schoolboys. There was a kind of stability, but there were three negative aspects to the family's years abroad.

they said...

"Russell Square is, under ordinary circumstances, a very nice place to walk in. If those troublesome railway vans and goods wagons would not come lumbering and clattering . . . through the square . . . on their way to King's Cross, 'La Place Roussell' would be as cosy and tranquil as 'La Place Royale' in Paris. It has the vastness of Lincoln's Inn Fields without its dinginess."—A "contemporary" review in *St. James's Magazine* of the Russell Square neighborhood the Allans called home

An Ailing Foster Mother

Frances, the foster mother Poe called Ma, suffered from an unending series of vague complaints—head colds, headaches, sore throats, croup, and catarrh. It is unclear how much of her poor health during these years was due to the climate—or, at any rate, was a psychosomatic response to a climate she found a lot less congenial than the one she had left behind in Richmond. As a result, she was often reclining and declining off in a separate place in the Allan home, and Poe lost some of his access to the woman who had rescued and coddled him. Ma became remote. The fear, of course, had to be that she would die—another mother lost. The possibility was unbearable, especially in a household where ambivalence was the most warmth the foster father could offer him.

An Ailing Business

Another source of trouble during the otherwise stable time abroad was the reason for the move in the first place—John Allan's business plans. At first, his expansion of Allan's tobacco enterprise into the London market prospered. But Allan was unable to escape a London business slump in 1819, and in a short time he found himself caught between demanding creditors and dissatisfied customers—and $250,000 in debt. It became clear to the entrepreneurial Allan that it was time to cut his losses and work out a debt repayment schedule that satisfied his creditors. Allan decided to move his family back to Richmond. The family returned in the summer of 1820, when Edgar was eleven.

A Stifling Education

For five years in British schools, Poe discovered his intellectual talents, his ability to excel in a rigorous school system, and his athletic prowess.

By the summer of 1820, when he was about to reenter the Richmond schools, the boy's relationship with formal education was strained. Master Allan was coming out of a system where rote memorization of texts was the standard of excellence. Little value was placed on encouraging a student's lively engagement with the material. How would that sit with a boy whose imagination and curiosity were already asserting themselves?

> "I myself did not see the contest; feeling little interest in feats of merely physical strength, or agility, when performed by rational beings. The speed of a horse is sublime—that of a man absurd. I always find myself fancying how very readily he could be beaten by an ass."—Poe on a foot race

Worshiping Edgar

In those years after the return from England in 1820, the Ellis and Allan families were thrown together frequently because the men were business partners and the women were cousins. A little younger than Poe, Thomas Ellis idolized the older boy, saying, "No boy ever had a greater influence over me than he had," adding that he was beautiful and brave. Thomas Ellis's anecdotes about the young adolescent Poe show a range of normal boyish escapades: hiding out, poaching, tramping through woods, scaring girls—thus emerging a star in the local pack of boys.

fact

One of Poe's childhood friends, Robert Sully, said Poe always included him in the boys' games when they were young, standing up for him against the teasing of the other boys. School was hard for Sully, who was deaf, so the smart, generous Poe helped him. Sully grew up to become a painter.

It was Poe who taught Thomas Ellis how to skate, swim, and hunt, although the lessons came with either a whipping for Edgar or a near-death experience for Thomas. The boys shot game birds on the Belvidere Estate, owned by a prominent local judge, and Edgar got a beating when word got back to John Allan. The swimming lesson Edgar gave his pal consisted of throwing Thomas into the river, and then—when it quickly became evident that self-preservation doesn't necessarily lead to skills—jumping in after him to save him from drowning.

Thomas was delighted when his idol won a local speech contest, and again when Edgar and a few school friends set up a tent for a stage in a vacant lot and charged the public a penny to watch their "thespian performances."

On one occasion, the Ellis parlor was set up with many card tables for the Gentlemen's Whist Club, a card game forerunner of bridge. The play was suddenly interrupted by a "ghost"—even then, bed sheets did the trick—and the crowd of card players was appropriately scared until the specter was finally cornered by a doctor, with help from none other than General Winfield Scott. Scott, known as "Old Fuss and Feathers," was a war hero who would go on to become a presidential candidate and famous tactician. His

Anaconda Plan to blockade the Confederacy would be instrumental in the Union victory in the Civil War.

It's characteristic of Poe that, even as his foes closed in, he faced them, never a victim of the fright he engineered—an unflappable bravery in the face of adversity. That night, defrocked, the high-spirited Poe laughed along with the others.

In all the years they knew each other, Thomas Ellis remembered only one "piece of meanness" perpetrated by Poe. One Christmas, the Ellis family was celebrating the holiday with the Allan clan. One of the toys was a segmented toy snake, connected by wires, the kind you can handle so it wiggles in a lifelike way. Apparently for Poe, the evening's entertainment was a classic boy tease—poking the snake at the Ellis's daughter, Jane, until "it almost ran her crazy."

> "Whist has long been known for its influence upon what is termed the calculating power; and men of the highest order of intellect have been known to take an apparently unaccountable delight in it, while eschewing chess as frivolous."—Poe on whist in *The Murders in the Rue Morgue*

Against a Powerful Current

Not an orphan, but not quite a son. Not a Brit, but not quite a Virginian. From the age of eleven until he packed up and went—exceptionally young at seventeen—to Thomas Jefferson's new university in Charlottesville, certain things about Poe were becoming clear. He was athletic, romantic, and literary. He was already trying to reconcile his considerable gifts with the deep insecurity that kept him from ever believing in himself. His feats came to matter keenly to him, maybe because with the insecurity that sapped him everywhere he turned, he had to struggle to achieve what more light-hearted boys did more easily.

Edgar was a swimmer and a broad jumper. Although his achievements—and his likeable nature—gave him some standing among the other boys, he still gained a reputation for aloofness.

His studies introduced him to the romantic ideals of Byron and Keats, and in some ways, he was already trying to emulate them. The summer he was fifteen, he swam six miles up the James River against a powerful current, an anxious schoolteacher following him in a rowboat in case he got into trouble. He likened this exercise to Lord Byron's famous feat. Byron was the first person known to swim the Hellespont, the hazardous one-kilometer strait between Europe and Asia. An element of risk heightened the experience and infused it with excitement.

they said...

"This institution of my native state, the hobby of my old age, will be based on the illimitable freedom of the human mind, to explore and to expose every subject susceptible of its contemplation."—Thomas Jefferson on his vision for his new university, which included ten pavilions in an academic village with a 7,000-book library as its centerpiece, 1820

With the Greek and Latin he learned in England—and continued in Richmond—he read stories about the feats of Greek and Roman heroes. With the "new" Romantic poetry of Byron, Shelley, and Keats, he had visions of an extravagant individualism. Classicist? Romantic? Something else? Potent new influences were seeping into the young adolescent Poe, and while he continued to excel at school, he was also beginning to see the possibilities for self-creation. His life was something he could make a breathing work of art—but how?

And then he met Helen, otherwise known as Jane Stith Stanard. She wasn't the girl next door or a student at a nearby girls' academy. Poe's Helen, the subject of his fourteen-year-old passion, was Jane Stith Stanard, the mother of one of his school friends. Jane Stanard had certain advantages as material for a young poet. She was a classic beauty; she reminded him of his dead mother, Eliza; as a married woman, she was deliciously unobtainable; and she showed a sincere interest in him and his potential. But late in April of 1824, Jane Stith Stanard died, and Poe, for a second time, lost a woman extremely dear to him. The death of his mother when he was two was the kind of loss that spread itself throughout his nature as he grew. The loss of Jane Stith Stanard occurred when he was fifteen, old enough to experience it on many levels—and mourn conspicuously.

Sulky and Ill-Tempered

These were pre-therapy days, and an adolescent boy in mourning was a difficult figure around the house. In just a few years Poe would write the poem that called Jane his Helen, "the glory that was Greece," to memorialize this idealized woman who had proved so devastatingly mortal. With Jane's death in 1824, another source of support went out of his life. During this time, John Allan commented in a letter to Edgar's brother, Henry, that his ward was "sulky & ill-tempered," but no mention was made as to the cause. In fact, Allan was beginning to feel ill-used by his foster son, claiming all his provisions for the boy had been unmet by any affection or gratitude. But Allan's business was still undergoing some financial hardship and these pressures may have limited his tolerance of Edgar during that time.

Edgar was fifteen, in the throes of adolescence. He lost someone else he loved, a woman whose belief in his artistic potential was something he had never experienced. Within one important year in his personal and artistic development, Poe met and lost his first real confidante and supporter. By the time Jane Stith Stanard died, her marriage was unhappy. Like Melville's Ishmael, who remarks thirty years later in *Moby Dick* that "there is a woe that is madness," her depression grew into what looked like insanity, which may also have been symptomatic of the brain tumor responsible for her death. The record is unclear.

"This lady, on entering the room, took his hand and spoke some gentle and gracious words of welcome, which so penetrated the sensitive heart of the orphan boy as to deprive him of the power of speech," wrote Helen Whitman, one of Poe's fiancées, remembering how he described Jane Stanard. "This lady afterwards became the confidante of all his boyish sorrows, and hers was the one redeeming influence that saved and guided him in the earlier days of his turbulent and passionate youth."

> "Did I, when an infant, sollicit [[sic]] your charity and protection, or was it of your own free will, that you volunteered your services in my behalf? It is well known . . . that my Grandfather (my natural protector at the time you interposed) was wealthy, and that I was his favourite grand-child—But the promises of adoption . . . induced him to resign all care of me into your hands."—Poe to John Allan

But, in addition to what this woman meant to him—many years later, in a letter to another female friend, he called Jane his "first, purely ideal love"—the death of his "Helen" is significant in another, more sinister way. It's the first appearance of the melancholy that defined much of his adult life. To the unsympathetic John Allan, the young man was sulky and ill-tempered, a kind of house devil. For the boy himself, though, Poe was beginning his acquaintance with a part of his own psyche that had nothing to do with the classical inspirations of Jane Stanard—a part of his soul that was deeply inconsolable, and that would eventually seek dangerous forms of pain relief.

Escorting the Marquis

Six months after the death of Jane Stith Stanard, Edgar served as a lieutenant in the Junior Morgan Riflemen Club of Richmond, a boys' volunteer company given the honor of escorting the old Revolutionary War hero, General Lafayette, during his visit to

Richmond. Lafayette was particularly dear to the citizens of Virginia's up-and-coming mercantile center because in 1781, upon orders from George Washington himself, he and 1,200 troops reached Richmond in time to defend it against Lord Cornwallis.

Nearly half a century later, President Monroe invited Lafayette to tour what were then the twenty-four states in the Union, and the old General arrived in New York City in August. In a charming coincidence, when Lafayette marched in the New York City parade honoring him, he scooped up a little boy from the crowd and carried him—Walt Whitman, age six.

His hero's tour lasted a year. By late October, Lafayette visited Williamsburg and inspected the sixty-five-gun frigate *North Carolina*. In Richmond, the parade included the Junior Morgan Riflemen and the reception featured forty veterans of the Revolutionary War. At some point during the festivities, he placed a wreath, while the uniformed Edgar watched, at the grave of "General" David Poe, calling his old comrade "a noble heart." Afterwards, the Marquis de Lafayette attended the horse races, and a week later he was the guest of former President Jefferson at Monticello.

they said...

"Before Mr. Poe came to New York, he traveled much, both at home and abroad; he had been partially educated at West Point, but his mind was neither mathematical, military, nor subordinate to soldierly discipline, as might have been conceived, and for this cause his relation therewith was dissolved, though he always retained the air inseparable from military training."—New York writer Elizabeth Oakes Smith, 1867

Many years later, Thomas Ellis, the son of John Allan's business partner, claimed "there was not a brighter, more graceful or more attractive boy in the city than Edgar Allan Poe." Thomas Ellis recalled how he was never prouder of his idol than the moment he saw him in the uniform of the Junior Morgan Riflemen, the unit handpicked by Lafayette himself to be his honorary bodyguard.

The procession followed Lafayette's carriage through Richmond to Capitol Square, where the General reviewed the "troops."

For Edgar, not yet sixteen, the occasion was his first, potent experience with his grandfather's military background, something of honor to a young man struggling with his own identity. The Poe side of the young writer's family would figure most prominently in Edgar's life and sense of himself in the coming years. There were actual relatives, stories, transmitted adventures, and reflected glories. As a grandson of General Poe, young Edgar resonated to dashing exploits, noble causes, and the opportunities for heroics he associated with military service—not to mention the splendid line item his grandfather made in Edgar's application for admission to West Point.

Chapter 3

Squaring Off

The academically talented Poe enrolled at the University of Virginia, where he excelled—for the one year he attended. Believing himself to be John Allan's heir, Poe gambled to increase an allowance he felt was too low but which his foster father believed would teach the boy the value of a dollar. Already the first inklings of Poe's literary talent as a writer were evident.

Not All the Work Was Hard...

Around the time of the Marquis's visit to Richmond, some new information came to Poe that sharpened the relationship with his foster father. Poe found out that the hard-working, churchgoing John Allan had managed—over several years—to take some time away from the concerns of his business to float some extramarital affairs and had several offspring living in Richmond. Wind of these developments reached Frances, who was devastated. Poe aligned himself with her.

Within six months, Poe dealt with the death of Jane Stanard, the discovery of his foster father's infidelity, and heightened questions about his own identity. His experience of Lafayette's visit as a Junior Morgan Rifleman reconnected the young man to his own biological family, the Poes. To the bitter and exasperated John Allan, his foster son was baffling and ungrateful; to Poe, the philandering moneymaker Allan was a hypocrite. Until this point in their lives together, the inadequacies of their father/ son relationship were tolerable—Allan provided the financial support, and Poe excelled at school and sports. Despite a real lack of warmth, the relationship superficially worked as long as the roles were clear.

they said...

"... you have not evinced the smallest disposition to comply with my wishes.... your Heart will tell you if it is not made of marble whether I have not had good reason to fear for you, in many ways. I should have been justly chargeable, in reprimanding you for faults had I had any other object than to correct them."—John Allan to Poe, 1827

But with the discovery of Allan's infidelity, Edgar made himself a more obvious opponent to his foster father, and the conflict between them escalated. It must have been a defining moment for the young writer, finding the secret underside of adult behavior there in his own home, feeling his own response, and finally standing up for what he valued—even flying in the face of his own self-interest—in this case, Frances Allan. Aside from putting on a uniform and marching behind Lafayette's carriage, aside from a six-mile "extreme sport" swim against a strong tide, aside from any challenge the young man had set himself, to confront his foster father about his affairs was touchingly adult.

But John Allan was no pushover. He countered Poe's dangerous knowledge with some of his own. Apparently, when Poe's mother died, the orphan came with the deceased Eliza's belongings, including some compromising letters. Although they were later destroyed (at Poe's wish), it is believed they mentioned the illegitimacy of Poe's younger sister Rosalie, and because of the letters, John Allan and Poe arrived at a standoff—indiscretion for indiscretion.

Who Wants to Be a Multi-Millionaire?

The idea of having a rich uncle who dies and leaves you a fortune at an opportune time is a dream that came true in Poe's life—only not to him. Edgar had no rich relatives, but John Allan did. Allan's uncle, William Galt, owned gristmills, sawmills, a tobacco business, a bank, plantations, and various real estate. A Scottish immigrant, Galt recognized in his nephew traits they both valued: a good head for business, respect for a dollar, and a ferocious work ethic.

It was Galt who gave John Allan and his friend Charles Ellis a job in the business, where the two young men got on-the-job training and an enviable head start in the Richmond mercantile world. Ellis and Allan became partners and moved on. Eventually, in 1825, William Galt moved on as well—permanently and dramatically—while sharing breakfast with his nephew John. He simply died where he sat. When the will was read, John Allan—coping with his wife's unending health complaints, conflicts with that ingrate Edgar, the complications of multiple infidelities, and the dissolution of his partnership with Ellis—inherited one third of the Galt fortune.

It was a staggering fortune, and in the short run, John Allan paid off his creditors and bought an elegant two-story brick house, Moldavia, on a hillside in Richmond. He, Frances, and Edgar moved in. The house boasted upper and lower wraparound porches, an octagonal dining room, and a mirrored ballroom.

fact

In today's currency, the Galt inheritance amounted to well over $13 million. With not quite $15,000 of that money John Allan bought Moldavia, the home of a well-to-do milliner, who had named it. Then a European principality, Moldavia merged in 1829 with another principality, Wallachia, to form modern Romania, and for the former owner, the name may have held romance.

What ensued were the most comfortable living circumstances Edgar would ever know. But the single longest stretch he enjoyed them were the first six months, until he packed up to go to the University of Virginia, sixty miles southwest of Richmond in Charlottesville. After that time, with the exception of a possible total of four months, on and off, he would never again live under John Allan's roof—nor would any of the fabulous Galt inheritance ever come into his increasingly threadbare pockets.

Edgar found happiness in the new house, specifically in a friendship with a fifteen-year-old neighbor, Sarah Elmira Royster. No one objected: after all, wasn't the smart, athletic Edgar John Allan's heir? What wasn't to like? Elmira and Edgar became secretly engaged. Maybe the secrecy appealed to the seventeen-year-old boy's sense of drama, or maybe on some level he sensed a strong parental disapproval coming his way. Off he went to the University of Virginia. But it didn't take long for the engagement to come out into the open. In the best tradition of melodrama, love letters were intercepted and the engagement was broken—by her parents, who now didn't think quite so well of the smart, athletic neighbor. What kind of life would

Elmira have had as the wife of a poor poet? Her family married her off to another man, Alexander Shelton, who had better prospects.

At Work on the Myth of Himself

Edgar Allan Poe's first notebook was himself. He was his own original raw material. Most of his fabrications—or what Huck Finn would call 'stretchers'—occurred when he was young, trying to find his way through the long periods of estrangement from John Allan. Once he was married and launched as a professional writer, the need to create a persona or pad a resumé lessened. He was a husband, a working writer grappling with financial hardship, discovering how real life gets in the way of the dream. But the desire to dramatize continued, and leaping onto the pages were the tragedian, the criminal, the philosopher, the detective—maybe just different potential Poes who would never actually don his black greatcoat.

> "Experience has shown, and Philosophy will always show, that a vast portion, perhaps the larger portion of truth, arises from the apparently irrelevant."—Poe on truth

Little White Lies

At the beginning of *The Adventures of Huckleberry Finn*, Huck lets readers know that Mark Twain's previous book is not altogether truthful. "There was things which he stretched, but mainly he told the truth." Huck's desire to set the record straight is playful on many levels: the work is fiction, in the first place; Mark Twain is speaking through Huck; and although Huck mentions these stretchers, he doesn't condemn them. By the time *Huck Finn* hit the book stalls in 1885, stretchers had been enjoying an American literary presence for quite some time. If you believe art imitates life, maybe that explains the American love for stretchers—tall tales and literary hoaxes—as the natural literary result of those American figures of the folk hero and the con man.

Until Poe arrived on the scene—not from his birth, but his late adolescence, when he was struggling to find his way—American tall tales and hoaxes were folksy and genial. You know the Headless Horseman wasn't really headless. You know Davy Crockett couldn't really whip his weight in wildcats. But in a new, independent nation 'stretching' free of the shackles of colonialism and orthodoxy, possibilities were as vast and teeming as the frontier that beckoned. The possibility of greatness, wealth, heroism, romance—it was all there in the American mind and literature. Spirits were high and exaggerations abounded. Personal histories were invented.

The Line Between Lying and Storytelling

In a time and place that was, in a way, just one big application—for a job, education, appointment, bank loan, mate—the tomfoolery of tall tales and hoaxes, where you always shared the joke with the jokester, changed. Those shadow lands in the land of opportunity held the temptation of self-promotion. The individual became the tall tale, became the hoax. To an ambitious and insecure young man like Poe, stretchers became alluring. Out of an imagination that would yield, in his lifetime, ten volumes of poetry, fiction, and essays, he began to write his first real creation—himself.

Despite what that raven croaked many years down the road, Poe was a foundling forevermore, one with rare gifts, a complex nature, and a foster father who provided for him—up to a point—but without ever loving him. His losses were real, and they ran deep. His talents were real, too—and they flourished. There is a borderland in Poe where there are no stakes marking the boundaries between truth and fiction.

Where the Devil Is My Frock Coat?

When the doors to the University of Virginia opened in 1824, its founder and architect, Thomas Jefferson, envisioned a center of learning to attract and develop the enlightened human mind. It's the Greek Revival-style library (not a chapel, you'll notice) that stands at the head of the campus, and it's significant that the university—Jefferson's fondest personal achievement—was unaffiliated with any church, unlike northern rivals Harvard and Princeton. The first class consisted of 123 students, mostly sons of the plantation gentry.

The Jeffersonian ideal of the enlightened human mind seemed to take a measure of good student behavior for granted. But into the "academical village" of rolling lawns and graceful, classical buildings came a rowdy bunch of antebellum plantation boys seeking some happy blend between college—philosophy, arts, foreign languages, science, law, and medicine—and college life.

> "Dixon made [a] physical attack upon Arthur Smith . . .—and a 'very fine fellow'—he struck him with a large stone on one side of his head—whereupon Smith drew a pistol (which are all the fashion here) and had it not miss'd fire, would have put an end to the controversy—"—Poe, describing a fight between two classmates in a letter to John Allan, 1826

They came from lives of privilege, where their place in the social order (thanks to a slave economy that seemed unassailable) was as dependable as a sunrise.

Poe arrived the second year, bringing with him his experience of the comforts of Moldavia and the reflected glory of the Galt inheritance. When nobody knows you, you can become anyone you please. Despite the acrimonious relationship with his foster father, Edgar led others to believe that Allan was one of the landed gentry, not just an immigrant merchant, and led others to believe he was Allan's adopted son and heir. His sense of his own prospects determined how he set himself up as a student of ancient and modern languages in Jefferson's academic village.

His quick mind responded not only to the intellectual stimulation but also to a sense of something in the air: both Poe and the new nation were still formulating their identities. It is symbolic that when Thomas Jefferson died that July Fourth, the young Poe attended his funeral at Monticello. As the generation of nation-builders was dying, the work of defining America and Americans was increasingly falling to younger hands. The nation was just one more adolescent individual trying to figure out what it was. Athlete, poet, heir, Richmond's answer to Lord Byron in every conceivable way, the young Poe, as a member of the second class to enter Jefferson's university, bought an expensive wardrobe and hired a personal valet (from a pool of local slaves) he could ill afford. Allan had given him less than half of the money Poe thought he needed to pay the fees and hobnob with the plantation boys as a social peer.

Empty Chairs and Broken Tables

When it came to his studies at the University of Virginia, Poe was first-rate, passing his French and Latin exams with highest honors. His shortcomings never spilled over into the realm of his intellect, his creative powers, or artistic integrity. But the truth of his orphaned beginnings was always something he tried to offset by walking the walk and talking the talk of the young Southern gentleman. The question is whether you can ever quite take the foundling out of the boy—especially when the foster father, for whatever reason, keeps the child's position ambiguous. Edgar was seventeen the one year he was enrolled at the University of Virginia—two years younger than his classmates—and maybe it was some combination of extreme youth, insecurity, or an imagination awakening to the chance of self-creation that led to his difficulties. It was here, in Jefferson's realized vision of a place for the enlightened human mind, that Poe got drunk and lost at cards often enough to rack up a debt of $2,000.

Despite the popular opinion that he was an alcoholic, firsthand accounts generally agree that he was constitutionally incapable of drinking great quantities of alcohol. Less than one glass of wine was enough to put him under. Chronic drunkenness on Poe's part wouldn't have escaped the notice of the faculty, the staff, or the officers of the university, and the records show no censures against his name—for anything. An occasional "frolic"? Absolutely.

It was the gambling debt that ended his university education just ten months after it

"The faculty expelled Wickliffe last night for general bad conduct—but more especially for biting one of the student's arms with whom he was fighting—. . . It was bitten from the shoulder to the elbow—and it is likely that pieces of flesh as large as my hand will be obliged to be cut out—He is from Kentucky"—Poe to John Allan

began. Edgar argued to an irate John Allan that gambling was an attempt to make his inadequate allowance go further. Allan refused to invest in any more education—or adventures in living beyond the boy's means—at the University of Virginia, and Edgar returned to Richmond. Perhaps he wanted to mollify "Pa," because he suffered the punishment of going to work in Allan's office.

fact

On the subject of his education, according to Poe he graduated from the University of Virginia with first honors. Although he did achieve highest honors in two classes, he actually left the university after one year, when John Allan refused to bankroll any further education.

The university librarian recalls visiting Edgar in his room on a cold night in December, watching him restoke the dying fire with some tallow candles and the fragments of a little table he had broken up for firewood. In a touching bit of sleuthing that would have made Poe's future detective, Auguste Dupin, proud, the librarian concludes it must have been Poe's last night in Charlottesville, because "having no further use for his candles and table, he made fuel of them."

Bleak Counting House

What must have felt like servitude to Edgar—toiling over the accounts in Allan's "counting house," a kind of Bob Cratchit before Dickens even conceived of him—lasted just two months. There would be a tradition of different sorts of day jobs among the great writers of this period in American literary history, jobs that must have felt like the absolute antithesis of any imaginative impulses.

Nathaniel Hawthorne worked for three years as a surveyor for the Port of Salem until he was fired. Herman Melville, for the final two decades of his life, worked as a customs inspector on the docks of New York City. Henry David Thoreau worked in a pencil factory—although maybe that job had *some* relevance for a writer.

Poe never in his mature adulthood—aside from his stint in the military—earned money at anything other than a writing-related job. This determined stance is part of his literary legacy. In choosing the financial hardships of making his lean way as a writer in American life, he quietly insisted that the making of literature was an honorable profession.

Poe's unhappy drudgery in Allan's counting house, and the uneasy peace between him and his foster father, ended when Poe's creditors showed up on Allan's doorstep and the older man erupted. He categorically refused to make good on any more

> "Simplicity is not always stupidity—and as a pendant to this proposition we may observe that, had we ourselves occasion to deceive your man of finesse, we should feel more certain of accomplishing our object by a course of undisguised frankness and truth, than by the most elaborate processes of cunning."—Poe on appearances

of Poe's debts, pretty effectively picking the scars off deep, old wounds for both him and Poe.

they said...

"I should be glad if you would write to me even as a friend, there can certainly be no harm in your avowing candidly that you have no money, if you have none, but you can say when you can pay me if you cannot now. I heard when I was in Richmond that Mr. Allan would probably discharge all your debts."—Edward Crump, one of Poe's creditors, writing to Poe about his outstanding debt

The indentured servant decamped, leaving John Allan's house, office, and authority behind. He went to stay with a round of local friends, leaving no forwarding address. By this time, Edgar had already been using a false name, Henry Leonard (plucked from his brother William Henry Leonard Poe), to confuse his creditors in Charlottesville. He and a friend made their way to Norfolk, where Edgar used a different false name, Henri Le Rennet—full of dashing romance—and sailed for Boston. His sidekick quickly reconsidered the adventure and returned home, so Edgar continued alone. The young, Southern gentleman-poet may have felt that Boston, the city of his birth, was a truer home than anything the Allans could provide—or maybe, as his own poetry increased, he wanted to throw himself into what was still the literary capital of the United States.

Several years later, San Francisco humorist Bret Harte visited Boston and commented that "it was impossible to fire a revolver without bringing down the author of a two-volume work." So the city had appeal for a growing writer. At any rate, Henri Le Rennet arrived with only a small sum of money his foster mother, Frances Allan, had slipped him.

Chapter 4

Setting Out

On his own, Edgar joined the Army and began his life as a self-proclaimed poet. Frances Allan died, leaving no buffer between John and Edgar, but the two men came together when Edgar enlisted his estranged foster father's help to get into West Point. Believing the troublesome lad had found a sensible career and abandoned poetry, Allan used his political pull. But West Point was not for Edgar Allan Poe, either.

The Byron of Boston

It must have felt like pure liberation to the young Poe, sailing out of Norfolk and into a future that felt tolerably hazy to the young Virginian. This was the period that later lent itself to his romantic fabrication that he had made a transatlantic voyage to fight for the Greeks in their War of Independence from the Ottoman Empire, which had ruled mainland Greece for approximately four hundred years. Maritime interests led the Greeks to greater wealth, education, and general awareness of European history in the making. There was the thrilling example of the French Revolution, and—distantly—the American. It was air and bread to the soul of the nineteenth-century romantic.

they said...

"... he will deserve to stand high—very high—in the estimation of the shining brotherhood. Whether he *will* do so, however, must depend, not so much upon his worth now in mere poetry, as upon his worth hereafter in something yet loftier and more generous—... to the magnanimous determination that enables a youth to endure the present ... in the hope, or rather in the belief, the fixed, unwavering belief, that in the future he will find his reward."—John Neal, in his early review of Poe's first collection of poems, 1829

By the time Edgar was old enough to set his own dramatic course—and create the persona of the young, soldierly Virginian poet—the war for Greek independence had already "claimed" that icon of the English Romantic movement, Lord Byron, in 1824. The hard-loving aristocrat called "mad, bad, and dangerous to know" by Lady Caroline Lamb had joined the rebel Greek forces, subsidizing them, drawing up battle plans with them, even commanding some of them, until he died of a fever, never seeing battle. His body was returned to England for burial, but his heart literally remained in Greece. All of this was powerful, heady stuff for the young Poe, who genuinely responded to the work of the English Romantic poets, especially Byron, Coleridge, and Keats.

The Byronic hero, drawn straight from the life and work of Lord Byron, found a home in the young Poe's soul, where the figure of the moody, introspective loner seemed to fit. In his own concoction of his idealized personal history, Poe didn't stop in Boston, instead making it all the way to St. Petersburg, Russia, where he was thwarted in his goal to throw himself in with the Greeks. Boston poet James Russell Lowell obviously bought the tale, since, many years later, he described Poe's abortive attempt to fight for Greek independence ". . . which ended at St. Petersburg, where he got into difficulties through want of a passport, from which he was rescued by the American consul and sent home."

Check Your Attic

Four months after the young Poe's arrival in Boston, a local printer—who also printed druggists' labels—published *Tamerlane and Other Poems*, Poe's first volume of poetry. It was a little forty-page volume with tea-colored covers. There is some disagreement about the total number of copies in this first printing—twenty, fifty, 200—but the whereabouts of only twelve copies of this first published volume are accounted for, housed in various libraries and private collections—one criminal, because the copy in the library at the University of Virginia was stolen. As recently as twenty years ago, one of these first volumes sold at Sotheby's in New York for $198,000. Considering it's his first published volume altogether, and that there was a very small print run, *Tamerlane and Other Poems* is probably the work by Edgar Allan Poe you'd most like to come across in your attic.

In the summer of 1827, the appearance of *Tamerlane* yielded no reviews and just a couple of notices in the local Boston press. In the Preface, Poe writes that the poems were all written when he was thirteen, and in the long poem, "Tamerlane," a deathbed narrative by the Mongol warrior, he ". . . has endeavoured to expose the folly of even risking the best feelings of the heart at the shrine of Ambition." This was a folly Poe himself avoided, managing to keep both love and ambition afloat in his life, even though it led to real and enduring financial hardship.

they said...

"... exceedingly boyish, feeble, and altogether deficient in the common characteristics of poetry, but then we have ... parts ... which remind us of no less a poet than Shelley. The author, who appears to be very young, is evidently a fine genius, but he wants judgment, experience, tact."—John Neal on Poe's early poems

So Henri Le Rennet, who always carried himself proudly and called himself "a Virginian," sent himself into exile from his Southern foster home and was busy establishing a life and career in Boston. The Cradle of Liberty became Poe's personal cradle of liberty, for those first couple of years out of Richmond. He was eighteen years old when this first book was published, and *Tamerlane* is another example of the young man's search for a personal identity, because the front cover gives the elusive non-name, "A Bostonian," as the author. Calling himself a Bostonian is interesting in many ways: it implies a lifelong identification with the city; it is uncharacteristically self-effacing; and it is an early example of Poe's delight in mystification.

"'Tis thus when the lovely summer sun / Of our boyhood, his course hath run: / For all we live to know—is known; / And all we seek to keep—hath flown; / With the noon-day beauty, which is all. / Let life, then, as the day-flow'r, fall — / The trancient, passionate day-flow'r, / Withering at the ev'ning hour."
—"Tamerlane." In this passage, Tamerlane returns to a vanished home and love.

What Huck Finn would call the stretchers of Poe's university days—John Allan's son and heir, the expensive wardrobe, the valet—were changing. As a free man out and about in the world, he could try on different names, and see where they took him.

Sometimes hiding is really just a way of showing something in a different way.

You're in the Army Now

On November 18, 1827, a twenty-two-year-old Private Perry, Battery H, First Artillery, arrived on the Brigantine *Waltham* at Fort Moultrie in Charleston Harbor, South Carolina. It had been a ten-day trip for the thirty privates in Battery H, reassigned from Fort Independence, the regimental headquarters in Boston. A private's pay was five dollars a month, but Private Perry, who was a capable, trustworthy sort, found his pay doubled during his time at Fort Moultrie—year one of his five-year commitment to the military.

fact
Even though Edgar Allan Poe "aged" himself four years in order to enlist in the Army without parental consent, many years later he took to shaving anywhere from two to four years off his actual age—which, in the case of the latter, was a pretty good trick considering his mother died two years before his falsified birth date.

Poe had enlisted in the U.S. Army about two months before *Tamerlane* was published. He was really only eighteen—not twenty-two—at the time. Until the end of the 1800s, the minimum age for enlistment was sixteen, and the new recruit, "Edgar A. Perry" as he called himself, met that requirement. But there was another rule he was hoping to avoid: anyone enlisting who was under the age of twenty-one had to have written parental consent. Still so fresh off the last break with his foster father—who believed Edgar had gone to sea "to seek his fortune," which shows Allan possible of either romance or cynicism—Poe probably wasn't anxious for any personal contact. So Henri Le Rennet, a Bostonian, became Edgar A. Perry that summer, and he aged four years with the stroke of a pen.

question

What did a person like Edgar Allan Poe do in the U.S. Army?

In an ironic touch, toward the end of Battery H's posting at Fort Moultrie, "Perry" worked his way into a job requiring blacksmithing and mechanical skills. What was his job title, this young man poised to become a major figure in American literature, this young man hard at work forging a persona? "Artificer."

The military life had always been attractive to Poe. Despite the deep disruptions in his early family life, his associations with the U.S. Army had always been positive. There was his grandfather, "General" Poe, honored by that Revolutionary War hero, Lafayette. There was the Poe's own experience in the Junior Morgan Rifleman Club. This family and personal history gave him an emotional foothold in the military, and the life appealed to whatever in his nature craved order, stability, and respect. Coincidentally, he served as the company quartermaster, responsible for food and supplies—the same duties as his grandfather, all those years before.

Thirty-five years after Poe's stay at Fort Moultrie, the U.S. Army decamped, moving to the stronger position of Fort Sumter, soon shelled by the Confederates in the opening salvo of the Civil War. But in 1827–28, peace was unbroken—in fact, it was maintained by stranglehold in Charleston, in the aftermath of the aborted slave rebellion led by Denmark Vesey five years earlier. The restrictive laws affecting communications and movements among free and enslaved blacks had no impact on the languid coastal lifestyle experienced by the young soldier Perry, who had plenty of free time for absorbing the atmosphere—all preparation for writing.

A Deathbed Battleground

Edgar made his whereabouts known to his family, and his letters during his two years in the Army reassure his foster father that he's reformed, has no vices, and is establishing an honorable future for himself.

Poe's stay in South Carolina lasted a year, after which he was reassigned to Fortress Monroe, near Richmond. It was the closest he had been to his foster family since his stormy departure, and it coincided with a serious decline in Frances Allan's health.

"Ma" had always been in frail health. She may genuinely have been chronically ill, but maybe her absences from the family scene—husband and foster son—had something to do with putting herself out of the way of any possible encounters with the risky business of childbirth. It could not have been a comfortable household with John Allan's infidelities and the increasing friction between John and Poe. Or maybe she had the malaise of other comfortable women—too little education offered, too much time on their hands. Without property, education, meaningful work, or the vote, women—who weren't raising children—felt largely ornamental. Her foster son Poe had given Frances joy. But after he was forced to leave the University of Virginia because "Pa" would no longer subsidize his education, Edgar disappeared in the late winter of 1827 when his relationship with John Allan blew up. The cavernous Moldavia must have seemed then like a mausoleum.

It must have been a hard time for this caring woman who responded to a newspaper ad eighteen years ago when the actress Eliza Poe died and her orphaned children were left homeless. Edgar was her doll, her toy, her only child—something of value in her life with a man whose ferocious work ethic supported her financially but whose leftover love could not satisfy her.

In one of Edgar's letters to his foster father, just three months before Ma died, he asks Allan to send him news about Ma's health, adding: ". . . it is only when absent that we can tell the value of such a friend—I hope she will not let my wayward disposition wear away the love she used to have for me." Whether Frances Allan ever received the message, no one knows. One of John Allan's classic responses to his foster son was not to respond at all. Months of silence would ensue, and Edgar's letters would become increasingly hurt and desperate, filling in the gaps.

When it became clear to Frances in February of 1829 that she was dying, she asked Allan to send for Edgar. Whether her husband's procrastination was a demonstration of his denial that she was dying or a malicious non-action designed to hurt Poe is unclear. But Allan's timing was such that Frances didn't get her dying wish, and Edgar didn't get to see her one last time before she died. In fact, by the time Poe was released for the funeral, she had already been buried. Frances Allan was gone in every possible way, whisked—even dead—from his sight. To top it off, the normally frugal Allan actually bought Edgar a new suit for a funeral he probably knew the boy would never get to attend.

fact

Frances Keeling Valentine Allan was buried at Shockoe Hill Cemetery, Richmond's first municipal cemetery, four acres of city-owned land set aside by the city council in 1820. Landscaped and park-like, the cemetery became the destination for picnics and other outings. John Marshall, fourth Chief Justice of the U.S. Supreme Court, is buried there—and during the Civil War, 220 Confederate and 577 Union soldiers were also laid to rest there.

Aftermath of Ma's Death

A year later, the wound was still fresh when Poe lashed out at his foster father: "If she had not have died while I was away there would have been nothing for me to regret—Your love I never valued—but she I believed loved me as her own child . . ." On the subject of John Allan, Poe's introspection dried up. He became obtuse. "Your love I never valued" can only be extremely hurtful to a man who—despite his major shortcomings—used to confide sadly to others that the boy seemed to bear no affection for him. But considering how tangled and emotional their relationship was, you have to wonder whether Edgar couldn't admit even to himself how much he really wanted his foster father's love.

Edgar slipped into his usual self-defeating pattern of alternately wheedling and berating John Allan. The fact that neither approach ever worked with the man didn't seem to get through

> "I could not help thinking that you believed me degraded & disgraced, and that any thing were preferable to my returning home & entailing on yourself a portion of my infamy: But, at no period of my life, have I regarded myself with a deeper Satisfaction—or did my heart swell with more honourable pride—"—Poe to John Allan from Fort Moultrie

to Poe. Allan was probably a man for whom action told the whole story: had Poe gone into law school and never written another poem, Allan might have been softer. Words alone—whether they were high-handed, injured, noble, or whatever—were only words.

West Point: Whatever It Takes to Get In

The Edgar Perry deception continued for two years. After a year at Fort Moultrie, Battery H was shipped north to Fortress Monroe in Chesapeake Bay. Edgar A. Perry had just been promoted to Sergeant-Major, the highest rank for a non-commissioned officer, and being stationed in Chesapeake Bay was like coming home. At that point, to advance he had to go to West Point and get a commission, but he was ambivalent about the Army. On the one hand, he was well suited to the military life, thriving with the structure and demands. On some level, he was a natural because it satisfied unmet needs and tapped into certain talents. His approval ratings were consistently high, and there was never any record of bad behavior. But the romantic, the artist in him was languishing. If he left military service, what were his prospects?

Getting Out of the Army

Partly because of his own competitive nature, his desire for respect, and his need to re-establish ties with his disapproving foster father, Edgar Perry decided to renege on the remainder of his commitment to the Army—about three years—and resume his true identity as Edgar Poe and apply to the U.S. Military Academy at West Point. For this, he needed the help of John Allan, and he gambled on the possibility that the older man would support this kind of pursuit. He was right. First of all, the Army wasn't like the University of Virginia, where the young Poe could use his furniture for firewood or close the door behind himself and go. Not fulfilling the five-year commitment could lead to a different kind of five-year stint—in prison. There was also the little matter of finding a substitute, someone willing to fill the vacancy left by the one cutting short the obligation. Poe found one "Bully" Graves to take his place but had to pay him seventy-five dollars. Apparently this was far more than the usual fee, but the deal was a private one cut between Poe and Bully, and Poe could pay only $25 up front—the rest covered by John Allan, who seemed willing to support Poe's desire to get out of the Army and into West Point. So the substitute was on board, but what about that discharge?

> "I have thrown myself on the world, like the Norman conqueror on the shores of Britain &, by my avowed assurance of victory, have destroyed the fleet which could alone cover my retreat—I must either conquer or die—succeed or be disgraced."—Poe to John Allan while trying to obtain Allan's help in being discharged from the Army

Young Poe's commanding officer was a friend of John Allan's, and he extorted a promise from the unmasked Edgar Perry that he'd reconcile with Allan in exchange for a discharge, no strings attached. For the usual complex reasons that typified the relationship between the ward and the foster father, the two found common ground in the West Point application.

For whatever deeply incompatible temperaments and values—and emotional hardwiring—these two had, they worked together to get Poe into West Point. It required substantial "spin" from both of them.

Applying to West Point

Admission to the military academy was competitive, and there was always a waiting list. At the time Poe applied, the Secretary of War let him know that there were forty-seven other candidates ahead of him. While he waited for enough dismissals, rejections, and withdrawals to occur to move up the list, Edgar enhanced his resumé. For one, it was John Allan's suggestion to exhume the quartermaster grandfather, "General" Poe, and make his Revolutionary War service an attractive detail in his application.

they said...

"...from the interest exhibited by the Secretary of War you stand a fair chance I think of being one of those selected for Sept....I cover a Bank check of [Virginia] on the Union Bank of Maryland (this date) of Baltimore for one Hundred Dollars payable to your order be prudent and careful."—Allan writes to Edgar during the time they worked together to get Edgar into West Point, 1829

Had they been around to see the West Point application, David and Eliza Poe, Edgar's biological parents, would have been amazed to learn that they had perished together in the Richmond theater fire of 1811. The truth was pathetic, but for West Point, well, something special had to account for the absence of the young man's birth parents. Fire it was, then, and a spectacular and famous one, with real loss of life. In that single dramatic explanation, Poe the applicant effectively squelched questions about his father's desertion, his mother's line of work, and his family's abject circumstances.

John Allan probably couldn't believe his own eyes when he found himself writing, in his letter of recommendation to the Secretary of War, that Poe was a perfect candidate for a commission—referring specifically to the boy's "honorable feelings" and "elevated spirit." Those honorable feelings had certainly clashed with his own—and "elevated spirit" is certainly a euphemism for what Allan would have seen as Poe's baffling wild behavior.

But you have to wonder what the admissions committee at West Point made of this apparent contradiction: in his application Poe wrote that he was the son and heir of John Allan of Richmond; John Allan, in his separate, supporting letter, said the boy was no relation to him whatsoever.

> "The examination for admission is just over—a great many cadets of good family . . . have been rejected as deficient. Among these was Peyton Giles son of the Governor . . . I find that I will possess many advantages & shall endeavor to improve them." Poe writing to John Allan upon arriving at West Point, 1830

The Sparring Resumes

It took about a year before his acceptance to West Point came through. During that painful waiting period, the peculiar cooperation that Poe and his foster father had managed to pull off, united in their West Point efforts, fell apart. Allan became convinced his ward had misled him about his prospects for a commission and disparaged Poe's attempts to publish his work. Poe, in turn, fell back into his old ways, accusing Allan of never supporting him enough financially. Finally the acceptance came, the young man went, and once again excelled.

At one point during his time at the military academy, Poe threw his acceptance into John Allan's face, claiming he had earned it himself. For whatever reason, the cadet Poe couldn't quite acknowledge the fact that it was his foster father's considerable political pull that had secured his appointment.

West Point: Whatever It Takes to Get Out

Had life back home at Moldavia stayed the same, maybe Poe would have stayed the course at West Point. The drills, parades, and formations were certainly familiar to him from his two years in the Army; and the considerable academic abilities he'd shown at the University of Virginia were represented at West Point as well. He distinguished himself in French and math.

fact

Poe and another cadet, Thomas Gibson, played a practical joke at West Point. They trussed up a freshly killed goose (a special dinner treat), and Gibson staggered into the barracks, wielding a bloody knife, and announced that one of the professors wasn't going to bother him any more. He flung the goose at the single candle, and in the dark, the horrified classmates took the object for the professor's head.

Poe was more than managing—he was excelling. And socially, as another cadet put it, if Poe had made no lasting friends, he had also made no enemies, and he was generally on good terms with his classmates. On the home front, John Allan remarried, and his new wife took a quick, deep dislike to Poe.

The writing on the wall was visible a mile away. The man Poe claimed had "taken a fancy" to him when he was orphaned, who practically begged the grandfather, General Poe, for permission to adopt him, was opening himself up to an entirely new family—one that might seem more worthy of all those Galt millions. Poe was right. He had only ever been mistaken in thinking Allan would leave him any inheritance. His own prospects looked murky. Was the U.S. Army a smart move—even as an officer—for a young man with no prospects and no hopes of an inheritance? The cadet decided it wasn't, and—spurred on by a growing sense of his own destiny as a writer—he decided to leave West Point.

Easier said than done.

Getting Expelled

Apparently there was no simple way of getting out—no cordial packing up and waving goodbye—and a cadet couldn't leave unless he was dismissed. After all the uncharacteristic effort John Allan had put into getting Poe an appointment, the cadet told Allan he was leaving. It was a move really descriptive of his later tale, "Imp of the Perverse," which argues an element in man that makes him act contrary to his own self-interest. Allan was uncommunicative. So Poe made himself an unfolding, living narrative by doing whatever he needed to get court-martialed and dismissed from West Point. The plot was uncomplicated. Apparently if a cadet failed to show up for roll calls, formations, drills, classes, and—oh, yes—church, these were grounds for dismissal.

He thought he had earned his way into the military academy, not taking Allan's efforts into account, but now he could honestly claim that he had earned his way out. Poe was court-martialed and dismissed, and on February 19, 1831—one month after his twenty-second birthday—Poe returned forever to civilian life, with mere cents in his pocket. It was an omen of his future as a professional writer in the United States.

Chapter 5

Finding Family

After years of difficulties with his foster father, Edgar Allan Poe found both an emotional and actual haven in Baltimore with Poe family members. There he experienced the tireless devotion of his Aunt Maria and her young daughter, Virginia—who would later became his wife. No longer a boy and without John Allan to support him, Poe entered the real world with only a keen sense of literature to help guide him.

Three Clemms Plus Three Poes

Eddie, Sissy, and Muddy formed the little constellation that brought Edgar Allan Poe the greatest happiness in all of his forty years. Poe first stayed with his Poe relatives when he interviewed for West Point in Washington, D.C., and shopped around his poetry. There he met with Secretary of War John Henry Eaton, who told him there were ten applicants ahead of Poe on the waiting list for West Point, but that he was confident a place would open up. Poe went to his Baltimore Poe relatives again in 1831, broke and homeless, expelled from West Point. Just how far Poe got on the twenty-four cents in his pocket when he left the military academy is a mystery, but he managed to show up in Baltimore at the home of a hard-pressed assortment of Poe relatives.

Now that he was homeless, Richmond seemed closed to him, and he needed a place to stay on a long-term basis. What he found was the only unconditional welcome he ever really received: five Poes living in cramped quarters on the top floor of a "doll's house" in Baltimore. The practical head of house was his aunt, Maria Clemm, a widow with two young children, Henry and Virginia. Elizabeth Poe, Poe's paternal grandmother, was also on hand—as well as his own brother, William Henry Leonard Poe, who had been living with their grandparents since 1811, when Edgar was taken into the Allan home.

they said...

"...men praise him as the "patron" of Edgar Poe. To my eyes he committed a grievous wrong. When he had once assumed the responsibility of this boy, it was his duty to carry it through ... It was ... [cruel] to cast him, defenseless as he was, upon the hard bosses of the world.... if this youth had become such a monster, he had been ripened under the very eye of his guardian."—Novelist Elizabeth Oakes Smith on John Allan

It was like the Micawber household in *David Copperfield*: poor, crowded, busy, and uncomplaining. Suddenly the dashing, extraordinary Edgar—grandson, nephew, cousin, brother—joined them. He found a place where acceptance was instantaneous. Unlike his status under John Allan's sizeable roof, with Aunt Maria—"Muddy"—there was nothing cold, ambiguous, or merely dutiful.

He had a family.

Henry and the Eighty-Dollar Debt

By the time Eliza died in December of 1811, her older son, who went by Henry, was already living with his paternal grandparents, the illustrious "General" and his wife. Rosalie, just an infant at the time of the mother's death, was taken in by a fine Richmond family, the Mackenzies, who kept and supported her until they lost their money in the Civil War—more than fifty years.

But who were Henry and Rosalie? What kind of relationships did these three children of actress Eliza Poe have with each other? Henry grew up in Baltimore, and although it's only 150 miles away from Richmond, access to his brother and sister there wasn't easy. Especially because Frances Allan, worried the Poe grandparents might make a claim on Poe and take him away from her, discouraged it. The great distance of five years in England helped the separation, but when the Allans returned to Richmond and the boys were older, the brothers managed to see each other twice by 1825.

> "I was in a most uncomfortable situation—without one cent of money—in a strange place & so quickly engaged in difficulties after the serious misfortunes which I have just escaped—My grandmother is extremely poor & ill (paralytic)[.] My aunt Maria if possible still worse & Henry entirely given up to drink & unable to help himself, much less me—"—Poe, thanking John Allan for some cash upon his first visit to his Poe relatives

Henry Poe, by all accounts, was a pale shadow of his brilliant younger brother—like the two William Wilsons Edgar later described in his famous story about the murder of a man's conscience. Both Poe brothers were pale, slender, dark-haired, graceful. But it was Edgar who carried himself with style. In Henry, it all came off as weak. Like his brother, Henry was a writer, but he wrote far less than Edgar, and nothing more than the conventional stuff of the day. His poems and travel accounts were published, along with a story called "The Pirate." These he drew from his extensive travels—on this score, Henry topped his brother—probably through a stint in the Merchant Marines. He had ports of call in places as far away as South America, the Near East, the West Indies, and the Mediterranean.

fact

Once the brothers reestablished their relationship, they shared "material" with each other, and may even have put their names to each other's work. Whether Henry had Edgar's permission to palm off some of Edgar's poems as his own is unclear, but nothing interfered with their good will, and their reunion as housemates under Maria Clemm's roof—until Henry's death, which was just five months after Edgar arrived after his expulsion from West Point.

Poe had trouble with alcohol and wrestled with it throughout his adult life; Henry, like their father David, was an alcoholic and already in sorry shape when Poe joined the family in Baltimore. He died in August 1831, possibly of tuberculosis or cholera. Ironically, the only "inheritance" Poe had from his brother Henry was a very unwelcome eighty-dollar debt. As the new "head of household," Poe became legally responsible for Henry's debts—and when he couldn't make good on the eighty dollars, Henry's creditors had Poe jailed. With no other alternative, he wrote repeatedly to his foster father, John Allan, for help. Finally, it came.

But not before Poe sat in jail for five weeks.

The Mystery of Rosalie Poe

Rosalie Mackenzie Poe—like the Allans, her foster parents added the family name when they had her baptized—made no travels, wrote no poetry, and had no real prospects for an independent adulthood. Like Poe, Rosalie was raised in Richmond. Although Rosalie outlived her brothers, dying in a church home when she was sixty-four years old, apparently she never progressed beyond the developmental age of a twelve-year-old. By all accounts, she was a plain, simple, affectionate sister who actually played with their little cousin Virginia, who was fifteen years younger. She loved and baffled Poe, who would often try to figure out why she wore hairstyles and dresses so out of fashion.

fact

Once, when he was reciting "The Raven" by popular demand at a gathering, Rosalie came up and sat on his lap at a point in the poem that pretty much equated her presence there with the birds above the "chamber door." The guests loved it. Poe was tolerant, and quipped that he'd take her along next time to act out the part of the raven.

It was Rosalie Poe—and not her brothers—who came with a mystery attached. Who was her father? There's certainly some doubt it was David Poe, Jr., who was apparently gone from the family a year before Rosalie was born. The inference is that Eliza Poe's "compromising letters" that came into John Allan's hands suggest an alternative paternity. The rumor at the time was that the handsome young actor John Howard Payne was the father. Payne was performing in Boston with Eliza at the time, but he spent the next twenty years on the London stage. If he was the father, it's possible he never even knew. His theatrical career eventually included writing for the stage, but Payne has two more remarkable high points in his successful life. He was the first American consul to Tunis and he wrote that enormously popular sentimental hit song, "Home Sweet Home."

55

The Devoted Muddy

Maria "Muddy" Clemm was a big, solid, nurturing type. As the need demanded, she took in lodgers, worked as a dressmaker, and even begged, writing discreet, baleful letters to any acquaintance she thought might come through. Muddy, that antithesis of the slight lovelies who died their way out of mothering Poe (Eliza, Jane Stanard, Frances), was his mainstay. She outlived all her children—including her Eddie and all her charges, dying in 1871 in the Baltimore Church Home and Hospital (where Eddie had also died). She had exhausted the largesse of friends and moved on, poor to the last.

Maria Poe Clemm, Mother-in-Law of Edgar Allan Poe

Reproduction of Daguerreotype, 1916

No one was more devoted to Poe than his Aunt Maria, "Muddy." Muddy deeply believed in Poe's talent and prospects, and offered what practical support she could by keeping the home front up and running, even on others' "gifts."

Virginia Clemm, the cousin Poe always called Sissy, was thirteen years younger than he, making her eight years old at the time he relocated to Baltimore after his West Point stint. Muddy's other child, Henry, is listed in the 1830 census but disappears after that.

"I am Ugly Enough"

There are eight known, authentic daguerreotypes of Poe, in addition to a few other painted and engraved likenesses. The originals are housed in several places—university libraries, historical societies, museums—and some have disappeared, presumably into private (and in one case, larcenous) collections. What's interesting is how varied even these photographic likenesses of him are. He parts his hair on the left, he parts his hair on the right. He has a trim mustache, he has no mustache. Long sideburns or none. In this respect, Poe doesn't differ too much from his contemporaries: look at photos, over many years, of Longfellow, Lowell, and Whitman and you'd swear they're a dozen different men instead of three. Portraiture was infrequent and formal, and the poses were not always natural or characteristic—or comfortable!

An undated portrait of Poe

But there's something about the vicissitudes in Poe portraits that seem somewhat annoying—as if you want to see someone, final, plain, indisputable portrait of him. Doesn't matter if Walt Whitman has a nimbus of white beard floating up around his face in one picture and bare cheeks and slouchy mustache in another. With Poe, you always want unequivocal answers, almost in direct contrast to his teases, mysteries, hoaxes, horrors—all his literary tricks that keep him disturbingly mysterious.

Poe's Portraits

One woodcut portrait in particular bewildered Poe. It showed a man lounging in a chair, looking fierce and supercilious. "I am ugly enough God knows, but not quite so bad as that!" he wrote to a friend. Six months later he was still scratching his (dark, wavy-haired) head about the same likeness, telling James Russell Lowell that it ". . . does not convey the faintest idea of my person." The following year finds him complaining once again to Lowell that the latest engraved portrait of him "scarcely resembles me at all"—nice to know, since the fellow depicted looks drowsy and dim-witted.

> ## fact
>
> Ironically, one of the earlier known likenesses of Poe was an engraving derived from an oil painting by Samuel Stillman Osgood, husband of one of Poe's "amours," Fanny. Osgood painted Poe around 1845, when he was thirty-six years old. Although mystery about the relationship between Poe and Fanny still swirls, Osgood himself contributed to the instability of the marriage by his own extramarital interests.

From the daguerreotypes and watercolor portraits, at least, you can get a general impression of Poe's looks. The man who was also known as The Raven has intense eyes, a tight expression, a broad forehead, and dark hair. The famous "Ultima Thule"—so called by his friend and romantic interest Helen Whitman, who found it a tragic likeness of a man pushed up against his Ultimate Limits— portrait of Poe is regularly chosen for book jackets and mugs and t-shirts because it seems to satisfy ideas about a suffering artist: his mustache is ragged, his mouth droopy, his eyes droopy in the other direction, his whole expression lopsided, pinched, vulnerable. This is the picture that has led a recent researcher to conclude that Poe was suffering from carbon monoxide poisoning. Is he drugged, demented, dying? Is what you're seeing the effects of too much grief, poverty, alcohol? For sure, it's a raw, provocative picture. What you have to dig deeper to discover, though,

Poe's "Ultima Thule" portrait Daguerreotype by W.S. Hartshorn, Providence, Rhode Island, November, 1848

is that it was taken in Providence, Rhode Island, just four days after he attempted suicide with an overdose of laudanum. Poe actually walked into a portrait studio to commemorate the ravages.

Eye of the Beholder

Firsthand accounts of Poe's general appearance throughout his life make fascinating reading. What's interesting is how divergent the observations are by people who actually knew him. There are some points of agreement, but on the topic of his eye color you get reports they were gray, blue, violet, or hazel. On the topic of his complexion, it was fair, it was dark, it was olive. Everyone seems to agree, however, that he was handsome, carried himself well, and had a beautiful voice. Also, his hair was curly. Although he adopted an all-black wardrobe that seemed almost military, some reports have Poe wearing a Panama hat, or a Spanish cloak, or gracefully swinging his hickory walking stick. Others add tantalizing comments about his ladylike hands, or his occasionally twitching upper lip, or—according to Thomas Wentworth Higginson, Emily Dickinson's mentor—that Poe's was "a face no one would feel safe in loving."

question

How tall was Edgar Allan Poe?
Poe himself noted his own height as 5'8".
General Ulysses S. Grant was also 5'8".
In 1840, the average height of a white American male was 5'5½".

Is some ways, a description of another human being almost says more about the describer than the described. Take, for example, the comment of Rufus Griswold, who was Salieri to Poe's Amadeus—a lesser critic, lesser writer, lesser editor. Here's Griswold on Poe's looks, in a famous, vindictive memoir that managed to do a century of harm to Poe. "In person, he was below the middle height, slenderly but compactly formed, and in his better moments, he had in an eminent degree that air of gentlemanliness which men of a lower order seldom succeed in acquiring." Griswold's comment is sly and deprecating, saying in effect it's amazing a creature from a degraded background can achieve so much. But he also literally belittles Poe, recording Poe's 5'8" height as below the middle height. Others, coming later, notice Griswold's attitude and other biographers and critics label him small, slight. Firsthand reports put him at anywhere from 5'6" to 5'8" tall—Muddy believing the first, the doctor who attended him when he died, the second.

Is the Melodrama All on the Inside?

What was the emotional life of the man who wrote about human beings on all sorts of edges? In his stories, you find reckless adventurers on precipices, analytical egotists solving crimes, and passionate egotists committing crimes. There are men and women who are willful and perverse. You find men and women whose emotional bonds are so strong they literally defy death. Poe's poems, too, tell stories—the themes of lost love and premature death are everywhere. But do the stories and poems give you the full picture of Poe? Was he really just writing the biography of his own emotional nature?

Without a doubt he drew from his own experiences to endow his characters with whatever emotional richness they needed for Poe to achieve his desired effect. Take the droll, canny Montresor in "The Cask of Amontillado." To write convincingly of this character's revenge on his enemy, did Poe draw on his private reserves of feelings toward the "literati" who injured him? A convincing story has to take an emotional truth and dramatize it, squeeze it. Maybe

"Of American female writers we must consider her the first. The character of her pen is essentially feminine . . . the delicate yet picturesque handling; the grace, warmth, and radiance; the exquisite and judicious filling in. . ."

—Poe on novelist Catharine Sedgwick, 1835

you assume Poe was no different from his confessional lunatics—how else could he write them?—because it's hard to see where the creator leaves off and the creation begins.

But they do.

Far from being the lunatic, demon, or drug abuser he's been called for more than 150 years, Poe had a small, caring household (cat, wife, mother-in-law included), and a spirit that shunned parties and preferred walks in the country. For a man who lived in major urban areas of early nineteenth-century America, he liked peace and quiet. He had impeccable Southern manners in that period before the nation blew apart in the Civil War, and impeccable artistic integrity. When it came to literature, he was an absolute purist. He had a vision of what lay ahead in the world, and he was determined it would include excellent writing from Americans. All these are true about the man Edgar Allan Poe, but you'd be hard pressed to find those qualities in what he called his "grotesques," those delicious little melodramas about crime and insanity.

Chapter 6

On the Runway of Fashionable Ideas

Poe spent his adult life primarily in four cities—Richmond, Philadelphia, New York, and Baltimore. The political climate of the times was fractious, with Andrew Jackson rallying the common man around him but alienating many in his own party. Poe was taken in by some of the fads of his day, including phrenology, which claimed to detect a person's character based on the feel of his or her scalp.

Before Cheesesteak

After he left West Point, Edgar Allan Poe spent more years in Philadelphia than in any other city. There was a long, uninterrupted stretch between 1838–1844 that was a period of heightened creative activity and a kind of domestic tranquility for Poe. At home—in each of the five houses they rented during this time—were Virginia, Muddy, and the beloved Caterina of the feline persuasion. Poe celebrated their uncommon stability by springing for some more expensive furnishings, including a piano and a harp for Virginia. Within the Poe family walls, life had settled into a daily round of contented housekeeping and writing in the evenings, after Poe returned from his day job.

> **fact**
>
> In 1830, Louis A. Godey started the first successful magazine directed at a female readership, *Godey's Lady's Book*. In addition to its fashion plates, dressmaking patterns, and sheet music for popular songs, it sought articles from the top American writers of the day. Poe published articles and reviews in *Godey's*, and the editors had to run a disclaimer distancing themselves from Mr. Poe's opinions—which had elicited complaints from those who had come to his "notice."

But the Philadelphia scene outside the various Poe family homes was quite different. Maybe it had something to do with its location, bordering Virginia and Maryland, making it more like a crossroads between North and South, both geographically and ideologically. Offshore there was the slave revolt aboard the Spanish ship *Amistad*. Onshore there was Philadelphia. If Boston was the young nation's intellectual hub, Philadelphia was its test kitchen: first public parks, public schools, lightning-rod, volunteer fire department, fire insurance company, workhouse, hospital, medical school, law school, medical clinic for the poor, theater company, scientific institution, North American Arctic expedition, Anti-Slavery Society, and U.S. Congress.

In nearly all things, Philadelphia was in the forefront of progress. Just four months after the Poes moved to Philadelphia in early 1838, an angry mob attacked Pennsylvania Hall, which had just opened as a forum for abolition and other important issues. During the opening ceremonies, abolitionist Angelina Grimké kept speaking while the mob hurled rocks through the windows of the hall. "What would the breaking of every window be? What would the leveling of this Hall be? Any evidence that we are wrong, or that slavery is a good and wholesome institution?" she asked.

The anti-abolitionist riot occurred just two days after Angelina Grimké's wedding, which was a racially integrated affair the local press reproved as too "amalgamated" for their liking. Angelina married Theodore Weld, another prominent abolitionist.

Grimké kept the audience's panic at bay that evening, but three days later, the rioters burned Pennsylvania Hall to the ground. It was four blocks away from the Poes. The day after, the mob burned the Shelter for Colored Orphans. It was here that the abolitionists realized the enemies to their cause weren't only in the South. By 1838, there were an impressive 100,000 members in various local branches of the American Anti-Slavery Society, which was founded in Philadelphia. Now they knew they could expect reactionary violence from Northerners who were threatened by what they perceived as disruptions to the comfortable old social order—less in response to abolition, possibly, than to having the "womenfolk" step out of the parlor and into leadership positions in public forums.

> "The fact is, in efforts to soar above our nature, we invariably fall below it. Your reformist demigods are merely devils turned inside out."—Poe on social reform

Philadelphia was a crucible for invention, innovation, and visionary activities and beliefs. All of it provided stimulation for Poe, who was busy establishing a professional identity. It was in this six-year Philadelphia period that Poe emerged as a literary critic, wrote his favorite ("Ligeia") and best ("Usher") stories, invented the modern detective story, and published his first story collection. But there was not enough work, in either editing or publishing, for Poe to maintain his little family, so he had to pick up stakes and move to New York City in 1844. In America, he believed, "more than in any other region upon the face of the globe to be poor is to be despised." Over the next decade, other writers—tired of a lack of support and the increasing homogenization of ideas—relocated to New York City.

If You Can Make It There . . .

New York, New York. What was the city like, especially in lower Manhattan, where Poe moved in the spring of 1844?

Aside from the two locations far uptown, including the Fordham Cottage, where Virginia eventually died, their New York years were spent in lower Manhattan and Greenwich Village.

Poe and Virginia were two blocks away from Washington Square Park. Just twenty years before Poe and Virginia arrived, the park served as a potter's field—quite an enormous one, really, considering 10,000 yellow fever victims are buried there. A surviving elm near the corners of Waverly Place and Macdougal Street was a hangman's tree for public executions, until 1835 when New York led the young nation in moving executions indoors and away from the public—regardless of whether the mob consisted of the down-and-outers or the elite. By the time the Poes arrived in the heart of Greenwich Village, the cemetery-gallows green space had been dedicated as a public park.

> " . . . their faces are all fashioned of brass, and they carry both their brains and their souls in their pockets." —Poe on the New York City cabbie of the 1840s

Although the park's history as a spot for public rituals was dimming, just a mile away from the Poes to the southeast was a related urban phenomenon known as Five Points. A rough neighborhood teeming with immigrants, Five Points was viewed from the outside as a terrifying "den of iniquity." To residents of Five Points, theirs was a rough-and-tumble working-class neighborhood. Overcrowding and poverty led to violence and crime. There was a drug trade, prostitution, and gambling. The cornerstone of the Five Points neighborhood was the old Brewery, which had become a tenement where, reportedly, a murder occurred every night.

Just a few blocks away was sculptor Anne Lynch's salon on Waverly Place, where the literati gathered—including Poe, until his reputation was so shredded by others' ill will that she closed her doors to him.

they said...

"I must tell you how much pleasure I took in reading your Tales and in knowing that they are a selection from seventy, all of which I hope to read. They are unsurpassed by any stories I have ever read in poetry of language and fire of imagination. More of them when I see you."—Anne Lynch, in a letter to Poe before he fell from her grace, 1845

The "official" start of New York bohemian life in Greenwich Village, where writers, artists, composers, and philosophers would gravitate and try to make a living, was just a few years away. Charlie Pfaff's beer hall at 653 Broadway became the meeting house for America's first countercultural "elite"—including the dead poet-storyteller Poe, that poor but brilliant artist who became the icon for the early set of Greenwich Village bohemians.

The Border State of the Mind

The Baltimore where Poe spent (on and off) fewer than five years living and not quite a week dying was in many subtle ways the true microcosm of pre-Civil War America. In Poe's day, historic Philadelphia, a literary center, was still a headline grabber for many important firsts. Ivy-covered Boston hummed along as the nation's intellectual incubator. Up-and-coming Richmond was emerging as a southern showcase. And New York was, well, New York—a metropolis in the making, the place of the American future, the magnet for artistic endeavors of all sorts, the young financial center—the "boss" of American entrepreneurism. Despite the dramatic class clashes in Philadelphia and the social problems arising from immigrant overcrowding in New York, it was Baltimore, Maryland, that was a kind of diorama of the American character in those decades before the Civil War shattered that pretty glass ornament of the new republic.

fact

Maryland was a border state through and through—a place of dualities of all sorts. Its Great Seal carries the motto, "Strong deeds, gentle words." Its northern boundary (shared with Pennsylvania) is literally on the Mason-Dixon line, drawn in 1767, representative of the North/South cultural divide the line came to symbolize.

Lay of the Land

Maryland is nearly split by Chesapeake Bay, separating the urban areas from the pastoral Eastern Shore. From its beginnings in 1729, Baltimore was a commercial center (shipbuilding was the principal industry), with its large, geographically protected port, and its railways, trafficking in tobacco and grain. Maryland—and Baltimore—were centers of commerce in more than goods. With its history, geography, and population, Maryland was the field for "commerce" in some of the most raw and conflicting ideas of the day.

The British attacked Fort McHenry during the War of 1812 in their attempt to clean out the "pirates" they believed Baltimore harbored. This battle, of course, occasioned Key's poem, "The Star-Spangled Banner." Baltimore was the scene of the first fatalities of the Civil War, when Southern sympathizers confronted a Union regiment. In 1863, the battle of Antietam was the bloodiest single day in the entire war.

Baltimore's Mighty Pens

Baltimore was the nursery for a new generation of writers who internalized the dualities of their place and time. While Poe was still a student, other "men of letters"—men of very different temperaments and tastes—found a home in Baltimore.

Byronic poet Edward Coote Pinkney's Baltimore roots included a father who served in the diplomatic corps. Though his father's career opened a world of possibilities for Pinkney, he eventually gave up Navy life for the role of starving Baltimorean poet. Like the younger Poe, Pinkney was powerfully drawn to the work of Byron, and his own unconventional work did not endear him to an audience of conventional (Southern) sensibilities.

> ## they said...
> "You have a pleasant and prosperous career before you, if you subdue this brooding and boding inclination of your mind. Be cheerful, rise early, work methodically—I mean, at appointed hours. Take regular recreation every day. Frequent the best company only. Be rigidly temperate both in body and mind—and I will ensure you . . . all the success and comfort you covet." —John Pendleton Kennedy to Poe, 1836

Fellow writer John Pendleton Kennedy's newspaper and magazine pieces found favor both north and south of the Mason-Dixon Line. Kennedy's success marked Baltimore as a place friendly to American literary development—and Kennedy himself would become a friend to Poe.

What's the Secret Handshake?

The America of the early nineteenth century was rife with intellectual activity, a loading dock for imported ideas. The cultural fashions of the day were donned, altered, cast aside. Independence from England had been secured two generations earlier, and the memories of that fight were fading as the older generation died away. Now there were all sorts of intriguing new questions to ponder. Some had to do with what the new nation could be, and some had to do with fixing what were already appearing as its mistakes. North/South sectionalism was becoming more noticeable, and the lyceum movement provided a public forum for abolitionist speakers to condemn slaveholding. With the increase in "media outlets," the hot new theories of the day got plenty of attention in newspapers, journals, magazines, and novels. Many of these new ideas centered around issues of sociopolitical philosophy and spirituality. In an age marked by tolerance of spiritual quests and questioning, there were glaring departures from the mainstream.

Poe had internalized none of the early American Calvinistic world view, and despite the Allans' conventional efforts to bring traditional religious faith to their foster child, Poe always seemed more interested in it as a curiosity than as any source of personal comfort or pathway to salvation. The devil, to Poe, was more a folk figure of limitless fun. Poe despised Romantic-era outgrowths like Transcendentalism. In terms of human misery and crime, he was far more interested in abnormal psychology than in the problem of evil. Always the independent loner, he was naturally suspicious of anything that attracted "the mob," even the mob of otherwise thoughtful, reasonable human beings. He didn't need to gravitate toward new ideas that were the product of imaginations other than his own. For him, his own imagination was a renewable resource.

Wear Your Whig Hat on Your Head

With the literal passing away of founding fathers and their immediate heirs, the American political inheritance was up for grabs. In the scramble for power, the political parties during the adulthood of Poe bear little resemblance to the two-party system that exists today. How much did Poe internalize the conflicting political philosophies of his day? Where did he stand? How much did it matter?

> "To declare a thing immoral . . . at all times, is one thing—to declare it immoral on Sunday, and therefore to forbid it on that particular day, is quite another. Why not equally forbid it on Saturday, which is the Sabbath of the Jew?"—Poe on Sunday saloon closings in an article, "Doings of Gotham," 1844

Poe wrote during a period of relative peace, where the War of 1812 was just a memory and secessionist talk had not yet started. Industrialization kept everyone busy, either attending to the possibility of wealth, or just plain earning a livelihood while others got wealthy. Politically, there were concerns about government itself, and the influence of Andrew Jackson began to polarize people. Old Hickory, that backwoods populist war hero, became a force to be reckoned with—and his presidency squared off against the landed aristocracy.

Under Jackson, suffrage increased to include all white males regardless of property ownership. The common (well, common white) man finally had a vote, and he pretty much voted for Andrew Jackson. Jackson absolutely believed in rewarding political loyalty with government jobs, a policy, of course, which consolidated his power. His policies caused a rift in his own party, which fractured and became two separate entities—the Democratic Party, which supported Jackson and the Whig Party, which opposed him.

Poe's Views

The nature of Poe opposed what he called the "democratical mob," and as a Virginian, he was not alone in this belief. The mob had the vote, and the mob was now working in Washington. Where would it all lead? If the western territories became free states, what would happen to the economy and way of life of the South? In Richmond in Poe's day, the emerging Whig Party was a strong force.

Poe contributed to a Whig magazine and was befriended by Whig mentor John Pendleton Kennedy. But Poe, despite some natural sympathies, was not a political activist, not even a political hobbyist. As a fervent artist, he made use of political issues occasionally, but a man absorbed by the rhythmical creation of beauty—no, Beauty—had his eyes locked more on stratosphere than political sphere.

> "I can see no objection to gentlemen 'standing for Congress'—provided they stand on one side—nor to their 'running for Congress'—if they are in a very great hurry to get there—but it would be a blessing if some of them could be persuaded into sitting still, for Congress, after they arrive."—
> Poe on politicians

The Will to Disenchant

When asked about his religious faith, Poe replied, "My faith is indeed my own." No further explanation. He was not a man who allowed what was accepted, unexamined, by the rest of society, into his life. He was too intelligent, solitary, and skeptical not to question the norms. If a church accepted the philandering John Allan, what could it possibly hold for the outraged, outcast Edgar? If a newspaper or a magazine could opportunistically pay a writer too little for the publication of his work—followed by nothing whatsoever for reprinting it—how could it hold itself up as a beacon of enlightened thought?

But if you cast a skeptical eye to your public institutions, where then do you turn your gaze? Poe had no interest in the reform movements of the day. He was an artist juggling his visions of excellence with serious domestic responsibilities. What he saw when he looked around were comfortable platitudes and unshakable complacencies of the entrenched upper classes.

Spiritual reformist zeal must have looked like the handiwork of the idle. Out of his deep, artistic nature, Poe was an adventurer into the "heart of darkness," the human mind, well before psychology became a discipline. He was not alone. Up in New England, Hawthorne identified his own enduring interest in what he called the foul repository of the human heart. Swirling around the greatest American writers of this period is a credulous optimism that must have seemed naive and dangerous to them. They heard others say Utopia was achievable—just go off and form a farming community with a few good friends. If these skeptics, these writers, had a suspicion there could be something self-deluded or self-serving in the advice to be a nonconformist, they could choose civil disobedience, find God in a blade of grass, or believe in their inner poet.

For a man as classically inclined as Poe, who had little use for the "mob" and whatever it swallowed whole, he had a real taste for the pseudoscientific trends—like phrenology and mesmerism—of the day.

> "No doubt, it is a very commendable and very comfortable thing, in the Professor, to sit at ease in his library chair, and write verses instructing the southerners how to give up their all with a good grace, and abusing them if they will not. . . ."—Poe on Longfellow's anti-slavery poems

Feel the Bumps On My Head

Forget bustles! In Poe's day, craniums were all the rage. Well over a century later, all you can do is scratch your cranium in wonder at the phenomenon known as phrenology, that belief that character and mental capability can be "read" in a sort of cranial Braille. The Viennese doctor, Franz-Joseph Gall, who first developed this theory, believed that the surface of the brain hosted twenty-six "organs," each serving as the seat of a mental faculty. Gall had it right in suspecting that mental functions like perception, intellect, emotions, and so on, were located in the brain, but it took quite some time before true scientists were able to discredit the

> "I am not personally acquainted with Judge Upshur; but I have a profound respect for his talents. . . .His head is a model for statuary—Speaking of heads—my own has been examined by several phrenologists—all of whom spoke of me in a species of extravaganza which I should be ashamed to repeat."—Poe to Southern novelist-lawyer-editor Frederick William Thomas on his own phrenological readings, 1841

notion that feeling the bumps on a man's head was either a way of judging his character or predicting his behavior. A highly developed faculty meant a more muscular "organ" which in turn created bumps in the skull over that particular area. A sample of Dr. Gall's taxonomy would include things like "philoprogenitiveness," "marvellousness," "cautionness," and "gustativeness." (Our fingers could expect to find a skull depression over Dr. Gall's own language organ.) A phrenological reading was called a cranioscopy and looked a lot like a good scalp massage.

Poe bought it, and apparently had several readings done.

Poe judged that through "well-directed inquiry, individuals may obtain . . . a perfectly accurate estimate of their own moral capabilities." From there he goes on to say this knowledge is useful in terms of directing an individual toward certain kinds of work. The problem with phrenology, of course—well, one of them—is how deterministic it is. Would an elevation in what Dr. Gall defined as "the murder organ" then mean a bank clerk could expect to move into

"... the surest and truest basis, indeed the only sure basis, of all medical knowledge—A blow legally struck at it, is a vital blow to the best and most important interests of the human family."—Poe, on human dissection, 1840

homicide? And, even more amazingly, would a bump in the skull over "the murder organ" in a man accused of a murder actually be used in evidence against him?

In terms of the "moral capabilities" mentioned by Poe, could he really have believed they were mappable on an individual's cranium? Later in his own century, of course, the field of human psychology emerged—which would have been profoundly interesting to a writer whose work was already taking on the subjects of emotional excesses and aberrant behavior. It was the drama of the mind that attracted Poe.

Chapter 7

The Work Begins

Edgar A. Poe was the first professional American writer, publishing first a volume of poetry and then taking jobs at various magazines to earn a livelihood. His unswerving dedication to this goal of being a professional writer destined him and his family to a life of poverty. Although his professional life was not entirely successful, Poe made friends among his peers and held on tight to his little family, Muddy and Sissy.

I Contain Multitudes

A bold liar? A delusional romancer? A chronic joker? A cruel hoaxer? A creative writer? Which of these was Edgar Allan Poe? If you think all, then ask yourself where those roles overlap. For a writer with a powerful imagination, the boundaries between truth and falsehood become blurred, breached, or erased. In a teller of tales, there is that constant boarder, that writing self working away inside. In "Song of Myself," Walt Whitman, another great nineteenth-century American writer—says, "I am large, I contain multitudes." So did Poe.

The "multitudes" are all the stuff of art—the locations, the ideas, the trappings, and the creatures that collide inside the writer, waiting to be made into art. Sometimes, in the hands of great writers, fiction is just the biography of those who have never lived.

> "The true genius shudders at incompleteness—imperfection—and usually prefers silence to saying the something which is not every thing that should be said. . . . Sometimes, dashing into a subject, he blunders, hesitates, stops short, sticks fast, and, because he has been overwhelmed by the rush and multiplicity of his thoughts, his hearers sneer at his inability to think."—
> *Poe on listening to genius, 1848*

Sometimes fiction is a form of autobiography. Was Walt Whitman born in the South, as he says in one place, or on Long Island—or somewhere else? How can he say he heard a story about the Mexican War told in Texas, when it's a place he never visited? Whitman, who was ten years younger than Poe, became all things on the page. Poe stepped off the page. Some of his fabrications came directly out of his insecurity—son and heir to John Allan, distinguished graduate of the University of Virginia, high-ranking military grandfather—but others came out of a belief that you can be anyone you choose to be, even under different names. In the expansionist America of the early 1800s, whom did Poe have in mind? What persona was he shooting for? Probably a New World version of Lord Byron, but there were already plenty of those. Coming as he did from a strong theater background—his poetry and tales have a rich theatricality about them—he played the part of Edgar A. Poe, Henri Le Rennet, and Edgar A. Perry exceptionally well.

For Whitman and Poe—not to mention Hawthorne's dark villages or Melville's watery wildernesses—the great metaphor for the first half of the nineteenth century in the United States was expansion. Spreading out. Making discoveries. Confronting the wild. What's outside that firelit circle of the known world, the parlors of Boston, the shipyards of New York, the stables of Virginia? For Whitman, everything outside that circle was beloved and celebrated. There was no such thing as the unknown, just the unsung. For Poe, what lay beyond that firelit circle was a shadowy figure, a worthy adversary, someone beckoning him out of that safe, lighted precinct. Himself.

First Published Story

In the spring of 1831, the Philadelphia *Saturday Courier* ran a story contest for a $100 prize and publication. In advertising their noble objective as the "Cause of LITERATURE," the newspaper showed a giddy enthusiasm for what the young Poe must have hoped was excellence. Poe submitted "Metzengerstein" and four other stories to the contest. None of the five won—in fact, the winner was a piece called "Love's Martyr" by Delia Bacon, chosen for what the editors called its "taste, genius and feeling."

Although "Love's Martyr" edged out Poe's entries, throughout the year the newspaper went on to publish them all—without paying the writer and probably even without notifying him. Commonly, work submitted to a contest for publication, regardless of the outcome, was then considered the property of the sponsoring newspaper. Later on, Poe took up the cause of protecting authors against this kind of loss of their rights to their own work. As a man determined to make a living as a professional writer in the United States, financial hardship politicized him. By the time the International Copyright law was enacted in 1898, he had been dead for fifty years.

Although none of his entries won the *Courier's* contest, they were the first of Poe's tales in print. They displayed some of the themes and interests of his later work, and his distinctive voice is also clear. "Horror and fatality have been stalking abroad in all ages," he begins "Metzengerstein." "Why then give a date to the story I have to tell?" It tells the story of a vicious young Hungarian lord who engineers the violent death of his hereditary enemy.

fact

Delia Bacon, a well-educated Connecticut scholar and educator of young women, was one of the first scholars to question the authorship of Shakespeare's plays. For a limited time, she even persuaded Emerson that Shakespeare was not one but several men. Hawthorne, who considered her gifted, rescued her from destitution and later recounted how she lost her mind while researching her Shakespeare theory in England.

Poe describes the ascent of the wicked young Baron Metzengerstein: "Upon the succession of a proprietor so young, with a character so well known, to a fortune so unparalleled, little speculation was afloat in regard to his probable course of conduct. And, indeed, for the space of three days, the behavior of the heir, out-heroded Herod, and fairly surpassed the expectations of his most enthusiastic admirers. Shameful debaucheries—flagrant treacheries—unheard-of atrocities—gave his trembling vassals quickly to understand, that no servile submission on their part—no punctilios of conscience on his own were, thenceforward, to prove any protection against the bloodthirsty and remorseless fangs of a petty Caligula."

In this first published tale, Poe worked with what would become some of his favorite materials: the first person narrator; a sense of timeless horror; the grab-the-reader-by-the-collar opening; and a philosophical, organizing idea he explores fictionally (here, the idea that human souls can set up shop in animals' bodies). In this first published tale, there are the "high Gothic" leavening: castles, blood feuds, florid descriptions; and a walloping dose of the supernatural—retribution, galloping across the page in the form of an avenging horse.

they said...

"If we were merely to say that we had read them, it would be a compliment, for manuscripts of this kind are very seldom read by anyone but the author. We have read these tales every syllable, with the greatest pleasure, and for originality, richness of imagery and purity of the style, few American authors in our opinion have produced any thing superior. . . ."—Review of Poe's stories in 1832 edition of the Baltimore *Saturday Visiter*

The First First Prize

What Philadelphia didn't give Poe in 1831, Baltimore did in 1833. But even this win wasn't uncomplicated.

The prize winning "MS. Found in a Bottle" begins with the usual arresting Poe prose: "Of my country and of my family I have little to say. Ill usage and length of years have driven me from the one, and estranged me from the other." The epigraph is French, and while it doesn't lay out the whole of Poe's underlying idea here, it does defend the narrator's honesty: "Who has no more than a moment to live has nothing more to dissemble." In other words: Why would I lie? The "writer" of the manuscript found in a bottle describes the immediate aftermath of a shipwreck: "By what miracle I escaped destruction, it is impossible to say. Stunned by the shock of the water, I found myself, upon recovery, jammed in between the sternpost and rudder. With great difficulty I gained my feet, and looking dizzily around, was, at first, struck with the idea of our being among breakers; so terrific, beyond the wildest imagination, was the whirlpool of mountainous and foaming ocean within which we were engulfed. After a while, I heard the voice of an old Swede, who had shipped with us at the moment of our leaving port. I hallooed to him with all my strength, and presently he came reeling aft. We soon discovered that we were the sole survivors of the accident. All on deck, with the exception of ourselves, had been swept overboard; — the captain and mates must have perished as they slept, for the cabins were deluged with water." The story is a tight, clever little tale that offers an original spin on "crossing over" to the underworld. No gondolier Charon, no River Styx for Poe. It is all supernatural shipwreck.

Edgar had submitted six tales from what he called his Folio Club collection—a collection that never made it into print in the final form he wanted—plus one poem, "The Coliseum," to a contest sponsored by the Baltimore *Saturday Visiter.* Apparently the judges initially decided Poe had won both contests, fiction and poetry, but then changed their minds, feeling such a "sweep" by one writer would be misunderstood by the readers. So they went ahead and awarded Poe the prize for fiction, and punted on the poetry prize, naming instead a poem submitted by John Hill Hewitt as the winner.

Hewitt was the editor of the Baltimore Saturday *Visiter.*

they said...

"... the author owes it to his own reputation, as well as to the gratification of the community, to publish the entire volume, (The Tales of the Folio Club). These tales are eminently distinguished by a wild, vigorous, and poetical imagination—a rich style, a fertile invention—and varied and curious learning."—The judges of the Baltimore Saturday *Visiter* contest, explaining why they chose Poe's "MS. Found in a Bottle," as the winner of the fiction prize, 1835

By this time, Poe was living in Baltimore in a household with an assortment of Clemms and Poes, and the prize money was welcome. But it must have been painful to the young writer to know that he had technically swept both categories, only to have one win—plus the prize money—snatched away. Hewitt later told an anecdote about being accosted on the street by the legitimate prizewinner, who asserted, "You have used underhanded means, sir, to obtain that prize over me." Outraged, Poe went on to accuse Hewitt of being an ungentlemanly cheat, at which point Hewitt punched him. Whether Hewitt had ladled on some of his own moonshine, who knows, but the incident does seem to touch on Poe's characteristically passionate response to what he deemed the unfair advancement of inferior artists. What he may have earned in addition to the fifty-dollar prize for "MS. Found in a Bottle" may have been a sock in the nose. However, a definite perk was the friendship of one of the judges, John Pendleton Kennedy, a novelist.

The Right Advice at the Right Time

John Pendleton Kennedy was fourteen years older than Poe and filled the father-figure vacancy nicely when Poe was twenty-four and all but estranged from John Allan. Kennedy was a man whose curriculum vitae read like the careers of several men. He was a practicing lawyer who was elected to Congress, where he served as Speaker of the House. As secretary of the navy in the Fillmore administration, he was instrumental in supporting expeditions to Japan and the Arctic. To no surprise, Kennedy was also interested in education—he consulted in the affairs of the University of Maryland. With whatever free time he managed to find in the lives he lived, he wrote four novels that received a fair amount of critical praise.

Kennedy, a man known for his kind and generous nature, recognized talent in Poe, and gave him both practical and moral support early on. Finally, it wasn't so much Kennedy's influence that helped the struggling Poe as his plain good advice. Although he approached his own Philadelphia publisher on Poe's behalf, the result was disappointing. Hard to sell a book of tales, they thought, but Mr. Poe should consider sending out his stories individually to magazines. No promises, but it might result in getting his name before the reading public.

It did.

Kennedy was a consistently supportive friend during this early period of professional (and emotional) uncertainty in Poe's life. It was through Kennedy's efforts that publisher Thomas White gave Poe an editorship at the *Southern Literary Messenger*, effectively launching what became his critical/editorial career—bringing with it a small but reliable income. But even Kennedy's influence wasn't a magic wand over the career of Poe. Poe's tales were considered brilliant but kind of odd and distasteful—and a book's worth of them was a hard sell for several years. Even after Kennedy's Philadelphia publisher issued an edition, it was unenthusiastic about any reprints. For Poe, no door was ever flung open. Openings came in inches only. Novelist and Congressman John Pendleton Kennedy came at a time when help was essential.

they said...

"Mr. Kennedy accompanied him to a clothing store, and purchased for him a respectable suit, with changes of linen, and sent him to a bath, from which he returned with the suddenly regained bearing of a gentleman."—Rufus Griswold, Poe's executor, describing (with dubious accuracy) the first meeting of Poe and John Pendleton Kennedy, 1849

Poe Finds a Bride

The combined Poe-Clemm household chugged along nicely until change inevitably intruded. John Allan died in 1834 and left his erstwhile foster son entirely out of his will. Poe's grandmother, Elizabeth Poe, died in July 1835. The pension she received, a crucial bit of money for the family, disappeared. Poe also removed himself from the household, taking a job with the *Southern Literary Messenger* in Richmond. He could do little but watch as another cousin, Nielson Poe, took a shine to Virginia and made some overtures about having her and her mother come to live with him. Neilson could offer more stability and a chance for Virginia to "come out" into society.

Edgar, who was still grappling with the prospect of an adulthood that was stretching out before him with relentless bills and an unstable professional writing career, panicked at the possibility of losing Sissy and Muddy, the only daily, emotional security in his life. From Richmond, he pleaded his case to Muddy in a letter, declaring, "I love Virginia passionately devotedly," apparently not even taking time to punctuate. What he says next is revealing: "I cannot express in words the fervent devotion I feel towards my little cousin. . . ." To Virginia herself he added: ". . . my own sweetest Sissy, my darling little wifey, think well before you break the heart of your cousin. . . ."

Poe prevailed, calling her his "wifey" before she even knew what was being offered.

Edgar Allan Poe and Virginia Eliza Clemm were married in a secret ceremony in 1835. A couple of sources claim Poe and Virginia lived together platonically for a full two years before they consummated their marriage. This first ceremony was secret because there were other family members who objected—apparently not to her age, but possibly to her choice!

fact

During Virginia's lifetime, Poe wrote no poems for her, and she "never read half" his poetry. About a year before she died, Poe had occasion to write to Virginia while he was out of town on business: ". . . My little darling wife you are my greatest and only stimulus now, to battle with this uncongenial, unsatisfactory and ungrateful life—"

As if the secrecy of that first ceremony in the fall of 1835 wasn't interesting enough, apparently the happy couple claimed Virginia was twenty-one—even though there was no law at that time against a thirteen-year-old marrying. Half a year later—she still wasn't even fourteen—they repeated the vows, this time publicly, with Poe's boss at the *Southern Literary Messenger* as witness. A double dose of marriage vows for the insecure Poe. Virginia continued to be a dark, ethereal, sweet, big-eyed, and all-accepting presence in his life—out on the street together (not in the society Neilson Poe had offered), Poe was all drama and Sissy pure understatement. She was his first audience as he read his new work in the evenings.

fact

An early Poe biographer kept Virginia's bones under his bed after the Fordham cemetery was destroyed, later donating them for reburial next to Poe. It wasn't until 1885, a full ten years after the rededication of Poe's grave, that Virginia's remains were interred with her husband's and mother's. Visitors to the graves are welcome daily from 8 A.M. to dusk. What used to be the Westminster Church is now a hall available for private events.

Poe's love for Virginia Clemm was as constant as his often self-destructive determination to work in nineteenth-century America as a professional writer. These two things—his work and his Sissy—got right to the essence of Poe. It was a complicated relationship, but all of his relationships were complicated, and at least the unlikely "domestic goddesses" of Muddy and Sissy provided him with a peaceful home.

Chapter 8

Filling the Pen with Prussic Acid

Journals and magazines provided natural "day jobs" for Poe, cut off from any inheritance. But his editorial work provided him with a forum for America's first real literary criticism. Not everybody was happy about it. Poe harbored a desire for his own literary magazine, a showcase for none but the best in contemporary literature. It was a dream that never came to fruition for several reasons, most of them having to do with Poe himself.

The Day Job

Poe had to support not only himself but his Clemm relatives, Muddy and Virginia, with whom he was establishing a household. In other words, Poe needed a "day job," and editorial work suited his temperament and his talents—it even sharpened them.

they said...

"... he seems sometimes to mistake his phial of prussic-acid for his ink-stand. If we do not always agree with him in his premises, we are, at least, satisfied that his deductions are logical, and that we are reading the thoughts of a man who thinks for himself, and says what he thinks, and knows well what he is talking about."—James Russell Lowell on Poe, 1845

Poe worked as an editor in each of the major cities where he lived—Richmond, Philadelphia, New York—except for Baltimore. By 1836, when he was hired as editor of the *Southern Literary Messenger* in Richmond, Poe had published three volumes of poetry and won first prize for his story "MS. Found in a Bottle"—all good credentials. His editorship of the *Southern Literary Messenger*, for which his boss Thomas Willis White paid him a salary of $800 a year, led to his opening salvo against the "literati" of New York and Boston.

In his position as the reviewer of new work, he started to develop critical theories and standards of literary excellence. He started to figure out what he valued. His critical essays ultimately constituted a large part of his authorship—and contribution to classic American literature. They are also probably the single best place to enjoy his dry, droll, and often corrosive sense of humor. His attacks against mediocre writers are downright funny. It was Poe who was really the first American literary critic and theorist.

Poe generously applauded fellow writers whose work he admired. He recognized the worth in a book called *Watkins Tottle*, praising the mysterious author, Boz: ". . . we know nothing more than that he is a far more pungent, more witty, and better disciplined writer of sly articles, than nine-tenths of the Magazine writers in Great Britain—which is saying much, it must be allowed, when we consider the great variety of genuine talent, and earnest application brought to bear upon the periodical literature of the mother country," Poe wrote. Little did he know that Boz was none other than Charles Dickens.

"Mr. Mathews once wrote some sonnets 'On Man,' and Mr. Channing some lines on 'A Tin Can,' or something of that kind—and if the former gentleman be not the very worst poet that ever existed on the face of the earth, it is only because he is not quite so bad as the latter. To speak algebraically:—Mr. M. is execrable, but Mr. C. is x plus 1-ecrable."—Poe on Cornelius Mathews and William Ellery Channing

The End of Editing

The cycle of hard work and poverty was already beginning, and Poe became dissatisfied with his salary. Boss and publisher Tom White had his own troubles: health problems, labor problems, and a sense that he was losing control of the *Messenger*. Besides, against a backdrop of a rising temperance movement, Poe's occasional lapses made White nervous, and Poe "retired" from his job.

they said…

"No man is safe who drinks before breakfast! No man can do so, and attend to business properly."—Thomas Willis White, to Poe after dismissing him for drunkenness, 1835

Most of 1837 and half of 1838 found Poe and his family struggling in New York, with little documentary evidence to shed much light on that period in their lives. They boarded with a bookseller, but aside from publishing one story, one poem, and a review of a travelogue, it isn't clear how Poe earned a living. It's likely he was working on *The Narrative of Arthur Gordon Pym*, which was published in 1838. By the time the Poe family relocated to Philadelphia, he was despairing of earning a living as a writer, and there's some suggestion that he tried his hand at printing and lithography. Finally, he found steady work in a literary field, and from 1839 to 1842 Poe was one of the editors of what began as Burton's *Gentleman's Magazine* and ended as *Graham's Magazine*.

His job was not uninterrupted.

His boss, Billy Burton, was a hearty sort of man, a comic actor, a theater manager—finally, a magazine publisher, making his Burton's the *GQ* of his day. Burton was a businessman, and he defended Poe's poor salary by claiming financial troubles.

fact

In one of his many articles on cryptography, Poe insists that secret writing is "an excellent exercise for mental discipline" with real significance for the general, the statesman, the traveler, the scholar—and the lover. In fact, the two cryptograms Poe published in 1840 in *Graham's* defied deciphering until 1992 and 2000—more than 150 years later!

The quality (or lack thereof) of American literature was a never-ending frustration for Poe. He continued to brandish his pen at second-rate American writers while being compelled to contribute gossip to the pages of *Burton's*. Billy Burton—who probably tired of handling his maverick editor, no matter how much his "prussic acid" reviews increased the magazine's circulation—actually sold the publication out from under Poe to George Rex Graham, publisher of the *Saturday Evening Post*. Graham hired Poe back at a higher salary than Burton had given him—and gave him an assistant, as well.

Although the money and the work were better, Poe became disgusted with what he called the "namby-pamby" nature of *Graham's*. During his tenure as its editor, the circulation of the magazine soared. His efforts lined the pockets of George Rex Graham, but Poe—once again—felt exploited. Finally, he left.

they said...

"'[we note] the arrival at St. Marks, of 33 Cuba bloodhounds. While the vessel was at sea, the cook having slaughtered a pig, the dogs, excited by the smell of the blood, broke from their confinement . . . and kept possession of the deck for several hours before they could be pacified.'"—*Charleston Courier*. Newspapers printed a sensationalized story stating that the dogs had devoured all the passengers. Poe referred to the *Courier's* version to set the record straight.

In Philadelphia, Poe met George Lippard, a young journalist who, like Poe, wanted to do more than pen newspaper articles. In a period that was a kind of "foothills" to the major literary epoch of Emerson, Thoreau, Whitman, Hawthorne, Poe, Melville, and Dickinson, George Lippard's work is overshadowed. He appreciated what was great in Poe, and his own best-known work in Gothic novels shows he and Poe were compatible creatures in terms of those artistically stimulating dark corners of human existence. Despite this, Lippard received only tepid encouragement from his idol regarding his literary efforts. Lippard's stories and novels were some of the most popular writings in their time, but they did not survive into subsequent centuries. Lippard remained a staunch supporter of Poe up to the end. In a spirited obituary after Poe's death, Lippard remembered his friend as "a harsh, a bitter and sometimes an unjust critic. But he was a man of genius—a man of high honor—a man of good heart."

By 1844, Poe and the family lived in Greenwich Village, and he became co-editor of the *Evening Mirror*—where "The Raven" appeared and launched the writer who had been working in the literary trenches for a dozen years already. He moved over to the *Broadway Journal* as editor, but by late in 1846, Poe, the dark darling of literary circles—with all the wrangling personal intrigues that came out of his fame—finished up his final editorship anywhere. What he wanted was a magazine of his own.

Tomahawk Man

When a caricature of Poe appeared in *Holden's Dollar Magazine* in January 1849, Poe had already been doing hatchet jobs on mediocre American writers for a dozen years. No surprise, then, that the caricature by Felix Darley depicts Poe in silhouette with a war bonnet, brandishing a dagger in one hand and a tomahawk in the other, nearly dancing with critical glee. It was a reflection of Poe's status in the world of literary criticism—a Tomahawk Man.

Poe already knew Darley's work from 1843, when the artist illustrated Poe's story "The Gold-Bug." The caricature in *Holden's* came just nine months before Poe died in Baltimore, and Poe was coming fresh off the pre-marital merry-go-round of failed romances. It was a time of tiresome and infuriating personal intrigues for Poe, who was always just trying to make a dollar—at that time, lecturing. A little verse accompanied the silhouette, lionizing Poe as both a writer and a critic.

Poed

Poe earned a reputation for his critical harshness, but there were times when he went off the critical rails, overvaluing the work of writers whose reputations barely made it out of that decade, let alone the nineteenth century. For sheer fun you have to hear a sample of Poe at work on what was both second-rate and unfairly praised—and, for the perpetual struggler, maddeningly successful. With these folks, he was merciless.

What Mark Twain later does on the subject of "Fenimore Cooper's Literary Offenses," Poe does in 1835 on the publication of a highly anticipated novel, *Norman Leslie*, by Theodore Fay, the editor of the *Evening Mirror*—and a member of the New York literary circle. Over several pages, Poe pricks every bit of puffery in this novel, then adds, "For a page or two we are entertained with a prospect of a conspiracy, and have great hopes that the principal characters in the plot will so far oblige us as to cut one another's throats," but Fay fails to deliver, excusing his characters' unfathomable actions by calling them "veiled in impenetrable mystery."

they said...

"My Dear Mr. Poe,—I thank you for your very kind notice of my poems, no less than for your kind and friendly note. . . . But I am exceedingly pained at the desponding tone in which you write. Life is too short . . . to give one time to *despair*. Exorcise that devil, I beg of you, as speedily as possible."—New York literary salon hostess Anne Lynch to Poe, 1845

On the novel *Stanley Thorn* by Henry Cockton, Poe distinguishes between " . . . men who can think but who dislike thinking; and . . . men who either have not been presented with the materials for thought, or who have no brains with which to 'work up' the material. With these classes of people 'Stanley Thorn' is a favorite. It not only demands no reflection, but repels it."

Critical Rants

Poe dismissed *Joseph Rushbrook, or the Poacher*, a novel by Captain Marryatt, quite succinctly. "Its English is excessively slovenly. Its events are monstrously improbable," Poe wrote in his review. Marryatt was significantly more long-winded; *Joseph Rushbrook* rambled on for fifty-one chapters in two bound volumes.

In his critique of *Zinzendorff, and other Poems* by Mrs. L. H. Sigourney, Poe complained, ". . . when the noble river is bedizzened out in robes of silver, and made to wash with its bright waters nothing better than curtains of velvet, we feel a very sensible and a very righteous indignation. We might have expected such language from an upholsterer . . ."

Although not all of the victims of Tomahawk Man were American, Poe tended to be especially tough on his American contemporaries. Jealousy? Probably not, because no one was quicker to appreciate truly fine work. He was tough because he

> *"What do they know about Shakespeare? They worship him—rant about him—lecture about him—about him, him and nothing else—for no other reason than that he is utterly beyond their comprehension. . . . As for their own opinion about him—they really have none at all.—Poe on Shakespeare, or really, Shakespeare worship*

deplored the provincialism he saw in the literature of the new republic. He wanted to cultivate reading tastes and high-quality literary artistry among American writers. He was after a kind of delayed, follow-up revolution from England, one that saw the development of an independent literature. What about the American character and experience was worth telling? This, to Poe, was what the writers of the nineteenth century needed to discover. But even the sacredness of that goal wasn't enough to make the critic in Poe compromise his standards. He cautioned against ". . . liking a stupid book the better, because, sure enough, its stupidity is American."

In and Out of *Stylus*

Edgar Allan Poe dreamed of a national literary magazine all his own. Something without fashion plates and dressmaking patterns. Something with the work of the finest writers of the day. Poe himself would found, publish, and edit the paragon of literary excellence.

Incubation

The dream developed over many years of editorial experience on other entrepreneurs' magazines. Poe always felt he knew better than the likes of Billy Burton or George Rex Graham. They were businessmen; what did they know—or care—about the development of American literature? In the interest of earning a living, Poe tolerated the recipes and sentimental stories and fashion plates that meant success in the marketplace. He understood, in a limited way, mass appeal: wherever he worked, circulation soared. But it had nothing to do with his strongest artistic longings. Poe was after an aristocracy of American literature: well-read, well-educated, full-time writers "speaking" to each other.

Early Stages

In the early 1830s he started kicking around the idea of a national literary magazine, but he back-burnered the project because he had to support his little household. Several years later found him in Philadelphia, rankling under the slick fluff of *Burton's Gentlemen's Magazine*, later *Graham's*. His editorial prowess and critical savagery wildly increased readership, and he began to explore his own magazine as a way out of editorial servitude and personal poverty. By providing a selective, Olympian forum, Poe felt he was taking the next logical step in elevating the quality of American stories, poems, and essays.

question

What did Poe call his pet project?
Poe initially dubbed his magazine *The Penn*. He later changed the name to *The Stylus*, in hopes of appealing to a broader geographic range.

As usual, lack of money halted Poe's efforts.

An aristocracy—especially an American one—is a fraternity with a small membership. Beyond the elite writers themselves, and a high-brow clientele whose tastes and education might enable them to get behind the work, who would support Poe's project? The fact that Poe envisioned a whopping 50,000 subscribers—well-educated males from the South and West—belies his regional bias and also gender assumptions. Poe also miscalculated the demand for poems full of classical allusions and the beautiful dead women who haunted him.

The Problem of Personality

Edgar Allan Poe, despite his constitutional appropriateness for the launching of *The Penn*, was not a good front man. He had a rather self-righteous attitude toward what even the well-educated American should be reading—not a successful approach toward finding financial backers, let alone subscribers.

Like the boy back in school, he had personal abilities that others admired, but appeared enough the stand-offish loner to keep others from moving closer. It was a kind of self-defeating charisma that only became more pronounced as he grew older. Out of the solitary part of his nature, came, ironically, both the "lab" for his extensive creative work, and the "isolation booth" that only antagonized people who otherwise might have been caring and helpful. Why support the pet project of a man who commandeers the literary ship of state, who sees his own role as seigniorial, who repeatedly disparages the work of the most beloved writers, and who might hit you up for a loan?

> "We now demand the light artillery of the intellect; we need the curt, the condensed, the pointed, the readily diffused—in place of the verbose, the detailed, the voluminous, the inaccessible. On the other hand, the lightness of the artillery should not degenerate into popgunnery—by which term we may designate the character of the greater portion of the newspaper press—their sole legitimate object being the discussion of ephemeral matters in an ephemeral manner."—
> Poe on the American mind, 1846

Poe's inability to get either *The Penn* or *The Stylus* up and running is another painful example of the chronic difficulties in his professional life.

As a young man, he had excelled in the military, advancing through the ranks, thriving with the inelastic structure, until a struggle with his foster father made him throw it all away. But the

"We might safely give, for $5, a pamphlet of 128 pp. and, with the support of the variety of our personal influence, we might easily extend the circulation to 20,000—giving $100,000[.] The expenses would not exceed $40,000— if indeed they reached 20,000 when the work should be fairly established. Thus there would be $60,000 to be divided among 12—$5000 per an: apiece."—Poe on the financial aspect of his dream magazine

deeply troubled relationship with John Allan created a pattern for Poe's interaction with authority figures—namely, publisher bosses and literary icons, who had a kind of artistic authority. For one so bright, he was oddly obtuse about *people*, especially when he was caught up in one of his single-minded pursuits.

For instance, having brutalized Washington Irving in print, he then turned around and asked Irving to throw his financial support behind *The Penn*. What Poe saw in *The Penn*, and later *The Stylus*, as a forum for "an honest and fearless opinion," others dismissed as the project of a difficult, cranky *magazinist* (Poe's word).

Finally, it didn't make any difference that he signed up a very good illustrator (Darley, who drew the Tomahawk Man caricature) or found a co-publisher, or even enlisted the help of a Georgian poet who actually came through with some subscribers. For complex reasons stemming from his childhood, Poe was histrionically wounded by anything less than unconditional love. Maybe the beloved *Penn/Stylus* was ultimately stillborn because, despite his courteous Southern ways, Poe never learned the art of diplomacy.

Chapter 9

The Pen Refilled

As a critic and reviewer, Edgar Allan Poe earned the label "Tomahawk Man." He had no patience for second-rate work and no compunctions about letting writers know. There were times he recognized true greatness—and times his usually sharp critical faculties were dozing. To earn extra cash, Poe tried the lecture circuit. It was still in its infancy, and it did not always show his best side.

Off the Rails

The best American novel according to Edgar Allan Poe was *George Balcombe, A Novel,* by Judge Nathaniel Beverley Tucker. This apparently Olympian novel is a story about a lost will, and covers quite a bit of ground between Missouri and Virginia. At one point, the title character confronts the villain in a scene Poe believes shows "the hand of a master": "'Shame upon you, sir. Would you palm such a bare-faced lie on me, as well as on that poor, confiding, generous, true-hearted girl? I will undeceive her instantly.' I shall never forget the grim smile in which something like triumph seemed struggling to free itself from the mire of degradation into which I was trampling him . . ."

Apart from a fifteen-year stint as a circuit judge in Missouri, Tucker was a lifelong Virginian and a professor of law at the College of William and Mary. A vocal defender of slavery, he wrote what was hailed as a "prophetic" novel, *The Partisan Leader,* which predicted Southern secession and a civil war as early as 1836.

> " . . . is there not a more lofty species of originality than originality of individual thoughts or individual passages? I doubt very much whether a composition may not even be full of original things, and still be pure imitation as a whole. On the other hand I have seen writings, devoid of any new thought, and frequently destitute of any new expression . . . I could not help considering as full of creative power." —Poe in a letter to Judge Nathaniel Beverley Tucker, 1835

But it was *George Balcombe* that dazzled Tomahawk Man, who also fell for what he called the "brilliancy" of Maryland poet Edward Coote Pinkney. A sample from Pinkney's poem "A Health," which records a toast: "I fill this cup to one made up / Of Loveliness alone, / A woman, of her gentle sex / The seeming paragon . . ." This stuff is so good, according to Poe, that had Pinkney been born in the North, he would have been considered "the first of American lyrists."

Maybe Poe felt something in common with this poet: boyhood years in London, a stint in the military, editorship of a journal, a melancholy nature—maybe even a cavalier, Southern sensibility, which Judge Tucker also shared. Was Poe "off" in his rapture over these Southern writers because it's human nature to like what you find familiar? Certainly his usually keen critical mind was dozing, but it didn't happen only when work by Southerners came to a stop under his nose.

> "There is no prevalent error more at war with the real interests of literature, than that of supposing these interests to demand a suppression, in any degree, of the feelings—whether of enthusiastic admiration, or of ridicule, or of contempt, or of disgust—which are experienced, . . . by the public censor of a book thrown open avowedly to the inspection of the public. He is circumscribed, by no limits save those of the book itself." —Poe on literary criticism

Poe called late Romantic poet Thomas Hood's "The Haunted House" ". . . one of the truest—one of the most unexceptional—one of the most thoroughly artistic" poems. When he decided this "thoroughly artistic" poem was too long to include in his lecture called "The Poetic Principle," Poe substituted a shorter poem by Hood, called "The Bridge of Sighs," which describes an Ophelia-like suicide drowning. The poet tells the people recovering the body to "Wipe those poor lips of hers / Oozing so clammily. . ." It's a remarkable "vigor" and "pathos" that Poe responds to in this poem.

But Pinkney, Tucker, Hood, and others Poe publicly praised didn't make it out of the nineteenth century.

You have an advantage over Poe in knowing precisely who, two hundred years later, survived. Within a year of Poe's death, *The Scarlet Letter* was published; within two, *Moby Dick*. You have to wonder how *George Balcombe* would have stood up against those two in Poe's estimation. In some cases, sectionalism—a kinship born of the antebellum South—shaped Poe's tastes. In other cases, a kind of temperamental compatibility, irrespective of "home," did. He felt a strong attachment to the great Romantic poets, those notorious loner-adventurer-artists. Maybe, for Poe, Hood wasn't quite outside the firelight of Byron, Keats, or Shelley.

When He Was Right . . .

. . . he was very, very right. Poe recognized the "majesty" of Coleridge. Elizabeth Barrett (Browning) showed "a happy audacity of thought and expression." Daniel Defoe was "fairly entitled to immortality." He spoke of Tennyson as the bridge between "Natural Art and Divine Genius." In everything he read, Poe looked for originality in the writer's attempt to create beauty—and beauty was the objective. When it came to poetry, and he always considered himself first a poet, he believed its home was the soul, something separate from mind, morality, or duty—separate even from truth. A poem must make a beautiful impression on the reader, making itself felt like "the dropping of the water on a rock."

they said...

"I have read your occasional notices of my productions with great interest—not so much because your judgment was . . . favorable, as because it seemed to be given in earnest. I care for nothing but the truth; and shall always much more readily accept a harsh truth . . . than a sugared falsehood.

I confess, however, that I admire you rather as a writer of tales than as a critic . . . I . . . dissent from your opinions in the latter capacity, but could never fail to recognize your force and originality in the former."
—Nathaniel Hawthorne in a letter to Poe, 1846vw

By the time Poe wrote his famous review of *Twice-Told Tales* and *Mosses From an Old Manse* in 1842, he had been aware of Nathaniel Hawthorne for a few years. Despite the publication quite a few years earlier of a first novel, *Fanshawe*, which became such a matter of self-disgust Hawthorne destroyed every copy he could get his hands on (including his own sisters'!), he had mostly been developing himself as a writer of short stories. This was how Poe knew him—on the page—as another New England literary "club" member. So imagine how strong his admiration for Hawthorne's stories must have been for Poe to overcome his own sharp prejudices against the writers of that region and call Hawthorne the American writer with "the purest style, the finest taste, the most available scholarship, the most delicate humor, the most touching pathos, the most radiant imagination, the most consummate ingenuity" of any writer of prose fiction in America.

> "Let a man succeed ever so evidently—ever so demonstrably—in many different displays of *genius*, the envy of criticism will agree with the popular voice in denying him more than *talent* in any. . . . Because universal or even versatile geniuses have rarely or never been known, *therefore*, thinks the world, none such can ever be." —Poe on the recognition of genius, 1849

Even if Hawthorne was "peculiar." And idiosyncratic. And his stories, Poe goes so far as to say, written to himself. In the stories of a man who had sequestered himself for twelve years in his famous "chamber" in his mother's house—hardly the act of a clubbish writer— Poe saw greatness, but he warns against the suffocation of the New England writing fraternity. When Poe wrote this review of Hawthorne's *Mosses* and *Twice-Told Tales*, Margaret Fuller was in the process of turning over the editorship of the Transcendentalist journal, *The Dial*, to Emerson. Poe may not have known this, so he probably had her in mind when he proposed that Hawthorne, in the interest of literary self-preservation, "hang the editor of *The Dial*." But Fuller was never an easy woman to dismiss, and six years later she would interpose herself into Poe's love life as part of a self-appointed group paying calls on Poe's lady friends, warning them off him.

As a literary critic, Poe occasionally overpraised—or skewered!—the unworthy, but his judgement was generally acute, and it's a measure of his greatness that he was able to move past his fixed opinions and acknowledge literary gifts whenever he found them. One of his comments about Coleridge goes: "he not only sacrificed all present prospects of wealth and advancement, but, in his inmost soul, stood aloof from temporary reputation." This kind of artistic integrity was extremely meaningful for Poe. After all, it defined his own life, as well.

The Longfellow War of 1845

Pity poor Longfellow.

He had the pedigree: descended from John and Priscilla Alden.

He had the education: Bowdoin College graduate.

He had the primo academic job: Harvard College professor.

He had the writing recognition: beloved American poet.

He had the wife: heiress Fanny Appleton.

He even had the house: historic Craigie House in Cambridge, Massachusetts—a gift!

He also had the relentless critical wrath of Poe, probably (deep down) for all of those same reasons. Although the lightning rod was invented in Philadelphia by Ben Franklin, it went on to be embodied in Boston in the skin of Henry Wadsworth Longfellow, who drew Poe's fire as early as 1839. Earlier, Poe had responded positively to an 1835 travelogue by Longfellow, calling it "rich" and "graceful." But four years later, Longfellow's *Hyperion* sparked something in Poe the critic—which set a course for all his future reviews of Longfellow's work—he lambasted the work as lazy and shapeless. In so many words he was saying Longfellow could do better.

Maybe Poe didn't know that *Hyperion* was a tender piece for Longfellow, who used it to describe Fanny Appleton's lengthy (seven years) and embarrassing reluctance to marry him. But even if he had known, Poe was never a critic swayed by the personal stories behind a writer's work. He was a purist.

"One of the most singular pieces of literary Mosaic is Mr. Longfellow's 'Midnight Mass for the Dying Year.' The general idea and manner are from Tennyson's 'Death of the Old Year,' several of the most prominent points are from the death scene of Cordelia in 'Lear,' and the line about the 'hooded friars' is from the 'Comus' of Milton." —Poe on Longfellow's literary pilfering

Over the next five years, his prickly attentiveness to anything Longfellow published was keen. For the most part—until the ultimate accusation of plagiarism in 1845—Poe was even-handed about this Northern icon. He always praised what he honestly believed was praiseworthy about Longfellow: his artistic skill, his genius, his vividness, his "idiosyncratic excellences," and something Poe referred to as his "ideality"—meaning, maybe, Longfellow's ability to lay out the ideal. But what he felt was Longfellow's tendency to be didactic, to use a poem as an opportunity to teach a moral, was "all wrong." For a poet to do so means he or she is saying that the aim of poetry is truth, which Poe himself long ago dispatched in favor of beauty. For Poe, truth was slippery, open to individual interpretation, and so not as fine a poetic goal as beauty.

The War of Words—All Poe's—Escalates

It was the publication of Longfellow's *Midnight Mass for the Dying Year* in 1840 that heated up Poe's attacks. When another critic called the poem an imitation or alteration of a poem by Tennyson, Poe retorted that it was "a bare-faced and barbarous plagiarism." He had fired an opening salvo. Over most of the year, letters flew back and forth in print—attack and counter-attack—and Poe dug in his heels. From his school days he had scorned anything smacking of plagiarism, so by the time he himself was writing poems and stories (and reviews), the issue was a particularly tender one for him. It was such a hot button, in fact, it's entirely possible he himself was using a pen name to represent the pro-Longfellow lobby in the pitched exchange of letters in print that dominated most of 1845. Poe cast his net wider when he referred to "the small coterie of abolitionists, transcendentalists and fanatics in general, which is the Longfellow junto—" Finally, rashly calling Longfellow the "GREAT MOGUL of the Imitators," he goes on to accuse the beloved Boston poet of achieving his status in American letters by "accident or chicanery." How that could have worked, he doesn't go on to explain.

> "*Had I accused him . . . of manifest and continuous plagiarism, I should but have echoed the sentiment of every man of letters in the land beyond . . . the Longfellow coterie. . . . Can it be considered either decorous or equitable on the part of Professor Longfellow to instigate against me the pretty little witch entitled Miss Walter; advising her . . . to pierce me to death with the needles of innumerable epigrams . . ."*
> —*Poe on Longfellow*

Rubbed raw by his own suffering—an ailing wife he could hardly support, a place in American literature he could hardly secure—Poe was probably unaware of the suffering in Longfellow's own life. Longfellow's first wife, Mary, died from a miscarriage. His second, Fanny, died horribly right before her husband's eyes when she dropped a lighted match she was using to melt some sealing wax and her dress caught fire. In his futile attempts to put out the fire and save her life, Longfellow was physically scarred. Longfellow's personal tragedies were not enough to soften Poe's critical pen, incited beyond any critical fairness by Longfellow's public successes.

What was Longfellow's response to the "war" that really only sealed Poe's alienation from certain friendships and literary circles? Longfellow stayed aloof from it in print, and sometime later only commented generously that he thought it came out of Poe's sensitive nature and "some indefinite sense of wrong." It makes an interesting footnote that, after Poe's death, two writers responded to the destitute Muddy Clemm's appeals for help: Charles Dickens and Henry Wadsworth Longfellow.

Step Up to the Podium

Over the decade he tried to sell enough backers on the idea of *The Stylus*, Poe was establishing an employment pattern: excelling in editorial positions, he grew increasingly disgusted with working for "the man," a figure he always saw as a cheap philistine. Even while he sought popularity by writing tales designed to reach wide audiences (the very "masses" his aristocratic nature spurned), he was fantasizing about himself at the head of an elite, premier American literary journal. He even worked an interesting middle ground, the lecture circuit, a good gig for the poised and arresting Poe, who was always at home on a stage.

fact

When the lyceum movement sprang up, there were certainly plenty of contemporary issues for its public speakers. Along the U.S.-Canadian border, hostilities escalated as Americans were caught in the middle between Canadian insurgents in their unsuccessful struggle for freedom from England. In Missouri, violence against Mormons ensued after the governor declared Mormons the "enemy." And in Washington, Congress continued its new tradition of tabling all anti-slavery resolutions.

Public lectures gained popularity just at the time Poe—always needy, always looking for writing-related work—was gaining a name for himself. It was time to step up to the podium in lecture halls wherever a crowd would gather, and earn the fee. It was the heyday of the American lyceum movement, a kind of prototype for adult continuing education. Ironically for Poe, who benefited from these opportunities to lecture on prose and poetry to what he must have considered "lay people," the lyceum movement began during the winter of 1838 in Boston, where it was merely another development in the region where higher education and the free exchange of ideas (hard-won from the earliest colonial times) was historic.

As literacy grew, so did the volume and variety of reading material. Not only could people read the buried treasure adventure "The Gold-Bug"—and try to solve the cryptograms—but they could come to a public hall and actually hear the author talk about the "Poetry of America." Lectures were a source of intellectual stimulation, occasions for social contact, and a form of entertainment. They were the natural outgrowth of a burgeoning middle class.

Where's the Hook When You Need It?

Poe's first lecture experiences went very well. He was captivating and even somewhat notorious. After a debut in Philadelphia, where he and his household were living, he borrowed a cue from his itinerant actor ancestors and took his act on the road, giving public lectures in Delaware and New York. With his pockets suddenly a little less threadbare, Poe was able to apply some of his lecturing income to finance an 1844 move east: to New York City. That metropolis rose before Poe in all its sprawling, inscrutable neutrality. He fell into his usual round of editorial jobs and critical flaming, and then it was the publication of "The Raven" in 1844 that launched him, effectively reviving lecture hall interest in the likes of Poe.

they said...

"... a Prospero, whose wand is one of wonderful properties. That he has faults, are beyond question, but these are such only as will be insisted upon by those who regard mere popularity as the leading object of art and fiction." —Southern novelist William Gilmore Simms on Poe, two months after the Boston lecture hall debacle

What happened on October 16, 1845, in Boston fueled the gossips, decorated the newspapers, and further deepened a North-

South literary divide that up until then had been at least gentlemanly, if not always dormant.

No one knows for sure whether it was Sissy's deteriorating health back home in New York, or his finding himself in the literary lions' den—Boston, the epicenter of so much of his own complicated responses as a professional writer—but the event was doomed by his altogether peculiar behavior during the lecture. What he presented to the audience (who had already suffered through an overly long address on China) was a bald look at the extravagances of his personality, ranging from relatively fawning praise of the New England writers he scorned, to his usual critical hobbyhorse—a high-handed diatribe against Henry Wadsworth Longfellow. As if these contradictions weren't enough, he went on to deliver to the audience, who had come to hear something new from The Raven himself, a dusty recital of his obscure, early, long poem, "Al Aaraaf." The evening, thankfully, ended, but it didn't slink away. Poe, never one to sidestep even the mildest rebuke, met criticism of his performance with some slashing comments against his old "enemies," who he saw as those unfairly entitled writers in that "frogpond" area of Massachusetts. He even went so far as to claim he had been lured to Boston just so he could be made to humiliate himself.

On that October night in 1845, Emily Dickinson was just a schoolgirl one hundred miles away in Amherst, but one of the poems she later wrote seems to apply to her melancholy Richmond

> "My Dear Griswold, Will you aid me at a pinch? . . . If you will, I will be indebted to you, for life. I have succeeded in getting the 'Broadway Journal' entirely within my own control . . . with a very trifling aid from my friends. May I count you as one? Lend me $50 and you shall never have cause to regret it." —Poe in a letter to Rufus Griswold, ten days after the Boston fiasco

contemporary, Poe: "Success is counted sweetest/ to those who ne'er succeed — / To contemplate a nectar / requires sorest need." The debacle at Boston's Odeon Theatre was the beginning of Poe's own personal "descent into the maelstrom" of despair and a tattered reputation.

Chapter 10

Salons and Busybodies

Literary salons were the gathering places of the day for professional writers and writing dilettantes. Edgar Allan Poe participated—but discovered they weren't always the high-minded enclaves he expected. By 1849, dislike for him ran deep in the salons where the second-rate writers he disparaged in print congregated. Poe's literary taste was frequently sublime, and he could see and describe what was rare and fine in other writers now hailed as great. But recognition of his literary criticism was as rare as commercial success for the still-struggling writer.

Sissy and Edgar in New York

Poe had high hopes and lyceum earnings in his pocket, catapulting himself into New York City, on the cusp of taking over from Philadelphia as the literary hub of America. His letter to Muddy, who waited behind in Philadelphia while Poe and Virginia got settled, was touchingly upbeat, detailing their journey and arrival at a boarding house on Greenwich Street in the Village. "Sis is delighted, and we are both in excellent spirits." He rhapsodizes about the meals, tolerates the "buggy" building, and reassures Muddy that Sissy has "coughed hardly any."

Sissy's health was a major issue by this point. In 1842, she had broken a blood vessel while singing—a symptom of the tuberculosis that steadily grew worse. Poe became a kind of prehensile work zealot, churning out stories, poems, essays, reviews, whatever he could get, to pay the bills and keep Virginia healthy. She didn't stay a child bride—she became a young woman with a dangerous illness. Maybe in some way she understood how absolutely inviolable her position in his life and heart were, because she always encouraged his friendships with other women, even though she wasn't always treated with respect by outsiders in return.

> "... admitting that 1500 of the Tales have been sold, and that I am to receive 8 cts a copy. . . . Deducting what I have received there is a balance of 60 in my favor. . . . So dreadfully am I pressed, that I would willingly take even the $60 actually due, (in lieu of all farther demand) than wait until February:—but I am sure that you will do the best for me that you can." —Poe, asking Duyckinck to intercede with his publisher after the 1845 edition, called simply Tales, was published

The Anointing of Edgar

Around 1847, Poe befriended a New York literary scholar by the name of Evert Duyckinck. Duyckinck held what was in effect his own literary salon, whose frequenters jokingly called themselves the "Knights of the Round Table." Along with his brother George, Evert Duyckinck was instrumental in furthering the careers of American writers of the mid-nineteenth century. Of all his literature-related hats—anthologist, encyclopedist, historian, biographer—the one Duyckinck didn't wear was that of a writer. Maybe this lack of any direct competition gave him a true impartiality when it came to the literary worth of whatever came to his notice. Both men, though, had their eyes on the promotion of a national literature. It was their approach that differed. Duyckinck was encyclopedic in every way, casting a wide net to draw in and compile as much new work by American authors as he could, and he wanted to give exposure to as many as possible.

Poe's deepest nature was anti-democratic—he was after a literary elite based purely on excellence and not on success in the commercial bazaars of American publication. Let history and the readership pronounce on the merits of the individual American writer, was Duyckinck's position. Don't waste my time, and don't risk letting the occasional best be sunk by the mass of the mediocre, was Poe's.

Duyckinck's Vision

Evert Duyckinck was an equal opportunity anthologist, but when it came to critical opinion in the literary trenches, he was incredibly astute. Not only didn't he miss real excellence, he wrote extremely articulate pieces about it—publishing, in the case of transplanted New Yorker Poe, several reviews. In Poe he publicly appreciated "a quickness of apprehension, an intensity of feeling, a vigor of imagination, a power of analysis, which are rarely seen in any compositions going under the name of 'tales . . .'" He came at Poe without prejudice and throughout this period displayed real critical acumen when it came to what was most original and noteworthy in Poe's work. To Duyckinck, literary criticism was never just an opportunity

113

to display his own cleverness or present as fact his own biased opinions—unlike other reviewers. Poe may have truly been America's first real literary critic, but Duyckinck added his own fair commentary to the mix. In addition, Duyckinck had the sublime good taste to recognize, early on, the genius of that lad Melville.

Intrigue with Fanny Osgood

Well, she was Poe's type. Big expressive eyes. Black hair pulled back in the style of the day. Fashionably pale skin. Slender, graceful, sensitive. Literary. When they met at a literary soirée in Greenwich Village in 1845, Frances Sargent Osgood and Poe had certain things in common: they were roughly the same age, married, and were published poets. Osgood's published poetry pretty much ran to the high sentimental type—flowers, motherhood, children—subjects believed appropriate for what Hawthorne called "scribbling women." But she had another, more renegade style and other subjects she reserved for her salon friends, and these poems were witty, even erotic, raising the issue of gender equality. Her marriage to the well-known portrait painter Samuel Stillman Osgood, was rocky, and she claimed she had to support her two young daughters by publishing—which accounted in large part for her commercial, sentimental poems. The flirtatious Fanny eventually fell for Poe.

American literary life at that time includes paper romances—courtships, intrigues, and affairs worked out in print. Sometimes the page was the only place they lived at all. In the case of Fanny and The Raven, it remains yet one more mystery in the life of Poe. It began one-sided, with Fanny sending cryptic love poems to Poe for publication in his *Broadway Journal*. He responded—hilariously—with a recycled poem, something at hand that would do in a pinch. Encouraged, she submitted more along the same line. In a move of unhappy coincidence almost Shakespearean in scope, he printed one of his own, titled "To F—" that was not in fact addressed to Fanny, but by then the New York rumor mill was grinding away.

What happened then was interesting: rather than backing off and letting speculation die, Poe and Fanny actually became friends. Close friends. How close is anybody's guess. In letters to others he praised her honor. In 1846, Fanny gave birth to a daughter, Fanny Fay, during a time she and her husband may have been estranged. Malicious rumors have claimed Poe was the actual father of the child, who died in infancy, but there is no conclusive evidence on the matter. The friendship was an open book when it came to Virginia Poe, who actually encouraged it, seeing something in Fanny that was worthwhile for her literary husband. He shared all of Fanny's letters with Muddy and Sissy. But the plot thickened.

> "In fancy, as contradistinguished from imagination proper, in delicacy of taste, in refinement generally, in naïveté, in point, and, above all, in that inexpressible charm of charms which, for want of a better term or a more sufficient analysis than at present exists, we are accustomed to designate as *grace*, she is absolutely without a rival, we think, either in our own country or in England."—Poe, writing in *Godey's Lady Book* on Frances Osgood's collections of poetry, 1846

Scandal

Like Virginia, Fanny Osgood had tuberculosis and she left the city for a while to recuperate. In 1845, 116,000 Americans died from tuberculosis, and plenty more were to follow. Into the void left by Fanny swooped another writer, Elizabeth Ellet, a poet who also wrote books on American women's history and "courted" Poe in print. The printed page was an interesting place for these relationships: a kind of testing ground where you could put your coded passions out there on the page, in some daring ways for public consumption, but which you could still control because they existed in the "no man's land" of a mere magazine.

Poe was unresponsive, and the spurned Mrs. Ellet undertook a smear campaign, careful to see that the innuendoes about his relationship with her perceived rival Fanny Osgood reached Virginia's ears, even going so far as to write anonymous, vindictive letters to Virginia. Although the rumors upset Virginia, she never doubted her husband.

> "The quick failure of Mrs. Ellet's five-act tragedy "... had little effect in repressing the ardor of the poetess ... Her articles ... have the disadvantage of looking as if hashed up for just so much money as they will bring. The charge of wholesale plagiarism which has been adduced against Mrs. Ellett, I confess that I have not felt sufficient interest in her works, to investigate—and am therefore bound to believe it unfounded."—Poe on Elizabeth Ellett's work, 1848

The "scandal" rippled. When Fanny Osgood returned to New York, she was appalled at the other woman's behavior, and she published a piece absolving Poe of any wrongdoing. Then the two women turned on each other, finally, lambasting each other in published poems. Fanny's defense of Poe was no match for the relentless, rejected Ellet, who persisted in her attacks on Poe until he died. For him, the result was disastrous. His reputation was tainted and he was excluded from the New York literary salons. Although Poe and Fanny never saw each other after 1847, his relationship with her—which he called an "amour"—is generally considered a meaningful one.

Frances Osgood died of tuberculosis in 1850, less than a year after Poe's own death. Her two daughters died of tuberculosis as well. About her poetry, Poe had this to say in the unfinished *Literary America*: "It may be questioned whether with more industry, more method, more definite purpose, more ambition, Mrs. Osgood would have made a more decided impression on the public mind. She might, upon the whole, have written better poems." Even when his heart was on the line, he couldn't utter anything he believed was untrue when it came to literature. How and why Fanny Osgood overlooked his comments is anybody's guess.

fact

That "Great White Plague," tuberculosis, which killed both Virginia Poe and Fanny Osgood, peaked in New England in 1800 when it accounted for 1,600 deaths per 100,000 people. By the end of the nineteenth century, tuberculosis was responsible for 10 percent of all deaths in the United States. As part of the movement to control the disease, sanitariums—where isolated tuberculosis patients were treated with fresh air and good diet—originated in upstate New York.

The Enemies of Love

By all rights, Margaret Fuller should have liked Edgar Allan Poe. She should have liked his keen intellect, his high critical integrity, his magazine work, his forays into new worlds in his stories, his depictions of strong (literally, death-defying) women, his genuine interest in the work of women writers—frankly, maybe even his looks and personal style, which would feel Southern-exotic to the Bostonian Fuller.

Maybe she did like him, up to a point, but for reasons you can only guess, Poe's dalliance with Fanny Osgood soured her on Poe to such a degree that she spearheaded a little group whose mission was to end the affair.

"I am fond of the society of women—poets always are; and I have found enough to play into my foibles and palliate my defects; but a true woman, with superior intellect and deep spiritualism, would have transformed my whole life into something better." — Poe, according to novelist Elizabeth Oakes Smith. It's an unusual point of view for the age in which Poe lived.

Elizabeth Ellet was part of the group, but her poison-pen letters were her own stealth operation. The high-minded Margaret Fuller never descended to that level. In fact, when it came to letters on the Poe/Osgood matter, Fuller's objective was to lobby for the return of Fanny's "incriminating" letters to the happily married Poe. To this end, Fuller showed up on doorsteps, which seems a bit "hands on" for a woman as high-minded as Fuller. For some reason, the relationship—never clear—between Poe and Fanny Osgood made Margaret Fuller act in uncharacteristic ways.

The scholarly Margaret was a public figure in Boston's intellectual life, with her wide-ranging talents. She was a linguist, translator, editor, an interesting and outspoken teacher, and a writer unafraid of addressing contemporary social issues. Along with Ralph Waldo Emerson, she started *The Dial*, the Transcendentalist magazine. Along with a few others, she founded the 200-acre Brook Farm Institute of Agriculture and Education, a commune.

they said...

"Unhappily he had no earnestness of character, no sincerity of conviction, no faith in human excellence, no devotion to a high purpose,—not even the desire to produce a consummate work of art,—and hence, his writings . . . are destitute of the truth and naturalness which are the only passports to an enduring reputation." —George Ripley, "father" of the (failed) Brook Farm experiment, on Poe, January 1850

In its five-year existence, the commune attracted some of the true notables of the day—including, briefly (you can see how communal life would interfere with his solitary nature), Nathaniel Hawthorne. Hawthorne used it as a model for one of his novels—and Fuller herself for one of the characters.

Despite the Transcendentalist philosophy that wafted throughout the farm, Emerson was mildly hilarious on the subject, calling the living experiment "the Age of Reason in a patty-pan." Always, for Emerson, the individual was key, not the individual as mere human unit. But the devotees of Brook Farm were the kind of serious thinkers whose involvement is finally more self-serving than they'd ever care to admit. This, in fact, was the heart of *The Blithedale Romance*, Hawthorne's novel on the Brook Farm community.

Margaret, Full of Contradictions

Margaret Fuller was a serious woman—or, and there's a difference here, a woman who deeply wanted to be taken seriously. In the America of the early nineteenth century, this was culturally no easy task, despite the lip service of her Boston literary cohorts. None of them could stand her. Not the usually generous James Russell Lowell, not the restrained Nathaniel Hawthorne—even the usually mild Emerson admitted to a troubling love/hate feeling for Margaret Fuller. When she was done irritating her countrymen, she went to England, where—interestingly enough—essayist Thomas Carlyle called the "strange, lilting, lean old maid not nearly such a bore as I expected." On closer acquaintance, Carlyle went on to call her heroic and courageous, which she was. Out of this acquaintance came a famous literary rejoinder. When Carlyle was told that Fuller announced, "I accept the universe!" he responded, "By God! She'd better!" In some ways, that anecdote gets to the heart of Fuller. If you have to declare that you accept the universe, it

". . . thoughtful, suggestive, brilliant, and . . . scholar-like—but . . . in their attainment too many premises have been distorted and too many analogical inferences left altogether out of sight. . . . Miss Fuller has erred . . . through her own excessive objectiveness. She judges woman by the heart and intellect of Miss Fuller, but there are not more than one or two dozen Miss Fullers on the whole face of the earth."

Poe on Margaret Fuller, 1846

implies that you really don't. Carlyle's comment is sheer common sense.

She was a paradoxical character, Margaret Fuller, which may help to explain why she was so provoked by the relationship between Poe and Fanny Osgood that she had to take an extremely active role in it. There she was, the public intellectual and social experimenter Fuller, messing in someone else's affairs. As a feminist, how could she reconcile the contradiction between what she believed about a woman's right to self-determination and her apparent pique at Osgood's involvement with Poe? Or—to put it another way—her pique at Poe's involvement with Osgood? Toward her, Poe vacillated, but not unreasonably: he praised her critical skills (which was no small thing, coming from him), but he also satirized her in one of his stories. In this respect, he had a lot in common with his Boston literary brethren—Fuller brought them all together.

In what Poe called "a silly and conceited piece of Transcendentalism," Fuller selected Longfellow and Lowell as the worst of American poets, referring to Longfellow as a "booby" and Lowell as "disgusting even to his best friends." Poe fired back: "*Why* she said it, Heaven only knows—unless it was because she was Fuller, and wished to be taken for nobody else."

Fuller—along with Elizabeth Ellet and other doorstep solicitors—succeeded in getting Poe to return Fanny's letters. We'll never know how much of a victory that seemed to the highly intelligent Fuller, who probably surprised herself on her feelings about this relationship.

There's an extremely significant footnote to her life. Just after her involvement in the Poe/Osgood matter, she sailed away to Italy, where she became the mistress of an Italian marquis and had a son. Eventually, she and the marquis got married, and on the return trip to America, all three drowned in a shipwreck off Fire Island, New York. These biographical details make an interesting comparison to her feelings about Poe and Osgood, considering the questions around the birth of "Fanny Fay," Fanny Osgood's third daughter. As for Poe, ground through the literary gossip mill—in print, in salons, and on his doorstep—he eventually swore off literary women.

Chapter 11

The Tell-Tale Heartthrob

The last years of Edgar Allan Poe's personal life were marked by tragedy and, oddly, romance. His beloved Sissy died in January 1847, a horrendous blow for the already depressed writer. But before too long he was appealing to other women for affection, generating varying degrees of enthusiasm among the ladies. Poe was attracted to "superior women," but his attempts to remarry failed—partly due to his own shortcomings, and partly to the hostile interference of others.

The Death of Virginia

While Virginia was dying in the drafty cottage in the Fordham section of New York City, a friend who came to visit was struck by the heartbreaking picture of her lying on her back on a bed that had its posters sawed off in order to fit into the room with slanting eaves.

they said...

"Mrs. Poe looked very young; she had large black eyes, and a pearly whiteness of complexion, which was a perfect pallor. Her pale face, her brilliant eyes, and her raven hair gave her an unearthly look. One felt that she was almost a disrobed spirit, and when she coughed it was made certain that she was rapidly passing away."—Mary Gove Nichols, on meeting Virginia Poe

Against the cold of the room and the death that was moving closer, all Virginia Poe had to keep her warm was the famous black greatcoat her distraught husband had wrapped her in—and, on her chest, the quiet warmth of the great, curled-up tortoiseshell cat, Caterina. One of their neighbors, a generous, divorced woman named Marie Louise ("Loui") Shew, provided help, money, and moral support. Muddy Clemm was a Biblical figure, gleaning vegetables from neighboring fields, a Divine right granted to widows, orphans, and strangers. The itinerant Poe household qualified as all three.

Virginia Clemm Poe died on January 30, 1847. She was 25.

Poe literally collapsed at Virginia's bedside the moment she stopped breathing, and according to eyewitnesses, he could never bear to look at her after she died. At the graveside he wore the greatcoat that had been Virginia's blanket on her deathbed. Not surprisingly, Poe became sick for months, suffering from depression and an irregular heartbeat—and drink. Loui Shew and Muddy nursed him.

There is only one known portrait of Virginia Poe: a watercolor by Loui Shew, showing the poor Sissy with her head turned, her lips curving, her skin alabaster, white linen covering her chest. She had just died.

Virginia's obituary, which appeared in two New York newspapers, invited her friends to attend her funeral three days later at the Dutch Reformed Church in Fordham. Aside from Poe and Muddy, fewer than a dozen people came to bury Virginia Eliza Clemm Poe, who even in death was dependent on charity. She was buried in clothes provided by Loui Shew, in the family vault of the Poes' landlord, John Valentine.

Loui Shew and Annie Richmond

Mary Louise Shew may have met Edgar Allan Poe as early as 1845 at a literary soirée in New York. She was already divorced when she responded to the call for help in 1847 when it became clear that Virginia was dying. In addition to the practical assistance she provided the Poes around the time of Virginia's death, afterward she was the absolute source of strength for Muddy Clemm and the despairing Poe. When she was alarmed by his physical illness, she took Poe to the city for medical care. When she was concerned at his despair, she took him with her to Episcopal services. (Poe tried earnestly to "walk the walk"—and failed.) When he languished over an inability to write anything new, she inspired him to write the poem that became "The Bells," even contributing the first four lines.

All this she provided without the least romantic interest in him—although after a while, he certainly started to feel something more than mere friendly gratitude. "Ah, Marie Louise!" he exclaims in one of the three poems he wrote for her. "In deep humility I own that now / All pride—all thought of power—all hope of fame— / All wish for Heaven—is merged forevermore / Beneath the palpitating tide of passion / Heaped o'er my soul by thee . . ." Unlike most of Poe's other female friends, the kind Loui Shew was apparently never tempted. When she finally remarried, it was not to Poe.

Whether Nancy Locke Heywood Richmond—the woman Poe called "Annie"—was ever tempted by Poe is another matter. Their relationship was harder to read than the apparent clarity Marie Louise Shew enjoyed when it came to her relationship with her famous friend. Poe met Annie, the wife of wrapping paper manufacturer Charles Richmond, in mid-July 1848, when he went to lecture in Lowell, Massachusetts. The fact that she was married didn't deter The Raven; after all, he was caught up in a period of emotional excess and simultaneous romantic entanglements.

Accounts differ: over several visits, he made repeated attempts to secure her as his wife; he viewed her as a "sister," a savior, his platonic love. To a man with a nature as complex as his, all could be true. In a letter to the unattainable Annie, Poe exclaims, ". . . I cannot live, unless I can feel your sweet, gentle, loving hand pressed upon my forehead . . ." In addition, in an absurd turnabout, after a half-hearted suicide attempt when he was despairing of ever persuading future love Helen Whitman to marry him, he wrote a powerful response to his own act, the poem "For Annie," chalking up the experience to ". . . the fever called 'Living' / That burned in my brain." The poem dreams of her kisses, her caresses, her love, and "the heaven of her breast." Finally, even the tolerant Charles Richmond had enough. Spurred on by the gossip of a jealous neighbor, Jane Locke, who had hoped to win the celebrated Poe for herself, Annie Richmond's husband put an end to the friendship.

A Second Helen

The year 1848 was the "Helen Year." Virginia had died the year before. Fanny Osgood had reconciled with her husband. Annie Richmond was happily married. And Edgar Allan Poe was getting nowhere with family friend Loui Shew.

He was working away, writing *Eureka* and finding backers for *The Stylus*. But mainly, he wanted to persuade Sarah Helen Whitman to marry him. The course of their relationship was the opposite of serendipity—which was strange when you consider how enthusiastic they were about each other's work and how much they had in common as friends. Helen Whitman was a bluestocking poet living in Providence, Rhode Island, and she and The Raven shared the same birthday, although she was six years his elder. She was a forty-five-year-old widow when Poe brought up the idea of marriage. What happened in 1848 between Poe and this second important Helen in his life is an excellent example of the wisdom of leaving well enough alone.

they said...

"He had some rare tropical birds in cages, which he cherished . . . giving to his birds and his flowers a delighted attention that seemed quite inconsistent with the gloomy and grotesque . . . writings. A favourite cat, too, enjoyed his friendly patronage, and often when he was engaged in composition it seated itself on his shoulder, purring as in complacent approval of the work proceeding under its supervision."—Helen Whitman on Poe's life in Fordham, 1860

The Whitman-Poe courtship began limpingly, based on a kind of "homework assignment." Planning a meeting at her salon for Valentine's Day 1848, Manhattan literary doyenne Anne Lynch requested original valentines from women she'd invited about any of the famous men who would be present. Although Anne Lynch was herself a published poet, she was more influential as a kind of literary socialite, inviting poets, actors, journalists, and industrialists into her parlor every Saturday night for literary camaraderie. Happily married, she was well educated and taught English, and Poe himself called her "equal to any fate." At her Valentine's Day gathering in 1848, Helen chose Poe, wrote the valentine, and they were off. What followed was a strange tug of war. While each enticed the other with love poems, both carried on a relentless vetting of the other's reputation, prospects, and nature.

Their common reluctance to commit was almost comical: he wanted a wife, and he wanted the intelligent Helen Whitman to be that wife, but his approach for much of the time was measured; she alternately worried about his reputation and the possibility that an intense younger husband might be the death of her. After all, she had a heart condition. Here is her passionate exclamation to him: "If I were to allow myself to love you, I could only enjoy a brief, brief hour of rapture and die—" Not to be outdone, he wrote that he would ". . . oh, joyfully—joyfully—joyfully—go down with you into the Grave." There were the malicious busybodies, of course.

The same crew responsible for the end of the Osgood affair resurfaced.

The Year of Courting Fruitlessly

There's no denying that Poe and Helen Whitman admired each other. Both were drawn to pop cultural things—phrenology, mesmerism, spiritualism. The intelligent and talented Helen, her flowing scarves defying the women's fashions of the day, held weekly séances at her Providence home, acting as human conduit to the spirit world. Later on, her intelligence led her to debunk these same occult practices.

Fanned by Helen's foot-dragging reluctance to marry him, Poe became more passionately attached to the idea. Which, ironically, only increased Helen's caution.

Letters arrived warning her off him. But throughout the frustrating year of 1848, they continued to be frank with each other, so he knew his enemies were calling him a drunk and a womanizer. "Ah, Helen, I have a hundred friends for every individual enemy," he told her, and pointed out that she didn't live among his friends. She was worried he had a romanticized view of her; how could he be sure that his feelings for her were true and not the emotional self-deception of the rebound? It had only been a year since Virginia had died.

With Fanny Osgood, the meddlesome literati did in the relationship. With Sarah Helen Whitman, it was finally—despite the best efforts of the meddlers—just Poe himself who did in the relationship. Helen agreed to marry him on the condition that he wouldn't drink. He tried. He couldn't. She called off the marriage. The emotional seesaw led to Poe's dramatic overdose on the train from Providence to Boston. But it was Helen Whitman who, after her ex-fiancé's death, consistently defended him, especially against the malign "memoir" by Rufus Griswold. Her book, *Edgar Poe and His Critics*, was not just a defense

"*. . . if you will have faith in me, I can & will satisfy your wildest desires. .*

. . Would it not be 'glorious', darling, to establish, in America, the sole unquestionable aristocracy—that of intellect—to secure its supremacy—to lead & to control it? All this I can do, Helen, & will—if you bid me—and aid me." —Poe in a letter to Helen Whitman, 1848

of the man she had known but also, really, a work of Poe scholarship. Helen—the "To Helen" of his second, 1848 poem—may not have married the man for whom she wrote forty poems, but in other, important ways, *she* came through.

In July 1849, Poe paid a last visit to Richmond, where he met Susan Archer Talley. She was quite a bit younger than he, but she grew up interested in him and loving his work, so meeting him socially was a significant event for her. Poe stayed at her mother's house the last night in Richmond, and the two of them took many walks together. When he sensed something deeply compatible in Susan Talley, he confided that his marriage to Virginia had not been "congenial," that he didn't find in her the kind of "intellectual and spiritual sympathy" that would have made him truly happy. Touring the empty house of a fine family Poe had known in his youth, Susan watched him take it all in, noting all the vacancy, noting where there had used to be violets. He pressed some flowers between the pages of a book. He and Susan Archer Talley talked books and writers, and she told him she was surprised at how highly he praised a certain woman writer. He agreed he had overrated her, admitting—with real insight—"I cannot point an arrow at any woman."

This woman with arresting looks—calm intelligence and a beautiful mouth—wrote several times about Poe. On his last night in Richmond, they were saying goodbye to each other on the steps of her mother's house. He was the last one to leave that evening, and as he lifted his hat to her and turned for a last look—truly a last look, because he died in Baltimore three months later—she wrote, "a brilliant meteor appeared in the sky directly over his head, and vanished in the east." Many years later, Susan Talley was captured as a Confederate spy and imprisoned. She met and married a Colonel Weiss and later had a son. She lived to be ninety-four.

"This is the only true principle among men. Where the gentler sex is concerned, there seems but one course for the critic—speak if you can commend—be silent, if not; for a woman will ne[v]er be brought to admit a non-identity between herself and her book . . ."—Poe on literary criticism of work by women writers, from "Marginalia," 1844

Return of the Girl Next Door

Sarah Elmira Royster, the child sweetheart who had been Poe's briefly betrothed during his moody Byronic adolescence, reappeared as an attractive widow in the final months of his life. If portraits tell the story, Elmira Royster didn't have Virginia's ethereal expressiveness or Fanny Osgood's inviting warmth or Helen Whitman's searching intelligence. Elmira wasn't literary. She was very much a girl of her times, and for a woman-in-waiting the times pretty much necessitated a "good" marriage and a predictable life. She had the inscrutable but slightly sad look of a woman who sensed maybe there was more out there, somewhere, but she didn't have the imagination or rebelliousness to go looking for it. It's a mild, long-suffering look.

Twenty years after the broken engagement, she was widowed and so was he. He was also courting Providence poet/mystic Helen

Whitman, mooning over Lowell, Massachusetts, married pal Annie Richmond, still pitching to the uninterested Loui Shew, and mourning the dead Sissy. It was probably this period poet W. H. Auden was referring to when he described Poe's love life as "crying in laps and playing house." It became a bit of a premarital horse race—except all but one of the contenders were running *away* from the finish line. The Annie and Loui relationships were going nowhere. Helen, after much dragging of feet, was also passing on marriage. The girl next door, Sarah Elmira Royster Shelton, stepped up.

fact

The childhood sweetheart accepted—and in record time, one month after the proposal. By late August 1849, the two were engaged—twenty-two years after he had first proposed! Poe presented the widowed Elmira with gifts: a hair ornament and a mother-of-pearl compact. He wrote poems. Muddy, who only wanted to see him married again, was delighted.

Elmira was now in a position to make all her own choices and determine her own destiny. What's especially intriguing about her decision to marry Poe—despite the ever-present whisperings about his reputation—is that it meant she would have to sacrifice her late husband's estate, according to Alexander Shelton's will. There was something about this Poe—and maybe the broken engagement only seemed like a twenty-year deferment to her—that made it all worthwhile.

But then he died.

Chapter 12

The Final Mysteries of Edgar Allan Poe

The days leading up to Edgar Allan Poe's death in October of 1849 remain mysterious. Did the creator of the detective story ironically meet a violent end? Was he really found unconscious in a Baltimore gutter? Whose clothes was he wearing? Did his demons finally get the better of him? What were his last words and what did they mean? What are the facts surrounding Poe's death and what is mere speculation?

The Habit of Melancholy

Despite the obvious advantages of his youth, Poe told Helen Whitman he did not have a happy childhood. He had a foster mother and aunt who loved him; a foster father who at least provided for him, in those early years, without hesitation; a strong intellect; the respect of his peers; a foothold in Richmond society; the expanding horizons of those years in England; an honorable family history; and tremendous talent. Some of these may also have been detrimental to him, and the deaths and desertions of key adults in his childhood and early adulthood certainly outweighed the positive aspects of his youth. To a person with a melancholy nature, gifts never come pure. Occasional sorrow and dark introspection swirl around advantages and attributes that others with more even or sunnier dispositions take for granted.

> "You speak of 'an estimate of my life'— and, from what I have already said, you will see that I have none to give. I have been too deeply conscious of the mutability and evanescence of temporal things, to give any continuous effort to anything—to be consistent in anything."—Poe to James Russell Lowell, 1844

In 1621, English physician Robert Burton wrote *The Anatomy of Melancholy*. It appeared in the style of a medical text, but it was unmistakably a witty examination of unhappiness. Melancholy, says Burton, is "an inbred malady in every one of us." Depending on the spirit of the times, it is a quality that is either tolerated, reviled, venerated, misunderstood, or even mistaken. What was then melancholy—which carried a kind of romantic panache—is now labeled clinical depression.

Was this the case of Poe? Was he, in fact, melancholy? From his stage-performer parents, he inherited a flair for drama. From his relentlessly poor circumstances and the failing health of his wife, he had reason to be anxious and fatalistic. From his distemper over the mediocrity in the American literature of his times, he was a fierce and gloomy critical presence.

Upon his death, several friends leaped into the journalistic void and wrote lengthy tributes and explanations of the dead man. Nathaniel Parker Willis, journalist and writer, recalled, "He walked the streets, in madness or melancholy, with lips moving in indistinct curses, or with eyes upturned in passionate prayers (never for himself, for he felt, or professed to feel, that he was already damned) . . ."

"It is not in the power of any mere worldly considerations, such as these, to depress me. . . . No, my sadness is unaccountable, and this makes me the more sad. I am full of dark forebodings. Nothing cheers or comforts me. My life seems wasted—the future looks a dreary blank: but I will struggle on and 'hope against hope.'"—

Poe to Annie Richmond, 1849

Helen Whitman, ex-fiancée and mystic poet, remembered "The exquisitely chiseled features, the habitual but intellectual melancholy, the clear pallor of the complexion, and the calm eye like the molten stillness of a slumbering volcano . . ." The artist, finally, becomes a canvas.

It's George Rex Graham, Poe's boss at *Graham's,* who makes the interesting point ". . . if genius be granted by nature to one whose mind is naturally, or by vicious education, warped to melancholy, eccentricity, waywardness, or any other irregular or ill-balanced condition, the genius will render that irregularity more conspicuous, and more dangerous both to the possessor and to others, than the same evil condition of mind would have been in an ordinary person." Graham clearly has no taste for melancholy—he takes a bit of a Puritanical stance, in fact—but does make an interesting distinction between how it appears in a genius as opposed to "an ordinary person."

A Demon in His View

Poe himself describes whatever dark vein in his nature shaped his adult life in a poem discovered by E. L. Didier, the editor of *Scribner's*, who published it in 1875.

Alone

From childhood's hour I have not been
As others were—I have not seen
As others saw—I could not bring
My passions from a common spring—
From the same source I have not taken
My sorrow—I could not awaken
My heart to joy at the same tone—
And all I loved—I loved alone—
Then—in my childhood, in the dawn
Of a most stormy life—was drawn
From every depth of good and ill
The mystery which binds me still—
From the torrent, or the fountain—
From the red cliff of the mountain—
From the sun that round me rolled
In its autumn tint of gold—
From the lightning in the sky
As it pass'd me flying by—
From the thunder and the storm—
And the cloud that took the form
When the rest of Heaven was blue
Of a demon in my view.—

Where had it been lying, this raw, plain self-analysis, this poem that might have demystified Poe at least a little bit to the general public? Was it slipped in with other papers, hidden for over twenty-five years? Maybe, finally, it wasn't meant for public consumption. Poe was an unfailingly proud man. For him, it's possible the poem

"Alone" revealed more than he was willing to share. Was it a well-lighted look at melancholy—or something else, something deeply separate in the composition of all artists—the place from which all original creative work comes?

In Half a Glass of Wine

Why overstate your bad habits? Why, in fact, state them at all? Two of the persistent beliefs about Poe are that he abused drugs and alcohol. Some of this Poe lore comes down over the last century and is based partly on his own letters and stories, and partly on the vengeful gossip of writers who didn't like him for personal or professional reasons. In the letters and stories, at least, Poe himself opines on the topic of drugs and alcohol, albeit with a whole lot of cross-pollination. The line between personal experience and the imaginative understanding of an experience gets blurred, and Poe's theatrical tendency to overstate his behavior asserts itself—either to enhance his mystique (to himself or others) or to express some sort of guilt or remorse.

> "To be thoroughly conversant with Man's heart, is to take our final lesson in the iron-clasped volume of Despair."—Poe on the heart of man

Explaining the Laudanum Episode

In a letter to Annie Richmond in 1848, Poe—despairing of ever being able to pull a second marriage out of a year of romantic intrigues—confessed to having swallowed an ounce of laudanum in an attempt to put himself out of his misery.

He got as far as unconsciousness, not having taken enough of the drug to meet his original goal. This is his only mention of drug use (although laudanum was used medicinally in those days), and even so, it's not clear whether it's just another bit of moonshine, designed to persuade Annie (or Helen Whitman, the object of his affection) of his love.

It is Poe's fictional narrators who self-medicate with opium, a choice the writer made to heighten the story's miasmic atmosphere and psychological rawness. Fifty years after Poe's most prolific period, Arthur Conan Doyle went so far as to give his detective hero Sherlock Holmes a cocaine habit, but no one ever supposed it was because Doyle himself had one.

question
What is laudanum?
Laudanum was a commonly prescribed medical drug in the nineteenth century. Derived from opium, it was used to treat an array of complaints ranging from insomnia to aches and pains.

Troubles with the Bottle

Alcohol, on the other hand, was clearly a problem. Poe wasn't a carouser or a barfly, and he didn't drink away whatever money he had. All it took, according to eyewitnesses, was less than a glass of wine. His father, David Poe, Jr., was an alcoholic, and so was his brother Henry. For Edgar, drinking was a complicated matter. It never took much to make him appear intoxicated. In a period fraught with tension between rollicking drunkenness and the Sons of Temperance, Poe wrestled with his own dislike of the loss of control drinking produced in him and the appealing image of the convivial Southern bon vivant he longed to be.

Fifteen years after he left the University of Virginia, Poe recalled his university days as "dissipated." Interesting, since there's no record to support it. He was implying a habitual state of near incapacitation, and it simply hadn't happened. Some classmates recalled how he'd feverishly down a glass of "spirits" all at once, in a kind of strange desperation—not at all the sort of hobnobbing geniality he was after. He did have the kind of pain he'd try to deaden with alcohol later on—occasionally. The greatest damage to his reputation in this regard was the result of multiplied inaccuracies, and the ill will of peers whose toes were feeling the tread of Poe's shoes.

It was only after his death that his experiences with alcohol and laudanum were sensationalized. But for a man who yearned for respect and admiration, Poe was philosophical on the subject of public opinion: "As for the mob—let them talk on."

they said...

"As an author his name will live, while three-fourths of the bastard critics and mongrel authors of the present day go down to nothingness and night. And the men who now spit upon his grave, by way of retaliation for some injury which they imagined they have received from Poe living, would do well to remember, that it is only an idiot or a coward who strikes the cold forehead of a corpse."—George Lippard, in his obituary of Poe, 1849

Pick Your Poison

It was murder. It was epilepsy. It was diabetes. It was his heart. It was rabies. It was dipsomania, hypoglycemia, delirium tremens brought on by end-stage alcoholism. In the sixteen decades since the death of Poe, the fact that the strange, inconclusive case of Poe's final illness still turns up in biographies and medical journals seems oddly appropriate for the father of the detective story. In 1999, a medical researcher from Johns Hopkins added carbon monoxide poisoning to the list, linking the sensations described in Poe's macabre tales—written in Baltimore and Philadelphia, where gaslights were used—to the symptoms of carbon monoxide poisoning.

The most common account of Poe's final days has him lying near death in a Baltimore gutter, an image that seems especially pitiful. The truth is close. On October 3, 1849, Poe's longtime Baltimore friend Joseph Snodgrass received a hasty note from a young printer who recognized the unconscious Poe down in the Fourth Ward, lying on a broad plank across some barrels. When Snodgrass arrived on the scene, however, he found Poe in a nearby tavern, Gunner's Hall, sitting stupefied and disheveled in an armchair. Snodgrass described his friend's appearance, "His clothing consisted of a sack-coat of thin and sleazy black alpaca, ripped more or less at several of its seams, . . . and pants . . . half-worn and badly-fitting, if they could be said to fit at all. . . . On his feet were boots of coarse material. . . ." Believing his literary friend to be so intoxicated he was nearly unrecognizable, Snodgrass managed to get Poe to Washington College Hospital, where he was attended by Dr. John J. Moran.

Dr. Moran later described his patient as haggard and dirty, noting that over the next three days Poe was alternately delirious and lucid, hot and cold—but not, Moran asserted, under the influence of "intoxicating drink." In the early hours of Sunday, October 7, the delirium subsided, and Poe uttered, "Lord help my poor soul!" Around 5 A.M., he died. The cause of death on record: congestion of the brain. This encephalitis could have been due to the exposure to the wintry weather Baltimore was experiencing then, considering how shabbily dressed Poe was when Snodgrass found him.

> "My sensitive temperament could not stand an excitement which was an everyday matter to my companions. . . . But it is now quiet four years since I have abandoned every kind of alcoholic drink—four years, with the exception of a single deviation, which occurred shortly after my leaving Burton, and when I was induced to resort to the occasional use of *cider*, with the hope of relieving a nervous attack."—Poe on the "alcohol issue" to his friend, teetotaler Joseph Snodgrass, 1841

But because Poe was buried two days later without an autopsy, his death will no doubt continue to intrigue scholars, biographers, and medical researchers. One young American novelist, Matthew Pearl, takes up the question of Poe's mysterious final days in his mystery, *The Poe Shadow* (2006). Interestingly, Pearl's previous novel, *The Dante Club*, was another historical mystery, this one featuring as "sleuths" those Frogpondians Poe disliked.

One thing is certain about Poe. The days before he died—great, blank pages of personal history—are finally nowhere near as interesting as the forty years he lived.

Reynolds! Reynolds!

Some of what Edgar Allan Poe (supposedly) said in the days before he died doesn't take much in the way of explanation. According to Dr. Moran, who was the only witness to his death, Poe declared his best friend would be the one who would blow his brains out. Then there were what Dr. Moran offered up as Poe's final words: "Lord, help my poor soul!"—the heartbreaking comment of someone in pain. But Poe deliriously invoked the name Reynolds in the hours before he died, and the identity of this Reynolds is still in question.

Just another mystery.

Just another puzzle.

With, probably, no solution—or, at any rate, no solution that will satisfy everybody. Theories abound. One guess is that Poe actually said "Herring"—the name of a distant relative—and Dr. Moran simply misheard him. Another posits the Reynolds Poe referred to was a local carpenter serving as a ward worker in Baltimore on election day.

The most common explanation for the identity of Reynolds is also the most intriguing one from a literary point of view. An explorer named Jeremiah Reynolds proposed an expedition to the South Pole to test Captain Symmes's Hollow Earth theory—Earth is hollow, and inhabitable by entering at the poles. The U.S. government refused to provide funding, so Reynolds lectured to raise money. He sailed away to the South Pole in 1829, where, of

"All—absolutely all the argumentation which I have seen on the nature of the soul, or of the Deity, seems to me nothing but worship of this unnameable idol. . . . At least, he alone is fit to discuss the topic who perceives at a glance the insanity of its discussion."—Poe on God, from "Marginalia," 1848

139

course, his team found impenetrable ice, no source of food, and plenty of good reasons to leave.

they said...

"... the sending out of one or two vessels on a voyage of discovery would not be attended with any very heavy demands on the public treasury, and would seem to be in strict accordance with the character and liberal policy which ought to be pursued by a government whose political existence is, in a great measure, dependent on the general intelligence of her people."—Jeremiah Reynolds in a petition to the Speaker of the House of Representatives, to approve his polar exploration

Reynolds's accounts of the voyage stirred the imaginations of two of the great American writers of the nineteenth century: Melville and Poe. Reynolds's description of Mocha Dick, a great white whale of the South Pacific that sank a ship, became the model for the masterpiece *Moby Dick*. And Reynolds's accounts of South Sea Indian encounters—and the mind-boggling wilderness of Antarctica— found an imaginative re-working in at least one of Poe's tales and his *Narrative of Arthur Gordon Pym of Nantucket*. To Poe, Reynolds was an adventurer in the realm of the metaphysical.

Poe defended Reynolds, taking offense at Congress's decision to entrust its Antarctic expedition to Charles Wilkes instead of Reynolds. "It is a great pity," Poe wrote, "that the control of this important enterprise was not given to its originator, Reynolds. He is, in every respect, as thoroughly qualified as Commander Wilkes is not. A more disgraceful—a more unprincipled—a more outrageous system of chicanery, never was put in operation, before the open eyes of an intelligent community, than that by means of which Mr. Wilkes was made to occupy the position, and usurp the undeniable rights of Mr. Reynolds."

In the hours before his death, is it more likely that Poe was calling out for a poll worker or a heroic figure who explored a harrowing region at the risk of his own life?

Chapter 13

Horrors!

L iterary anthologies capture some of Poe's stories, but not all of his stories are well known. What kind of a writer was Poe? Did he play by his own rules when he wrote stories? How did his circumstances influence his writing, and what did his stories reveal about him? Was horror an element in everything he wrote?

An Island in the Sea

Among the papers of Rufus Griswold, Poe's literary executor, were four manuscript pages in Poe's handwriting. They were the beginnings of a new story, which Poe hadn't titled yet, leaving only white space at the top for later inspiration. Generally taken for the story he had been working on at the time of his death, it's in the form of a diary, and the first-person narrator (classic Poe) records his arrival at his new job as lighthouse keeper. Except for his dog, Neptune, he is alone, having taken the solitary job as a way of getting some of his own writing done. Because of the setting and central image, these final fragments of Poe's work are called "The Light-House." From the clues Poe offers, you can speculate that a storm will destroy the light-house—and possibly the keeper—and that the dog carries the diary to safety. But who knows? It's just another mystery in Poe's tales—this one interrupted by his own death.

> "It seems to me that the hollow interior at the bottom should have been filled in with solid masonry. Undoubtedly the whole would have been thus rendered more *safe*:—but what am I thinking about? A structure such as this is safe enough under any circumstances. I should feel myself secure in it during the fiercest hurricane that ever raged—"—Poe lays down some foreshadowing as his narrator explores the lighthouse

"The Light-House" makes a good backdrop for a closer look at Poe's work. In some ways, that last story seems a poignant comment on his entire writing life: fragmentary, unfinished, and in some ways unknowable. Poe is his own solitary narrator, and like the one in the story, he has made a potentially dangerous choice in the cause of art. Like the lighthouse keeper, he has placed himself in this "island in the sea," buffeted by the waves of poverty and public opinion—in other words, the world. The beauty of the lighthouse, of course, is the light, and all that signifies for a man adrift. For Poe, the light is art. The last line gives you a classic, ironic undercutting by Poe, as the narrator explores his new "home" and discovers that "the basis on which the structure rests seems to me to be chalk."

Master of Horror

"During the whole of a dull, dark, and soundless day in the autumn of the year, when the clouds hung oppressively low in the heavens, I had been passing alone, on horseback, through a singularly dreary tract of country, and at length found myself, as the shades of the evening drew on, within view of the melancholy House of Usher." Poe received ten dollars from Billy Burton, the owner of *Burton's Gentleman's Magazine*, for "The Fall of the House of Usher," in 1839. It is generally considered his best story. The fact that he was the editorial assistant at Burton's magazine did nothing to sweeten the pot, although Burton did introduce the thirty-year old writer to the Philadelphia literary circle.

fact

Poe claimed a long-standing publishing history with two British journals he wasn't at liberty to name. This is a curious bit of mystification, since the mission of any publication is to build a readership—and get some name recognition.

A year later, while still working for Burton, Poe made an agreement with Lea & Blanchard, Philadelphia publishers, to publish his first collection of tales—including "The Fall of the House of Usher"—in a two-volume edition called *Tales of the Grotesque and Arabesque*. It was a dismal deal for Poe: he got his copyright and twenty contributors' copies, and the publisher got all the profits. Poe agreed to these unfavorable terms because he believed the collection would increase his appeal to magazines, which were turning out to be his principal source of income. In spite of the collection's positive reviews, Lea & Blanchard admitted it never made a profit on the publication.

None of Poe's stories has received more critical attention than "Usher." Why? What explains the durable appeal of this particular story? James Russell Lowell, one of Poe's contemporaries (although part of that Boston literary elite Poe scorned), gets at it when he says this story ". . . has a singular charm for us, and we think that no one could read it without being strongly moved by its serene and sombre beauty. Had its author written nothing else, it would alone have been enough to stamp him as a man of genius, and the master of a classic style." The plot concerns the narrator, who is invited to the ancestral home of his boyhood friend, Roderick Usher, where he discovers his old friend in a state of what used to be called nervous exhaustion, waiting for what he is convinced will be a crisis, something so terrifying he will die from fear. He and his twin sister Madeline—a cataleptic who sinks into death-like states—are the last of their long line of Ushers, and all around the narrator and the hypochondriac Roderick the house seems just about to breathe its "mystic vapor." The house, too, is waiting.

The following passage provides a good look at the four characters central to the story—the nameless narrator, Roderick, Madeline—and the mansion itself.

"I learned, moreover, at intervals, and through broken and equivocal hints, another singular feature of his mental condition. He was enchained by certain superstitious impressions in regard to the dwelling which he tenanted, and whence, for many years, he had never ventured forth—in regard to an influence whose supposititious force was conveyed in terms too shadowy here to be re-stated—an influence which some peculiarities in the mere form and substance of his family mansion, had, by dint of long sufferance, he said, obtained over his spirit—an effect which the physique of the gray walls and turrets, and of the dim tarn into which they all looked down, had, at length, brought about upon the morale of his existence.

"He admitted, however, although with hesitation, that much of the peculiar gloom which thus afflicted him could be traced to a more natural and far more palpable origin—to the severe and long-continued illness—indeed to the evidently

approaching dissolution—of a tenderly beloved sister—his sole companion for long years—his last and only relative on earth. 'Her decease,' he said, with a bitterness which I can never forget, 'would leave him (him the hopeless and the frail) the last of the ancient race of the Ushers.' While he spoke, the lady Madeline (for so was she called) passed slowly through a remote portion of the apartment, and, without having noticed my presence, disappeared. I regarded her with an utter astonishment not unmingled with dread—and yet I found it impossible to account for such feelings. A sensation of stupor oppressed me, as my eyes followed her retreating steps. When a door, at length, closed upon her, my glance sought instinctively and eagerly the countenance of the brother—but he had buried his face in his hands, and I could only perceive that a far more than ordinary wanness had overspread the emaciated fingers through which trickled many passionate tears.

"The disease of the lady Madeline had long baffled the skill of her physicians. A settled apathy, a gradual wasting away of the person, and frequent although transient affections of a partially cataleptical character, were the unusual diagnosis. Hitherto she had steadily borne up against the pressure of her malady, and had not betaken herself finally to bed; but, on the closing in of the evening of my arrival at the house, she succumbed (as her brother told me at night with inexpressible agitation) to the prostrating power of the destroyer; and I learned that the glimpse I had obtained of her person would thus probably be the last I should obtain—that the lady, at least while living, would be seen by me no more."

Part of what elevates this story above Poe's other horror stories is the presence of a normal narrator. There is no confessional psychopath, just a pal who arrives because his distressed friend needs him and who behaves in recognizably human ways. He stands in for all of the rest of us, who simply have to watch the events of the story unfold. Poe believed a short story should have "a single effect," in which every word has to count, something short enough to be read in a single sitting.

In earlier stories, you see that goal at work in lurid prose that creates a voice of extreme mental illness, rushing headlong toward a conclusion that feels horrific and inevitable. But in "Usher," the reader isn't manipulated quite so much. What you have instead is a kind of family drama endgame, a story where all the hysteria and heightened fears have almost a modern feel to them.

Adventures in Cryptography

"The lanterns having been lit, we all fell to work with a zeal worthy a more rational cause . . ." When Poe, living in Philadelphia, won a $100 prize from the *Dollar Newspaper* for "The Gold-Bug" in 1843, he was trying to get financial backing for a new national literary journal, having resigned his "day job" at *Graham's Magazine* nearly a year before.

Like he did with "The Raven" a year later, Poe set out to write something with popular appeal without giving critics and reviewers anything to scoff at. He succeeded, bringing to his story set on Sullivan's Island, one of the sea islands off Charleston, South Carolina, (where he was stationed for a year at Fort Moultrie) elements that would sell. Like *The Narrative of Arthur Gordon Pym*, it's a boy's adventure story, only more minimalist, with a hunt for Captain Kidd's buried treasure in a semi-exotic location. The eccentric treasure hunter, a freed slave, and the sidekick narrator conspire to figure out the clues. Parchments, invisible ink, cryptograms, skeletons, doubloons, and fabulous jewels—they're all here. In the following passage,

> "Few persons can be made to believe that it is not quite an easy thing to invent a method of secret writing which shall baffle investigation. Yet it may be roundly asserted that human ingenuity cannot concoct a cipher which human ingenuity cannot resolve."—Poe on secret writing, 1841

the team sets off, much to the chagrin of the narrator, who doubts his treasure-hunting friend's sanity:

"With a heavy heart I accompanied my friend. We started about four o'clock—Legrand, Jupiter, the dog, and myself. Jupiter had with him the scythe and spades—the whole of which he insisted upon carrying—more through fear, it seemed to me, of trusting either of the implements within reach of his master, than from any excess of industry or complaisance. His demeanor was dogged in the extreme, and 'dat deuced bug' were the sole words which escaped his lips during the journey. For my own part, I had charge of a couple of dark lanterns, while Legrand contented himself with the scarabaeus, *which he carried attached to the end of a bit of whip-cord; twirling it to and fro, with the air of a conjuror, as he went. When I observed this last, plain evidence of my friend's aberration of mind, I could scarcely refrain from tears. I thought it best, however, to humor his fancy, at least for the present, or until I could adopt some more energetic measures with a chance of success. In the mean time I endeavored, but all in vain, to sound him in regard to the object of the expedition. Having succeeded in inducing me to accompany him, he seemed unwilling to hold conversation upon any topic of minor importance, and to all my questions vouchsafed no other reply than 'we shall see!'*

"We crossed the creek at the head of the island by means of a skiff, and, ascending the high grounds on the shore of the main land, proceeded in a northwesterly direction, through a tract of country excessively wild and desolate, where no trace of a human footstep was to be seen. Legrand led the way with decision; pausing only for an instant, here and there, to consult what appeared to be certain landmarks of his own contrivance upon a former occasion.

"In this manner we journeyed for about two hours, and the sun was just setting when we entered a region infinitely more dreary than any yet seen. It was a species of table land, near the summit of an almost inaccessible hill, densely wooded from base to pinnacle, and interspersed with huge crags that appeared to lie loosely

upon the soil, and in many cases were prevented from precipitating themselves into the valleys below, merely by the support of the trees against which they reclined. Deep ravines, in various directions, gave an air of still sterner solemnity to the scene."

In a way, the puzzle of "The Gold-Bug" prefigures the more sophisticated criminal puzzle Poe grows into later with "The Murders in the Rue Morgue" and his other detective tales. "The Gold-Bug" was a warm-up for Poe, who discovered that his analytical mind and impressive puzzle-solving ability could find some action in the literary marketplace. Even before the popular success of "The Gold-Bug," Poe promised a year's subscription to *Graham's*, where he was editor, to anyone who could solve one of his own cryptograms. But the response was so overwhelming, finally, that he had to withdraw the offer. Here again, because no copyright law yet existed to protect writers' interests, Poe never made a cent beyond the $100 prize he was paid for "The Gold-Bug." The story went on to sell 300,000 copies.

"Infinite Supremacy"

". . . the play is the tragedy, 'Man,' / And its hero, the conqueror Worm."

By 1838, Poe, ever the Southerner, was beginning to react to what he perceived as the clubbishness of the American literary scene. For scene there was, and Boston had it. Out of that elite circle of writers and thinkers came the movement that defied the idea of movements, Transcendentalism. Two years before Poe wrote "Ligeia," for

"It is not to be supposed that Cryptography . . . as the means of imparting important information, has gone out of use at the present day. It is still commonly practised in diplomacy; and there are individuals, even now, holding office in . . . various foreign governments, whose real business is that of deciphering."

which he was happy to get ten dollars from the *American Museum of Literature and the Arts,* the Transcendental Club sprang up on the Boston literary scene where the members could hobnob to discuss theology, philosophy, and literature. They published themselves in their own journal, and some went on to experiment with utopian living in a commune, which only lasted a few years.

fact

The publication of the Transcendental Club was called *The Dial,* a kind of literary "sun dial" measuring the American cultural times, and it was published on a shoestring budget for four years. A subscription cost three dollars a year for four 136-page issues that promised contributions from writers who championed social justice and intellectual freedom.

Ralph Waldo Emerson expressed the central idea of Transcendentalism, which insists ". . . on the power of Thought and of Will, on inspiration, on miracle, on individual culture." This was grist for Poe.

Creation of Ligeia

Poe goes to great lengths to establish the intense Ligeia as a woman of unusual learning—not to mention other faculties. "I have spoken of the learning of Ligeia: it was immense—such as I have never known in woman. In the classical tongues was she deeply proficient, and as far as my own acquaintance extended in regard to the modern dialects of Europe, I have never known her at fault. Indeed upon any theme of the most admired, because simply the most abstruse of the boasted erudition of the academy, have I ever found Ligeia at fault? How singularly—how thrillingly, this one point in the nature of my wife has forced itself, at this late period only, upon my attention! I said her knowledge was such as I have never known in woman—but where breathes the man who has traversed, and successfully, all the wide areas of moral, physical, and mathematical science? I saw not then what I now clearly perceive, that the acquisitions of Ligeia were gigantic, were astounding; yet I was sufficiently aware of her infinite supremacy to resign myself, with a child-like confidence, to her guidance through the chaotic world of metaphysical investigation at which I was most busily occupied during the earlier years of our marriage. With how vast a triumph—with how vivid a delight—with how much of all that is ethereal in hope—did I feel, as she bent over me in studies but little sought—but less known—that delicious vista by slow degrees expanding before me, down whose long, gorgeous, and all untrodden path, I might at length pass onward to the goal of a wisdom too divinely precious not to be forbidden!"

"Ligeia's" Meaning

This tale gives you the gorgeous, intellectual Ligeia, who seems to believe death is just a failure of will; and the Byronic, opium-dependent narrator husband who reports the results of Ligeia's great experiment, setting the stage by describing her erotic attachment to him. "That she loved me I should not have doubted; and I might have been easily aware that, in a bosom such as hers, love would have reigned no ordinary passion. But in death only, was I fully impressed with the strength of her affection. For long hours, detaining my hand, would she pour out before me the overflowing of a heart whose more than passionate devotion amounted to idolatry. How had I deserved to be so blessed by such confessions?—how had I deserved to be so cursed with the removal of my beloved in the hour of her making them? But upon this subject I cannot bear to dilate. Let me say only, that in Ligeia's more than womanly abandonment to a love, alas! all unmerited, all unworthily bestowed, I at length recognized the principle of her longing with so wildly earnest a desire for the life which was now fleeing so rapidly away. It is this wild longing—it is this eager vehemence of desire for life—but for life—that I have no power to portray—no utterance capable of expressing."

Will Ligeia beat the death rap? And if so, how? Poe is making arch, deadpan fun of the Transcendental mystique of the will as one of man's great faculties—the way to triumph over mere matter, the way to approach the mystery of the divine.

> "*After reading all that has been written, and after thinking all that can be thought, on the topics of God and the soul, the man who has a right to say that he thinks at all, will find himself face to face with the conclusion that, on these topics, the most profound thought is that which can be the least easily distinguished from the most superficial sentiment.*"—*Poe on the Divine*

Countering what must have seemed to him an insufferably naive optimism that money and a secure social position could buy, Poe takes on this cult of the individual by using—of all things—Gothic devices to show the horror of it. Esoteric learning, castles, exotic locales, narcotic dreams, the mysteries of life and death, all render uncomfortable the vague Transcendental mystique of Ligeia. And so, in Poe's hands, the tale becomes a horror story, and it is so infernally deadpan and over the top that it's easy to take it at face value. In an 1846 letter to Evert Duyckinck, Poe calls this tale "undoubtedly the best story I have written."

No wonder "Ligeia" was his personal favorite of his seventy-three tales. It is in some ways a declaration of war.

The Feng Shui of Edgar Allan Poe

One of the clearest places you find that stark difference between what Edgar Allan Poe expressed luridly on the page of a story, what he declared cleanly on the page of an essay, and what he actually lived is in home décor. His creative imagination spun out garish extravaganzas of color and form, but did they reflect his own personal taste? The man who believed the objective of poetry was the creation of beauty actually paid a lot of attention to matters of taste. How men and women dressed both themselves and their homes counted. These were the ways in which poets and non-poets alike could demonstrate a belief in the value of beauty. When it came to beauty, there was nothing "mere" or "sheer" about it. It was an organizing principle, a manifest destiny of man's soul. No wonder

Poe liked Keats, the English Romantic poet who tells you in "Ode on a Grecian Urn" that "Beauty is truth, truth beauty,"—That is all / Ye know of earth, and all ye need to know."

The love of what's beautiful, to a man with Poe's spirit, is no superficial trait. It's part of the artistic spring out of which good work—even the desire to attempt good work—comes. It eases troubles, cancels failures. Beauty exists. For the Transcendentalists all those miles away from Poe in Boston, it resided in what the spirit can touch in contemplation of nature and divinity. For Poe, not satisfied with letting beauty shimmer just outside his reach, it was something he wanted to bring close. It was, in some ways, the surest, finest weapon against death, because "An immortal instinct, deep within the spirit of man is . . . a sense of the Beautiful." It is an immortality that speaks powerfully to the likes of Poe.

In a story like "Ligeia," he goes into great detail to describe the "bridal chamber" the narrator shares with the brilliant, willful Ligeia. It is a suffocation of decorative pieces, a "phantasmagoric" display of strange sensuous elements that seem monstrous. Hanging brass censers, opulent and massive tapestries, a wall of Venetian glass that was tinted so the sunlight and moonlight make everything in this vast, pentagonal-shaped room look ghastly—oh, and don't overlook the Egyptian sarcophagus standing in the corner. Antiquity invades. And it smothers.

So much bad Feng Shui going on in Ligeia's bridal chamber, but no matter; pretty soon she's going to have more important things to think about. Like coming back from the dead.

Welcome to Poe Interiors

The "interior" of the story "Ligeia" is Poe at his most lurid. He wants to impress you (literally) with bad art. But in his piece "The Philosophy of Furniture," published in 1840, he takes advantage of the printed page to say a few things in the matter of American taste. "It is an evil growing out of our republican institutions," he says, "that here a man of large purse has usually a very little soul."

The result is that Americans do it up big, insisting in their decorative choices that bigger is better, bigger is richer. The richer you are, the bigger the bed or the dresser has to be. You have the dough to be opulent, and everyone with smaller purses can keep their puny opinions to themselves. Poe Interiors arrives to lend a consulting hand. Curtains? Forget them if your furniture is formal. If it isn't, too many curtains are "irreconcilable with good taste." Carpets? Nothing in the striped, rainbow, kaleidoscopic line. Glass? Watch out for those demons, glitter and glare. What you're after is a mild, cool light with warm shadows. Don't even talk to him about cut-glass. As for glitter, "children and idiots" like flickering lights, so he advises against chandeliers.

Poe is being droll in this essay on interior decorating, but he cannot resist an opportunity to sting the American equation of wealth with opulence. And just because he's jesting doesn't mean he doesn't speak the truth as he sees it. Home mattered tremendously to him, and he was a man with a highly developed sense of aesthetics. How he felt about beauty in life and poetry penetrated into the home as well.

question

What did Poe's home look like?

"So neat, so poor, so unfurnished, and yet so charming a dwelling I never saw. The floor of the kitchen was white as wheaten flour. A table, a chair, a little stove that it contained, seemed to furnish it perfectly. The sitting-room floor was laid with check matting; four chairs, a light stand, and a hanging bookshelf completed its furniture."—Mary Gove Nichols, on visiting Poe in Fordham

Poe didn't want the grotesque furnishings of "Ligeia."

He didn't even need the tasteful choices of "The Philosophy of Furniture."

In furnishing a home with two people who loved him more than anyone else in the world, he had more beauty around him than he could possibly need.

Chapter 14

Tiger by the Tale

From among Edgar Allan Poe's seventy-three tales, which is the longest, the shortest, the most autobiographical? Out of his own personal history and the popular ideas of the day, Poe found story ideas, but see what they became when they made contact with his rich imagination.

Edgar Allan Poe, Meet William Wilson

"Men usually grow base by degrees. From me, in an instant, all virtue dropped bodily as a mantle," Poe declares via the narrator in 1839's "William Wilson."

Like Poe's favorite, "Ligeia," written around the same time, "William Wilson" takes on that Transcendental sacred cow, the human will. In the Lady Ligeia, it is like a muscle she exercises to get her back into life. In "William Wilson," which is really a crime story in advance of Poe's trilogy of detection, the Dupin stories, the will is a diabolical force—quite far afield from the Transcendental sense of the will as that energetic part of man that can carry you straight to the divine. But the story "Ligeia" was droll; Poe was slathering Gothic devices all over his material. Perhaps because the subject engaged him more deeply, Poe wrote "William Wilson" as one of those first-person confessionals that became his trademark.

question

What makes a work "Gothic"?

Look for medieval settings—castles, catacombs, and crypts figure large—supernatural elements, weather gone crazy, melodramatic language, and what we now call "fem jep," or damsels in distress. Think of Gothic as Romance on steroids—caught in an underground passage in the wee hours of the morning.

The Story Behind "William Wilson"

The narrator, William Wilson, describes his increasingly antagonistic relationship with a classmate at his boarding school. This other boy, also named William Wilson, is so superior in every way to the narrator that their rivalry becomes intense. The narrator, a willful boy, became a "mastermind" at school, but discovered he had no power over the rival William Wilson. The two were identical. Over the years at prep schools, college, and beyond, the narrator's rival always turns up as the finer incarnation of himself.

In this passage, during the boarding school days, the narrator decides to study his nemesis while the other sleeps. In it, he only has a glimmer of understanding of who the other William Wilson is.

"It was upon a gloomy and tempestuous night of an early autumn, about the close of my fifth year at the school, and immediately after the altercation just mentioned, that, finding every one wrapped in sleep, I arose from bed, and, lamp in hand, stole through a wilderness of narrow passages from my own bedroom to that of my rival. I had been long plotting one of those ill-natured pieces of practical wit at his expense in which I had hitherto been so uniformly unsuccessful. It was my intention, now, to put my scheme in operation, and I resolved to make him feel the whole extent of the malice with which I was imbued. Having reached his closet, I noiselessly entered, leaving the lamp, with a shade over it, on the outside. I advanced a step, and listened to the sound of his tranquil breathing. Assured of his being asleep, I returned, took the light, and with it again approached the bed. Close curtains were around it, which, in the prosecution of my plan, I slowly and quietly withdrew, when the bright rays fell vividly upon the sleeper, and my eyes, at the same moment, upon his countenance. I looked, and a numbness, an iciness of feeling instantly pervaded my frame. My breast heaved, my knees tottered, my whole spirit became possessed with an objectless yet intolerable horror. Gasping for breath, I lowered the lamp in still nearer proximity to the face. Were these—these the lineaments of William Wilson? I saw, indeed, that they were his, but I shook as with a fit of the ague in fancying they were not. What was there about them to confound me in this manner? I gazed—while my brain reeled with a multitude of incoherent thoughts. Not thus he appeared—assuredly not thus—in the vivacity of his waking hours. The same name; the same contour of person; the same day of arrival at the academy! And then his dogged and meaningless imitation of my gait, my voice, my habits, and my manner! Was it, in truth, within the bounds of human possibility that what I now witnessed was the result of the habitual practice of this sarcastic imitation?

Awe-stricken, and with a creeping shudder, I extinguished the lamp, passed silently from the chamber, and left, at once, the halls of that old academy, never to enter them again."

The gulf between them widens as the narrator, bedeviled by his inability to understand what's happening to him, is driven into increasingly bad behavior—the "other" William Wilson even exposes him as a cheat at cards!

Finishing the Story

Up to this point, the story is an exploration into the criminal mind as it develops. Toward the end, the narrator finds the will to free himself—in any way he can—from what he believes is his tormentor. He feels justified. "Double" stories like "William Wilson" were popular in Poe's day, before the advent of modern psychology that studied these internal warring impulses as part of the same individual. In the 1800s, that other self actually became another, separate character—there's the example of Dr. Jekyll and Mr. Hyde. But in the hands of Poe, the narrator is not the "good twin," the one dogged by the reprehensible and baffling "Other." It's the outshone, lesser self who moves toward increasing criminality, who Poe chooses to narrate this story about man's violence against his own conscience. What an American choice it was! In an era that saw the rise of popular interest in rascal tales, Poe was in the vanguard of writers looking at the seamy undersides of those American forms of the hoax, the tall tale, and the con game.

After years of eluding his tormentor, the other Wilson, something changes in the narrator's view of his own predicament.

"Thus far I had succumbed supinely to this imperious domination. The sentiments of deep awe with which I habitually regarded the elevated character, the majestic wisdom, the apparent omnipresence and omnipotence of Wilson, added to a feeling of even terror, with which certain other traits in his nature and assumptions inspired me, had operated, hitherto, to impress me with an idea of my own utter weakness and helplessness, and to suggest

an implicit, although bitterly reluctant submission to his arbitrary will. But, of late days, I had given myself up entirely to wine; and its maddening influence upon my hereditary temper rendered me more and more impatient of control. I began to murmur, to hesitate, to resist. And was it only fancy which induced me to believe that, with the increase of my own firmness, that of my tormentor underwent a proportional diminution? Be this as it may, I now began to feel the inspiration of a burning hope, and at length nurtured in my secret thoughts a stern and desperate resolution that I would submit no longer to be enslaved."

This tender, mistaken belief in his own injury sets the stage for his own ultimate action against his double.

"William Wilson" is most clearly autobiographical in the sense of what Poe draws on from his own youth: Dr. Bransby's school in England, where he excelled at Greek, Latin, and athletics (in fact, the headmaster in the story is actually called "Dr. Bransby"). The narrator's drinking and gambling—what he calls "my miserable profligacy"—are revved-up versions of Poe's time at the University of Virginia. But you have to wonder whether "William Wilson" isn't also a kind of psychic autobiography of a writer who was already experiencing a kind of split between the unwavering commitment to live the life of a professional writer at any expense, including health, comfort, and ordinary friendships—and the simple yearning for a haven-like home where he could be just "Eddie."

Imagining a New Frontier

Everything in *The Narrative of Arthur Gordon Pym of Nantucket*, Poe's longest work of fiction, is excellent. No lurid descriptions, no over-inflated prose. In *Pym*, even writing as a young man in his late twenties, Poe shows himself a prose master. Everything here is workmanlike, carrying you swiftly through the story, and very often beautifully. Why then did he once refer to *Pym* as "a very silly book"?

It's an interesting quirk of Poe's nature that he scoffs at his greatest works and rhapsodizes over his lesser.

Inspiration for *Pym*

In his mind, it takes no great ingenuity to unravel a puzzle created for the very purpose of unraveling, as he does in the detective tales. Maybe what he came to consider "silly" about *Pym* is the exuberant stacking up of boyhood seafaring adventures he previews for the readers in the book's subtitle, which promises an account of mutiny, butchery, shipwreck, various sufferings, famine, deliverance, capture, massacre—and all that's before the real "distressing calamity" that occurs even farther south.

they said...

"A more impudent attempt at humbugging the public has never been exercised . . . Mr. Poe, if not the author of Pym's book, is at least responsible for its publication . . . We regret to find Mr. Poe's name in connexion with such a mass of ignorance and effrontery."—Billy Burton, in a review of *Pym* in 1838, a year before hiring Poe as the editor of his *Gentleman's Magazine*

Here's a sample from *The Narrative of Arthur Gordon Pym.* Having survived a mutiny at sea, the young narrator and a few others are adrift. After many days of despair, they sight another ship, which seems to be their last hope.

"She had evidently seen a good deal of rough weather, and, we supposed, had suffered much in the gale which had proved so disastrous to ourselves; for her foretopmast was gone, and some of her starboard bulwarks. When we first saw her, she was, as I have already said, about two miles off and to windward, bearing down upon us. The breeze was very gentle, and what astonished us chiefly was, that she had no other sails set than her foresail and mainsail, with a flying jib—of course she came down but slowly, and our impatience amounted nearly to phrensy. The awkward

manner in which she steered, too, was remarked by all of us, even excited as we were. She yawed about so considerably, that once or twice we thought it impossible she could see us, or imagined that, having seen us, and discovered no person on board, she was about to tack and make off in another direction. Upon each of these occasions we screamed and shouted at the top of our voices, when the stranger would appear to change for a moment her intention, and again hold on towards us—this singular conduct being repeated two or three times, so that at last we could think of no other manner of accounting for it than by supposing the helmsman to be in liquor.

"No person was seen upon her decks until she arrived within about a quarter of a mile of us. We then saw three seamen, whom by their dress we took to be Hollanders. Two of these were lying on some old sails near the forecastle, and the third, who appeared to be looking at us with great curiosity, was leaning over the starboard bow near the bowsprit. This last was a stout and tall man, with a very dark skin. He seemed by his manner to be encouraging us to have patience, nodding to us in a cheerful although rather odd way, and smiling constantly so as to display a set of the most brilliantly white teeth. As his vessel drew nearer, we saw a red flannel cap which he had on fall from his head into the water; but of this he took little or no notice, continuing his odd smiles and gesticulations. I relate these things and circumstances minutely, and I relate them, it must be understood, precisely as they appeared *to us.*

"The brig came on slowly, and now more steadily than before, and—I cannot speak calmly of this event—our hearts leaped up wildly within us, and we poured out our whole souls in shouts and thanksgiving to God for the complete, unexpected, and glorious deliverance that was so palpably at hand. Of a sudden, and all at once, there came wafted over the ocean from the strange vessel (which was now close upon us) a smell, a stench, such as the whole world has no name for—no conception of—hellish—utterly suffocating—insufferable, inconceivable. I gasped for breath, and turning to my companions, perceived that they were paler than marble.

But we had now no time left for question or surmise—the brig was within fifty feet of us, and it seemed to be her intention to run under our counter, that we might board her without her putting out a boat. We rushed aft, when, suddenly, a wide yaw threw her off full five or six points from the course she had been running, and, as she passed under our stern at the distance of about twenty feet, we had a full view of her decks. Shall I ever forget the triple horror of that spectacle? Twenty-five or thirty human bodies, among whom were several females, lay scattered about between the counter and the galley, in the last and most loathsome state of putrefaction! We plainly saw that not a soul lived in that fated vessel! Yet we could not help shouting to the dead for help! Yes, long and loudly did we beg, in the agony of the moment, that those silent and disgusting images would stay for us, would not abandon us to become like them, would receive us among their goodly company! We were raving with horror and despair—thoroughly mad through the anguish of our grievous disappointment."

Pym, the Inspiration

Pym is a rip-roaring sea tale that actually sets the standard for the adventure story—think about the works of later Victorian writers Robert Louis Stevenson and Jules Verne. But *Pym* is also the direct ancestor of one of the most majestic novels in American literature. Just twenty years after Poe's "narrative" came out, Herman Melville, who admitted he was inspired by Poe's story, published *Moby Dick*, which turns some of the metaphors and characters of the earlier work into a towering novel of great beauty and depth. It began with Poe, who was too good a writer to simply put mindless heroics on the page. *The Narrative of Arthur Gordon Pym* shows whatever is most human in all the harrowing adventures: the brotherhood that defies stereotypes and self-interest, the treacheries that defy brotherhood, and the final mysteries that link brothers to something greater and relentlessly unknown. Hostile? Benevolent? It depends, deliciously, on the individual reader.

Poe looked very closely at the tentative steps into the moral wilderness of the American frontier—including the eastern forests—made by earlier writers like Washington Irving and James Fenimore Cooper. Always on the prowl for commercial appeal, and possessing an imagination that sprang at his own glimmering novelties, he saw the potential for relocating the stuff of American fiction to a vast new wilderness—the sea.

Short and Sweet

"Ye who read are still among the living, but I who write shall have long since gone my way into the region of shadows," begins "Shadow—A Fable." This tight little two-page tale, published in 1835, describes a "year of terror" in the eighth century, when the plague swept across Greece. Gathered in a hall fortified against any intrusion—meaning plague and death—from the outside are the narrator and six others, carousing hysterically in response to the terror beyond their walls. Everything about this story prefigures the longer tale, "The Masque of the Red Death," which Poe would write several years later. In "Shadow," he's experimenting with his materials, doing a sketch for what would become the later, more fully developed work. In this earlier version, Poe makes use of many of his favorite devices: a heavy, claustrophobic atmosphere with luridly described furnishings; death personified; an intense tone brought about by the repeated use of *terror* and other ominous words; and the headlong rush to the terrible conclusion. That conclusion is strangely milder and more touching than it is in that later story, "Masque." It's as if Poe decided to ratchet up that "single effect" he believed a good short story should achieve.

For such a brief story, "Shadow" quickly achieves the oppressive atmosphere that became one of Poe's signature devices. "Black draperies, likewise, in the gloomy room, shut out from our view the moon, the lurid stars, and the peopleless streets—but the boding and the memory of Evil, they would not be so excluded. There were things around us and about of which I can render no distinct account—things material and spiritual. Heaviness in the atmosphere—a sense of suffocation—anxiety—and above all, that terrible state of existence which the nervous experience when the senses are keenly living and awake, and meanwhile the powers of thought lie dormant. A dead weight hung upon us. It hung upon our limbs—upon the household furniture—upon the goblets from which we drank; and all things were depressed, and borne down thereby—all things save only the flames of the seven lamps which illumined our revel. Uprearing themselves in tall slender lines of light, they thus remained burning all pallid and motionless; and in the mirror which their lustre formed upon the round table of ebony at which we sat, each of us there assembled beheld the pallor of his own countenance, and the unquiet glare in the downcast eyes of his companions. Yet we laughed and were merry in our proper way—which was hysterical; and sang the songs of Anacreon—which are madness; and drank deeply—although the purple wine reminded us of blood."

It's interesting, too, to note that just five years after "Shadow" appeared in the *Southern Literary Messenger,* Poe changed its subtitle from "A Fable" to "A Parable." What's the difference? Both are short forms of writing for the purpose of instruction. However, a fable uses supernatural elements (sometimes, talking animals) to illustrate a truth, and a parable tells a story to illustrate a moral attitude. The truth in "Shadow—A Fable" is that death comes. Maybe the moral attitude in "Shadow—A Parable" is that you need to acknowledge the power of the dead, and our continuing connections to them. Which is better?

Devilishly Funny

None of Poe's seventy-three tales has the kind of genial warmth or rollicking wit of anything by, say, Mark Twain. Poe wrote some of his stories with a kind of avenging glee, but his humor was extremely personal and was not the sort that invited folks to sit around a wood stove and enjoy a bit of storytelling fellowship. He relished his own hoaxes in stories like "The Balloon-Hoax," "The Unparalleled Adventure of Hans Pfaall," "The Facts in the Case of M. Valdemar," and "Von Kempelen and His Discovery," and laid down just the right combination of authoritative voice and ersatz "facts" that fooled the public in these so-called accounts of a hot air balloon flight across the Atlantic, another to the moon, death delayed by mesmerism, and the process of turning lead into gold. But hoaxes are the practical jokes of literature, and even when Poe was writing, they left readers feeling more ridiculed than entertained.

fact
Poe's hoax, "The Journal of Julius Rodman," was mistaken for a true account of an expedition over the Rocky Mountains prior to Lewis and Clark's. An excerpt found its way into the *Congressional Record*, where it was published as fact.

This miscalculation of others' responses to him was characteristic of Poe. He expected his most searing criticisms of other writers to serve, really, as correctives: now go off and do better work. By bitterly haranguing his foster father, John Allan, over his failure to offer enough money, love, or moral support, it's as if he fully expected Pa to correct this unacceptable behavior—you're absolutely right, Edgar, so sorry, now let me set you up in fine style forever. His good friend Susan Archer Talley once remarked about him that ". . . in knowledge of human nature he was, for a man of his genius, strangely deficient." In many ways, the gambling debts he racked up at college because he was a bad card player were really a tell-tale shortcoming: Poe couldn't tell when the other guy held better cards.

Satan's Makeover
Oddly enough, his stories with any of the warmth of real humor are the ones featuring the devil. What makes his warm humor here so interesting is that in a writer with a taste for Gothic horror, you would think he would mine all the possibilities for evil in some

165

outsized figure of the devil. It's good material in the classic line. The finest writers of this period in American literature were rethinking the problem of evil, and Poe was no exception. Hawthorne, for example, cast the figure of the devil in more shadowy, ambiguous ways, suggesting that Old Scratch's true habitat was the heart of man. In Melville, evil is entirely man-made, even as man is left trembling at an indifferent universe.

In Poe, the devil is belittled, even while acknowledging his powers. Poe makes him a figure of fun. In fact, Poe makes him a true American original, a shape-shifting kind of character—yet another American con man?—in that good old classic American form, the tall tale. Maybe that accounts for the good-natured fun in Poe's "devil tales."

"The Duc De L'Omelette"

The story in this group that works the best is "The Duc De L'Omelette," published in 1832 in the *Saturday Courier*. It's a tight little frolic that pits His Grace, a French duke of the most sublime tastes, against His Majesty, the devil. Everyone triumphs somehow in this urbane duke's triumph over a devilish card player so bad even Poe himself could have beaten him. The story has a typical Poe shortcoming: bring along a French/English dictionary if you intend to read it. Maybe because the tale is short, Poe manages to sustain the frothy humor, and there's none of the bite you find in so many of his satires and hoaxes.

The effete Duc, having died, finds himself in the Devil's chambers. Unafraid, he is indignant when the Devil orders him to strip. "'Strip, indeed! very pretty i' faith! no, sir, I shall not strip. Who are you, pray, that I, Duc De L'Omelette, Prince de Foie-Gras, just come of age, author of the 'Mazurkiad,' and Member of the Academy, should divest myself at your bidding of the sweetest pantaloons ever made by Bourdon, the daintiest *robe-de-chambre* ever put together by Rombêrt—to say nothing of the taking my hair out of paper—not to mention the trouble I should have in drawing off my gloves?'"

The Devil is also indignant. "'Who am I?—ah, true! I am Baal-Zebub, Prince of the Fly. I took thee, just now, from a rose-wood coffin inlaid with ivory. Thou wast curiously scented, and labelled as per invoice. Belial sent thee,—my Inspector of Cemeteries. The pantaloons, which thou sayest were made by Bourdon, are an excellent pair of linen drawers, and thy *robe-de-chambre* is a shroud of no scanty dimensions.'" What ensues is a gentlemanly game of cards for such trifles as pantaloons and souls.

For the most part, Poe's humor stiff-arms us. It shows, for sure, how very clever and well-read Poe was, but it doesn't draw the reader in. In some ways, what Poe found funny is often at the reader's expense. With humor at its greatest, you share in the joke.

You Animal, You

Animal magnetism. Not quite the same as charisma, although you can see how a charismatic hypnotist might have a great rate of success. Poe used many of the fads of the era in his writing, and mesmerism did not escape his pen.

In the otherwise rational eighteenth century, Vienna in the late 1700s was apparently a hotbed of pseudoscientific thought and practice. Animal magnetism rocketed Viennese Dr. Franz Anton Mesmer into the limelight. He believed illness was caused by blocked magnetic fluids in the human body. Typically, a session with Dr. Mesmer could include sitting with your feet in magnetized water while he circled around in colorful robes, waving a magnetized pole to dislodge the blockage in your magnetic flow. Later refinements of mesmeric technique found many sufferers sitting together around a "baquet," a vat of water, with feet submerged, holding on to a metal pole. When all the laughing, crying, and convulsing began, the cure was pronounced. After such a cathartic conclusion to the theater of suggestibility, patients swore they were healed of whatever ailed them. As Dr. Mesmer's work continued and he grasped at sophistication, gone were the vats of water and metal poles (and, presumably, colored robes). No props were necessary. Getting that magnetic flow going again was a matter of the willpower the practitioner exerted over the patient. Pretty soon, a new phenomenon was reported: a

167

somnambulistic state, a trance. Followed, of course, by a cure. In the uptight, button-down, corseted and stayed Victorian era, it's not hard to understand the appeal of any activity that not only accepts histrionics but actually looks for them as a sign of success.

they said...

"It requires from me no apology, in stating, that I have not the least doubt of the *possibility* of such a phenomenon; for I did actually restore to active animation a person who died from excessive drinking of ardent spirits. He was placed in his coffin ready for interment."—Boston charlatan Robert H. Collyer, writing to Poe after being hoodwinked by Poe's story "The Facts in the Case of M. Valdemar," 1845

The uncontrollable laughing and crying was pure catharsis. And almost orgiastic—with a doctor's prescription. Maybe it's no wonder something like Mesmerism and Gothicism hit the scene at the same time. Both are alternative reactions to the sexual repressiveness of the age. Think of the frighteningly knowing, penetrating, devouring control of Count Dracula. First comes the trance.

Poe, always interested in the unexplored regions of imagination, wrote several tales in which mesmerism is mentioned. When an idea had something to do with the human mind, he was interested, hands down. Phrenology, mesmerism, spiritualism, even cryptography—the secret-loving mind devises codes that tantalize. The best known of his mesmerism tales is "The Facts in the Case of M. Valdemar," which happens also to be one of his hoaxes since the story is presented as a piece of reportage. Spiritualism attempts to "penetrate the veil" between life and death and provide a way (a "medium") through which the dead can speak to us. In Poe's "Valdemar" story, he describes what happens when a dying man is mesmerized. In this case, there's no comfortable medium acting as an intermediary between the living and the dead, which certainly helps keep the lid on all the awe and fright in the room. In Poe's case, the pre-death trance enables the dead man to address those gathered around, face to death mask. The story had a thrilling effect on readers everywhere. Elizabeth Barrett Browning, whose work Poe admired, found herself in a state of "disorder" over the story, wondering if it was true.

You have to wonder how much credence Poe would have put in the work of Dr. Franz Anton Mesmer had he known Mesmer twice committed "The Great Sin" in Poe's view: plagiarism. Mesmer's dissertation plagiarized another's work on how human health is affected by the planets, and he appropriated the work of a Jesuit priest/healer named, of all things, Dr. Hell, who had already cottoned to the curative properties of attending to magnetic blockage and flow.

"We see it stated in some of the papers that thirty-two physicians of St. Claireville, Louisiana, and its vicinity, have threatened to refuse medical attendance to any one who shall support the bill before the Legislature of that State, making disinterment of the dead for dissection a State Prison offence. This is undoubtedly a bold stand, but one which may well be justified."—Poe on scientific progress, 1840

Chapter 15

One-Shot Deals and "Rejects"

There were detours in the creative output of Edgar Allan Poe. He was a nimble and versatile writer, but there were limits even to what he could do. He tried his hand at a stage play, a philosophical treatise, and a textbook on malacology (mollusks). Not all of his work found instantaneous acceptance—as evidenced by his elegant "rejects," later recategorized as successes.

He Sells Seashells . . .

*The Conchologist's First Book: Or, A System of Testaceous Malacology, Arranged Expressly for the Use of Schools,*1839. Haswell, Barrington, and Haswell. No, it's not Poe's satire on natural science, or Poe's epic poem on searching for whelks or scallops. Ever on the prowl for writing jobs, Poe agreed to help his Philadelphia neighbor, naturalist Thomas Wyatt, publish a revision of his book on seashells. Wyatt's earlier book was a longer, much more costly edition that didn't sell well, so Wyatt and the publisher wanted to offer a slimmer, more affordable version of the book that would appeal to the textbook market. And, possibly sensing what lay ahead, they cynically believed they could deflect cries of "foul" by adding the sheen of a somewhat famous writer's name. For fifty dollars, Poe came on board.

"The study of Conchology, . . . when legitimately directed, and when regarding . . . the habitations, wonderfully constructed, of an immensely numerous and vastly important branch of the animal creation, will lead the mind of the investigator through paths hitherto but imperfectly trodden, to many novel contemplations of Almighty Beneficence and Design."—Poe on mollusks, in his Introduction, 1839

In terms of original work, Poe contributed the preface and the introduction, and he added his translation of a piece by French zoologist and paleontologist Georges Cuvier. Because his analytical mind couldn't help but scrutinize anything it came across, he tinkered with the taxonomy itself. Everything else was paraphrased from other writers—which he acknowledged.

Wyatt omitted his own name from this lean version, making Poe the "front man" for the book. The book appeared as entirely his own work—or, actually, the plagiarized work of Scottish naturalist Captain Thomas Brown, whose *The conchologist's text-book, embracing the arrangements of Lamarck and Linnaeus, with a glossary of technical terms,* had appeared in 1833.

Howls went up.

- Irony #1: Edgar Allan Poe, scourge of plagiarists everywhere, was himself accused of plagiarism—and it would not be the last time. Twelve years later, Poe's friend Henry Chivers accused the writer of "The Raven" of plagiarizing Chivers's poem about the death of his daughter, which Poe himself had published three years prior. The meter and patterns of rhyme are virtually the same, but Poe's most popular poem—which took him just a month to write—is a more original and dramatic piece than the conventional expression of loss in "The Lost Pleiad" by Chivers.
- Irony #2: Wyatt's textbook on seashells was a commercial hit, selling out in two months. Poe's true creative work was published in ten volumes during his lifetime, but the conchology book was the only book bearing his name to see more than a single edition during his lifetime.

By 1845, *The Conchologist's First Book* was in its third edition. As usual, Poe never made a penny more than his original fifty-dollar fee on what was his biggest commercial success.

And the Razzie Goes To . . .

At twenty-six, Edgar Allan Poe was living in Baltimore, publishing poetry and tales, enjoying quiet domesticity with the Clemms, and trying his hand at various courtships. On the brink of adding "critic" to his curriculum vitae, he was open to all things literary, and apparently he began to wonder whether he was a dramatist.

Since the result was *Politian*, the answer was no. Eleven clanking scenes in a Shakespearean line were all it took to show the shrewd Poe that his gifts did not lie in writing for the stage. The theatrical talent that came to him from his mother's side found a different sort of outlet—in the daily dramas of his life, the luxurious "sets" of his tales, and the quick, emotional responsiveness found in all his work. But it's clear he felt lumbered by his material in *Politian*, his only drama. His source for this revenge tale is an actual murder case in 1825 termed "The Kentucky Tragedy" by the press. The case involved a girl who married a lawyer and made him swear to kill the man who had seduced her before she was married. He did, after a few warm-up attempts, protested his innocence, was nonetheless convicted, and on the eve of his execution both he and his wife took an overdose of laudanum (is this where Poe got the idea?). She dies, he lives, but only until the hangman gets him. Unbelievably, this story served as inspiration for several writers aside from Poe, including William Gilmore Simms and Robert Penn Warren.

fact

"The Kentucky Tragedy" was a murky affair. Despite the avenging husband's insistence that his murder of the seducer (who, incidentally, was the Attorney General of Kentucky) was an act of honor, elements of the case made it look more like the result of long-standing political infighting. The "affair of honor" defense becomes less convincing when you consider the fact that the victim was stabbed in the middle of the night seven years after the seduction.

The first thing Poe did with this story was move it to the Italian Renaissance. Not even names like Lalage, Castiglione, and Politian, or peerages, monks, and moonlight could turn this stuff into a silk purse. Because the plot is just final crisis, all the dragging feet and swords along the way simply mark time until the inevitable conclusion. Consequently, there's a lot of posturing, tough talk, exclamation points, and speeches that go, "Ha! coward!" and "Scoundrel!—*arise and die!*" Approach this play in a giddy mood and you might take it for farce. At one point, you feel poor, avenging Politian is turning on Poe himself, when he challenges, "Draw, villain, and prate no more!" Poe, mercifully, runs him through.

Edgar Allan Poe Explains It All

"I design to speak of the *Physical, Metaphysical and Mathematical— of the Material and Spiritual Universe; of its Essence, its Origin, its Creation, its Present Condition, and its Destiny.*"

All that in 143 pages. A year and a half after Virginia died, Edgar Allan Poe came out with *Eureka*, his attempt to explain it all—seemingly to others, but really to himself. The author of "The Raven" and "The Gold-Bug" was suddenly concerned with things like mass, matter, nebulae, clusters, gravity, and infinity. In his effort to understand a cosmos that by 1848 must have come to seem inexplicably malign to him, he focuses, Dupin-like, on these mysteries and ends up making the proposition, "*In the Original Unity of the First Thing lies the Secondary Cause of All Things, with the Germ of their Inevitable Annihilation.*" His own emotional fatalism is couched there in the language of science and philosophy: the "germ of their inevitable annihilation."

fact

Poe's *Eureka* scoops the Big Bang theory by eighty years. It wasn't until 1927 that Georges Lemaître, a Belgian priest, asserted that the explosion of an atom (the Big Bang) sometime between 10 and 20 billion years ago was responsible for the creation of the universe.

As much as Poe tries to talk the talk in what he oddly subtitles "A Prose Poem," *Eureka* is fascinating far less as a philosophical treatise than as a heartbreaking document of a highly intelligent artist trying to subdue his own wayward reality. Man is a baffling, intractable creature—the author himself included. Life brings success and health and ease to the enemy, and hardship and disease and ruin to those you love. You shout into a void that never closes, never fills in. You send your best efforts out into the marketplace, where they're trammeled. Is it any wonder, then, that Poe looked up at the stars, that gateway into a vast unknown that, compared to anything he had known on Earth, could only be friendlier?

The following excerpt from Section 2 of *Eureka* gives you a sense of many things about Poe's writing toward the end of his brief life: the astuteness of his imagination, the breadth of his intellect, the riveting earnestness behind all his underlinings—and, in his attention to intuition, how close he came to the Transcendentalists he scorned.

"We have attained a point where only Intuition *can aid us; but now let me recur to the idea which I have already suggested as that alone which we can properly entertain of intuition. It is but* the conviction arising from those inductions or deductions of which the processes are so shadowy as to escape our consciousness, elude our reason, or defy our capacity of expression. *With this understanding, I now assert that an intuition altogether irresistible, although inexpressible, forces me to the conclusion that what God originally created—that that Matter which, by dint of His Volition, He first made from His Spirit, or from Nihility, could have been nothing but Matter in its utmost conceivable state of—what?—of* Simplicity.

"This will be found the sole absolute assumption *of my Discourse. I use the word "assumption" in its ordinary sense; yet I maintain that even this my primary proposition is very far indeed from being really a mere assumption. Nothing was ever more certainly—no human conclusion was ever, in fact, more regularly—more rigorously deduced; but, alas! the processes lie out of the human analysis—at all events are beyond the utterance of the human tongue. If, however, in the course of this Essay I succeed in showing that out of Matter in its extreme of Simplicity all things* might *have been, we reach directly the inference that they* were, *thus constructed, through the impossibility of attributing supererogation to Omnipotence.*

"Let us now endeavor to conceive what Matter must be, when, or if, in its absolute extreme of Simplicity. Here the Reason flies at once to Imparticularity—to a particle—to one *particle—a particle of* one *kind—of* one *character—of* one *nature—of* one *size—of*

one form—a particle, therefore, "without *form and void*"—a particle positively a particle at all points—a particle absolutely unique, individual, undivided, and not indivisible only because He who created it by dint of His Will can by an infinitely less energetic exercise of the same Will, as a matter of course, divide it.

"Oneness, then, is all that I predicate of the originally created Matter; but I propose to show that this Oneness is a principle abundantly sufficient to account for the constitution, the existing phenomena, and the plainly inevitable annihilation, of at least the material Universe.

"The willing into being the primordial Particle has completed the act, or more properly the conception, of Creation. We now proceed to the ultimate purpose for which we are to suppose the Particle created—that is to say, the ultimate purpose so far as our considerations yet enable us to see it—the constitution of the Universe from it, the Particle."

Not even twenty years later, to Walt Whitman that upward glance wasn't explained by a "learn'd astronomer's" calculations and ramblings. For Whitman, it was a glance that sped past any human analysis and lodged at a place of great emotional truth when he gazed "in perfect silence at the stars." But Whitman had a different nature, and Poe needed to be a "learn'd astronomer" in *Eureka*, enlisting the help of his analytical mind to make sense of a world that otherwise only felt like endless pain.

The Fate of *Eureka*

Poe expected Putnam to publish 50,000 copies of *Eureka*. Putnam published 500, and it's unclear how many of those sold at seventy-five cents a copy. It is an intense piece, Poe's "prose poem," which despite the subtitle doesn't really contain any more poetic devices (rhyme, rhythm, imagery, sound repetitions) than his other work, where there are plenty. In some ways, it contains even less. *The Narrative of Arthur Gordon Pym* is much more "poetic" in terms of its imagery and metaphors than anything in *Eureka*, so what about this book of philosophy makes Poe urge readers to consider it a prose poem? He declared that, having written *Eureka*, he couldn't imagine writing anything else, anything more, anything better. As a writer, he was content. For the moment.

Poe Tackles Transcendentalism

Maybe in his own mind this work was guided by a sense of such exalted beauty he had never before seen—and the object of any poem should be the rhythmical creation of beauty. In *Eureka*, the rhythms are cosmic, and the beauty he sees is sublime. But therein lies the problem—only Poe detects the beauty.

Ironically, readers were thrilled and overpowered by stories he dashed off to make a buck. Poe, on the other hand, was thrilled and overpowered by a treatise that pretty much sank without a trace. Henry David Thoreau could have succeeded with something like *Eureka*. Thoreau rhapsodized about nature and was hailed as a great individualist. However, people liked Thoreau, and Edgar Allan Poe was no Thoreau.

When folks had a look at this book, Poe was disparaged as a pantheist, someone who worships the divine in nature. Poe disputed the charge. If anything, passages in *Eureka* make him sound like the Southern chapter of the Transcendentalist Club. He talks about ". . . that cool exercise of consciousness, from that deep tranquillity of self-inspection, through which alone we can hope to attain the presence of this, the most sublime of truths, and look it leisurely in the face."

"It is a deeply consequential error this:—the assumption that we, being men, will, in general, be *deliberately* true. The greater amount of truth is impulsively uttered; thus the greater amount is spoken, not written. But, in examining the historic material, we leave these considerations out of sight. We dote upon records, which, in the main, lie; while we discard the *Kabbala*, which, properly interpreted, do *not*."—Poe on where to look for truth

Poe's Philosophy

Interspersed with ideas about nebulae and matter, he fires off comments on the divine will and the heart divine. Human beings yearn, says Poe, for the infinite. An "absolute Unity" is the "source of All Things." He sees universal cycles and rhythms, which he loses in starchy terms like "agglomeration" and "dissolution," wherein he finds hope: ". . . we can readily conceive that a new and perhaps totally different series of conditions may ensue; another creation and radiation, returning into itself; another action and reaction of the divine will." New and perhaps totally different. There is always— for both universe and man—the possibility of change. Behind all the cycles and rhythms is the Heart Divine.

> **they said…**
>
> "…the searching analysis, the metaphysical acumen, the synthetic power and the passion for analogical and serial development of ideas according to preconceived law . . . exemplified by Mr. Poe to a degree unsurpassed in this country, at least, so far as we are acquainted."—John H. Hopkins's account in the New York *Evening Express* of Poe's lecture on "The Universe," 1848

For a man derailed by the death of his wife and the exhausting tangle of his personal and professional relationships, Poe's only philosophy book is a poignant attempt to reconcile himself to forces he can neither understand nor change. In *Eureka*, you hear a sustained cry, an Existentialist bellow—and a heartbreaking statement that reaches down the long years to readers who are very far away: "And now, —" Poe says, "—this Heart Divine—what is it? *It is our own.*"

The Fever Called Living

When you get to look back at the total literary output of a major American man or woman of letters, you view that career as a success. That's the final reckoning that comes from a distance of many years—in Poe's case, a distance of more than a century and a half. A body of work—no more, no less, all done—takes on the air of artifact, something you can study, something you can understand as meaningful and valuable because it has survived, and it's good. You have the benefit of the big picture. But during the writer's working lifetime, especially one as fraught with drama as Edgar Allan Poe's, that "body of work" was all still a work in progress. A story, a poem, a review—separate little pieces that had to find their own way in a mercurial marketplace. Some stories and poems got into print, but didn't bring much to Poe in terms of notice or money. Some brought cash prizes, but, in the absence of any copyright protection, nothing more. Even when some were printed, publication alone didn't necessarily make Poe himself love them any better (for example, his calling *Pym* a "very silly book," or "The Conqueror Worm" "hurried and unconsidered"). There were a couple of poems that Poe had to send around a few places because publishers weren't clamoring. His poems "For Annie" and "The Bells" were "rejects"—but not permanent ones.

they said...

"There is talent unquestionably in these fanciful speculations.... But the vital element of sincerity is wanting. The mocking smile of the hoaxer is seen behind his grave mask. He is more anxious to mystify and confound than to persuade, or even to instruct...."—Epes Sargent, editor of the Boston *Transcript*, in a July 1848 review of Poe's Eureka

In "For Annie," published in 1849, just six months prior to Poe's death, Poe writes of ". . . the fever called 'Living'/ That burned in my brain." On November 3, 1848, on a train going from Providence to Boston, Poe swallowed an ounce of laudanum in an unenthusiastic suicide attempt prompted by his despair over his failing relationship with Helen Whitman. It's interesting to note that the poem that erupts from this one-time event in his life is not addressed to the lady in question, but to Annie Richmond. Poe's sorrowing mind turns to his young married friend in Lowell, Massachusetts for comfort.

He explains to her (and, obviously, to us) that he was driven to despair by that "fever called Living"—and living, of course, exceeds even failed relationships. What's especially poignant about this poem "For Annie" is that the content so beautifully matches its form. It's a breathless, feverish poem filled with the kind of heartbreaking repetitions—especially of Annie's name, which becomes a kind of mantra for the sufferer—that are nearly hypnotic.

"Think—oh think for me—before the words—the vows are spoken, which put yet another terrible bar between us— . . . Can you, my Annie, bear to think I am another's? It would give me supreme—infinite bliss to hear you say that you could not bear it—"—Poe to Annie Richmond less than two weeks after the suicide attempt, 1848

With a Little Help from His Nurse

"The Bells" was published in 1849, a month after Poe's death. The poem dealt with the titular instruments and all their functions, from raising the alarm to celebrating a wedding.

Poe was depressed.

It had been two years since Virginia's death. When the widowed husband went into a long decline over the winter following Virginia's death, his old friend Loui Shew nursed him. As he started to recover, he needed to write—write something—but claimed histrionically that he had nothing to write about, and that he couldn't write, anyway.

Was he inspired somehow by the very bells of nearby Grace Church that he complained were irritating him? At any rate, Loui Shew set down a challenge on a piece of paper: "The Bells," she wrote, "By E. A. Poe." His interest piqued, he wrote out seventeen lines, and continued to work on the poem for several months. Like

"*Kindest—dearest friend—My poor Virginia still lives, although failing fast and now suffering much pain. . . . Her bosom is full to overflowing—like my own—with a boundless—inexpressible gratitude to you. Lest she may never see you more—she bids me say that she sends you her sweetest kiss of love and will die blessing you[.]"—Poe to Loui Shew just before Virginia's death, 1847*

"For Annie," where the halting speech and murmured repetitions help convey a feverish state of mind, "The Bells" moves across the page with clanging music in its wake as Poe describes the pealing bells that accompany Christmas, weddings, fires, and funerals. You don't need notes on a staff to hear the music—and the increasing drama—of "The Bells." Musicians as different as Sergei Rachmaninoff and Phil Ochs have set the poem to music.

"For Annie" and "The Bells" are elegant rejects that show—besides their own beauty—the lingering insecurity of the writing life, where any one success is no guarantee of any other. Being at the height of his powers didn't guarantee Poe a quick acceptance for any of his new work; and, despite even the boost to his reputation that came with the earlier, popular successes of "The Gold-Bug" and "The Raven," apparently Poe wasn't seen as being any more "bankable" than ever. What's interesting about the destinies of these two rejects, aside from the irony that they're among his most famous, is that they appeared at the extremes of Poe's own personal pendulum—one out of suicidal despair, the other out of creative lethargy.

Chapter 16

Reaching for Beauty—
The Great Poems

"The Raven" put Edgar Allan Poe on the literary map once and for all. It was a success when it was published, and it remains one of his most well-known efforts. Students read the musical poem "The Bells" and the stately "To Helen" in their anthologies. But Poe's own favorite among his poetry was one you have probably never read.

"Israfel"–Timeless Poetry

What does it mean for something to be "the best"? Can everyone always agree? Does the best always stay the best? Does it necessarily start out the best? Although "the best" sounds like a permanent honor, it's really more vulnerable to change than anything else. "Israfel" was written in 1831, in that period when Poe knew that West Point and the life of the professional soldier was not for him but before he embarked into whatever that foggy future held and gathered a mixed bag of critical reviews.

Everyone's a Critic

During Poe's lifetime, one reviewer dismissed "Israfel" as ". . . unworthy the talents of E. A. Poe." Another reviewer, Thomas Dunn English, called it ". . . a very pretty specimen of fiddle-dee-dee." English was reviewing Poe's collection, *The Raven and Other Poems*, liked "The Raven" pretty well but lumped all the others together as chosen by Poe just to "fill up the book."

This was the sort of criticism Poe had to endure regarding his own writing.

fact

"Israfel" was one of the few poems Poe included in his 1831 collection. To underwrite the book Poe drummed up 131 subscribers among his cadet class at West Point, who paid $1.25 each in high-spirited anticipation of more of what they had come to expect from that versifier Poe—namely, jabs and jibes at officers and other cadets. What they got for their money—besides Poe's dedication to them—was the obscure "Al Aaraaf" and other poems.

Over time, the reputation of "Israfel" has improved. According to one critic, its "poetic rapture" outdoes Shelley. According to another reviewer, it has joy, radiance, and ecstasy. And, of course, there's always a dissenter, who called it "trashy." Generally, the farther you get from the year Poe wrote it, this poem about the Islamic Angel of Song is considered a masterpiece.

Gaining Popularity

Halfway between then and now, during World War I, a Canadian poet named Marian Osborne wrote her own poem on the angel Israfel, expansively describing the effect of Israfel's song, played on his heartstrings, which form a lute. The song silences everything in nature, air becomes holy prayer, and the despairing are comforted. Osborne's version of this angel folklore seems to fit the deep uncertainty of her times. But Poe's taut lyric strikes the kind of timeless and universal note that has led to a revised critical opinion. He picks up on one of Israfel's aliases as "The Burning One," and refers in the poem to Israfel's fire, which becomes a metaphor for the kind of passion that leads to creation.

question

What is the folklore about the angel Israfel?

In Islamic folklore, Allah sends Israfel, Azrael, Gabriel, and Michael on a quest to the four corners of the earth to secure the dust from which Adam, the first man, will spring. Of the four, only Azrael, the Angel of Death, succeeds. But it's the sensitive Israfel, the Angel of Resurrection and Song, who daily peers into Hell and grieves for the damned.

Poe moves completely beyond any predictable description of this angel actually playing the heart-instrument; in Poe's hands, the heart is a "trembling living wire" that responds without any help from the musician's fingers. The human poet yearns for an exchange with this angel whose source of song is organic. How would it go? Mark Twain once mused about what you'd get if you could crossbreed a human and a cat, concluding it would improve the human but would deteriorate the cat. An earthbound Israfel would suffer in this place where "flowers are merely flowers"—but the heaven-sent poet would thrive, and "a bolder note than this might swell/From my lyre within the sky."

In a self-reflexive poem interested in the nature and activities of the artist, Poe's "Israfel" is valuable because it glistens with the artist's perpetual struggle to create what's powerfully beautiful. The unresolvable tension for the artist is between the transient and the permanent—and where art falls. Ironically, even the Angel of Song, Israfel, who has the perfect instrument and heaven for inspiration, isn't immortal: in folklore, he's one of four angels destroyed on Judgment Day.

"Instant" Success

Quoth the ravin': "'Prophet!' said I, 'thing of evil! Prophet still, if bird or devil!—'"

Finally, just ten days after his thirty-sixth birthday, Edgar Allan Poe became a famous man. The man who had been writing at his chamber desk for two decades became an overnight sensation.

they said...

"The worth of 'The Raven' is not in any 'Moral,' nor is its charm in the construction of its story. Its great and wonderful merits consist in the strange, beautiful and fantastic imagery in which the simple subject is clothed. . . Added to these is a versification indescribably sweet and wonderfully difficult . . . 'The Raven' is a gem of art."—John Moncure Daniel, editor of the Richmond *Examiner*, September 1849

In his critical essay, "The Philosophy of Criticism," he uses the poem as a kind of how-to for aspiring poets, describing the very deliberate choices he made that he hoped would give "The Raven" universal appeal. At every turn he chose the crowd-pleaser. Best tone? Melancholy. Best subject? Death. Best refrain? A single word ("nevermore"). Best choice for uttering the refrain? A raven—"a bird of ill-omen"—because for some reason, he couldn't picture a human voicing the refrain. The raven may have been rapping, tapping at his mind since he had told a friend he had liked Dickens's *Barnaby Rudge*, but felt the raven underutilized. At any rate, all the ingredients went into the cauldron of his creative mind, which produced "The Raven," a fairly long poem that tramples on his own belief that a good poem shouldn't exceed an arbitrary one hundred lines.

What's "The Raven" about? What else? A lover mourning the loss of his dead love, Lenore (rhymes with "nevermore"). In an age reeling with an interest in such things as spiritualism, the occult, and mesmerism, the lover's superstitious agitation at the bird's one-note response to all his questions—it's as though he's working a Ouija Board—must have seemed familiar and thrilling.

The result?

Poe became sexy.

fact

Poe's "command performances" to recite "The Raven" were American drawing room affairs. He was still the man who couldn't resist the grandiose statement when it came to the recognition of his talent. After the enormous popularity of "The Raven," Poe made the deadpan claim that Queen Victoria had summoned him to London to recite the poem for her.

Literary women and women who fancied themselves literary plied him with love letters and published overt, languishing pieces addressed to him. A kind of antebellum Johnny Cash, he preferred dressing all in black, which may have increased the confusion the ladies of the day were having in telling him apart from his inscrutable bird creation. In drawing rooms he was referred to in pathetic code as "The Raven," and Poe found himself suddenly endowed with—well, sex appeal. Mystique. *It*.

Although the popular success of the poem still didn't pull Poe out of poverty, at least It was something.

A Favored Theme in a Favorite Poem

In his 1831 poem "Irene," which he later retitled "The Sleeper", Poe shows most convincingly the perils of rhyme: "The lady sleeps: oh! may her sleep/As it is lasting so be deep—/No icy worms about her creep. . ."

In a letter in 1844 to fellow poet James Russell Lowell, Poe wrote, "I think my best poems, 'The Sleeper', 'The Conqueror Worm', 'The Haunted Palace', 'Lenore', 'Dreamland' & 'The Coliseum'—but all have been hurried & unconsidered." For an artist as meticulous as Poe, this sounds like false modesty, especially because he's just said these are his best. But two years later, "The Sleeper" bolts upright once again out of the pile, when Poe, responding warmly to his admirer George W. Eveleth's appreciation of the poem, calls the poem better than "The Raven." "'The Raven,' of course, is far the better as a work of art—but in the true basis of all art 'The Sleeper' is the superior," Poe wrote. Poe seems to be saying that "The Raven" is a better poem, but "The Sleeper" uses more truly artistic materials. He doesn't name any of his poems as his favorite, but you can assume a strong attachment to the ones he mentions to Lowell. In both "The Sleeper" and "Lenore" you find exactly what Poe called the most fitting subject of poetry—the death of a beautiful woman.

fact

Poe's favorite poem is a textbook example of prosody and poetic devices. "The Sleeper" consists of four stanzas of iambic tetrameter (four "beats" with the accent on the second syllables) and rhyming couplets: "At midnight, in the month of June, / I stand beneath the mystic moon." He also uses personification (as in the "ruin's breast") and alliteration (as in "mystic moon" and "dewy, dim").

Considering how the death of a beautiful woman made itself felt in his own life—Eliza Poe, Jane Stanard, Frances Allan—it's no wonder he was so drawn to expressing that kind of loss in poetry (and, for that matter, prose). In some ways, "The Sleeper," which describes a beautiful woman on her bier by the sea, resembles "Ligeia," Poe's favorite story. Whenever death is the subject in a poem, Poe goes classic, bringing to bear all the meter, rhyme, and poetic devices he knows in order to do a kind of cavalier honor to his most sensitive subject. He's very much a poet of his time and place in the death poems; it's where he runs the risk of sounding most like other poets. But there are poems where he steps out from behind all his learning and painstaking composition and states powerful ideas in language very nearly modern. In Emily Dickinson and Walt Whitman, the two greatest voices in nineteenth century American poetry, you hear rich economies and a shimmering sensuousness. You hear original power. Poe was capable of the same sort of thing, and in some of his poems, achieved it. But those were not his favorite.

Ode to Jane

One of Poe's finest (and most famous) lines is in his 1831 poem "To Helen": ". . .the glory that was Greece, / And the grandeur that was Rome." This poem, his most anthologized, is also considered by many to be his best. One of Poe's jokes was that he wrote this poem when he was fourteen, when he first met Jane Stanard, but it shows an artistic maturity that makes it more likely a product of the twenty-one-year-old he would have been just before the publication of this third volume of poetry—still young! Calling himself a "weary, way-worn wanderer," Poe is a load of world-weariness when Helen returns him, really, to himself. And it's not just her beauty, it's her manner, her poise, that reminds him of "the glory that was Greece/ And the grandeur that was Rome." Whatever—whoever—can connect him in this way to classical civilizations restores him.

Until the day Robert Stanard brought his new friend home, Poe had been exercising his adolescent love on girls his own age. This resulted in the kind of grand poetic utterances that leave you wondering what could possibly have prompted them: "Oh feast my soul, revenge is sweet/Louisa, take my scorn—" But even his teachers picked up on Poe's "tender heart," so the entrance of Jane Stanard into his life provided the young Romantic with his first real, worthy subject.

A consistently warm woman like Jane Stanard made more sophisticated work possible, and the final form of that inspiration percolated for a long time. In her he was able to see (and no doubt embellish) an ideal. No more tortured adolescent rhymes. Compare his final curses on the probably unaware Louisa: "Curs'd was the hour that saw us meet / The hour when we were born"— nothing particularly new in either thought or expression here—to what the inspirational Helen evokes. It took seven years for the poem, "To Helen," to appear, and it's become Poe's most anthologized poem.

When the poem was first published in 1831, it read "the beauty of fair Greece, / And the grandeur of old Rome." By the time it was reprinted in *Graham's*, ten years later, Poe had revised the poem, and it appeared in his next published collection of his poetry (*The Raven and Other Poems*, 1845) in its final form. Poe once claimed to his friend Susan Archer Talley that he had written "To Helen" when he was ten years old—a few years before he even met its inspiration, Jane Stanard! But certainly what led to the elegant rewrite was an artistic maturity that would be unlikely in either a boy of ten or an adolescent of fourteen.

Poe's Helen is the embodiment of everything eternally serene, caught framed in a tableau of timeless beauty that spans all times, all places. She becomes Psyche, the Greek concept of the soul, and in a mere nine words—"Ah! Psyche, from the regions which / Are Holy Land!"—the young Poe makes a sublime connection between what you see, what you make of what you see, and how it lies finally in that holy zone of the human imagination.

"Rhythmical Creation of Beauty"

During the year Poe was waiting to hear whether he was admitted to West Point, he managed to interest a Baltimore publisher in this second volume of his poetry, *Al Aaraaf, Tamerlane, and Minor Poems*. But the young Poe, already calling himself "irrecoverably a poet," had to ante up the $100 it cost to print the volume. Because he and his foster father had achieved a practical peace while they had worked together on his West Point application, Poe appealed to him for the printing costs. However, Poe never quite learned that his writing and publishing poetry was never going to be anything other than a hot button issue for John Allan. No matter how the young man tried to "legitimize" his artistic activity to the older man—for example, reassuring him that the scandalous Lord Byron was no longer his role model—nothing worked. Allan refused, and Edgar had to come up with the money himself.

> "*Al Aaraaf* is a tale of another world—the star discovered by Tycho Brahe, which appeared and disappeared so suddenly—or rather, it is no tale at all. . . . I have supposed many of the lost sculptures of our world to have flown (in spirit) to the star '*Al Aaraaf*—a delicate place, more suited to their divinity.*"—Poe to John Neal, 1829

The title poem, "Al Aaraaf" is an ambitious 422 lines long, written when Poe was a teenager. He was working with a few ideas that caught his fancy. One: Al Aaraaf is the place in the Muslim perception of the afterlife that is neither heaven nor hell, where there is neither punishment nor reward. Another: In the sixteenth century, a Danish astronomer discovered a new and brilliant star that disappeared as suddenly as it had appeared. A final idea, one that persists throughout his writing life: the charismatic tug of beauty. Together, these make the strands of a poem that is very difficult. It's freighted with footnotes that, ironically, try to explain in untranslated French, Latin, and Spanish some of the poem's more obscure references. The reader could use more footnotes or less obscurity; neither choice is appealing.

they said...

"... of its object we have yet to be informed; for all our brain-cudgelling could not compel us to understand it line by line or the sum total—perchance, and we think we have hit it, it alludes to . . . the falling star."— critic John Hill Hewitt's response to *Al Aaraaf* in an 1830 article in the Baltimore weekly, *Minerva and Emerald*

Still, the beauty of Poe's longest poem is the early glimpse you get into his attitudes toward art and ideas that he shows even as early as nineteen. Many years later Poe said the purpose of poetry is the "rhythmical creation of beauty." Taking beauty as his subject matter in "Al Aaraaf," and trying to create it on the page itself, he works with some of his prized material. The poem shows the astonishing range of his acquisitive mind, and you see what thrills him: the self-preservation of unusual flowers, the group behavior of fireflies, the sound of approaching darkness, Egyptian ideas, Hindu ideas, phenomena of all sorts. At nineteen, all his learning is applied too thickly in "Al Aaraaf," but he may even have had a sense of this—he later came to the conclusion that a long poem is an impossible thing.

In the Margins

And here it is: "Last night, with many cares and toils oppress'd / Weary, I laid me on a couch to rest—" Poe was fifteen when he jotted down this little couplet on one of John Allan's business records. Was he spending time in Allan's office? By the time in November that these Ellis & Allan records were filed, presumably for tax purposes, certain events had occurred in Poe's life. The beloved Jane Stanard had died the previous spring, sending him into an emotional tailspin; it had become clear to both John Allan and Poe that the foster son was heading toward literature, not business; the young man had found out about his foster father's infidelities; and just a month before, in his military club uniform, he had escorted General Lafayette and connected with his Poe past. Apart from that proud occasion with Lafayette, 1824 was a difficult year for Poe.

The couplet he called "Poetry"—which actually seems more descriptive ("here's a poem") than an appropriate title for a two-line poem about profound fatigue—is interesting in a couple of ways. It shows how his mind went naturally to poetic expression in even the simplest of things—as fleeting, say, as dashing marginal comments on work pages. It also shows an early tendency toward self-dramatization, and the kind of weighty Romantic listlessness that shows up in some of his later stories. This couplet, written the same year as the elegant "To Helen," is also the oldest surviving poem in his own hand.

He Wrote It for *Me!*

"Annabel Lee" was published just two days after Poe died in Baltimore. He had tinkered with the poem over the course of several months while he was caught up in the romantic desperation that characterized the two years following the death of Virginia and his attempts to find a second wife. His love life during that era became a kind of horror he never actually put on the page, with the simultaneous courtships, vicious meddling, and spectacular failed romances. All was drama—even public at times—and nothing worked.

- Virginia died pathetically—cold, poor, and in pain from tuberculosis.
- Helen Whitman, a poet six years older than Poe, finally listened to enough whispers that she broke off the engagement.
- Annie Richmond broke off her friendship with Poe (who oddly saw himself as her suitor) when her husband finally insisted.
- Elmira Shelton, Poe's childhood sweetheart, agreed to marry him, even though it meant she would have to forfeit three-fourths of her late husband's estate.

All of these intense, erratic courtships made for quite an inner life out of which the stately and serene "Annabel Lee" appeared. It's another poem about the death of a beautiful woman, and in this one the poet, who sounds like a troubadour plying a ballad, longs for the pure, childlike love he had known with Annabel Lee. "But we loved with a love that was more than love— / I and my Annabel Lee—"

fact

"Annabel Lee" continues to capture artists' imaginations. On her 1967 album *Joan*, Joan Baez sang about both "Eleanor Rigby" and "Annabel Lee," and it's not difficult to find connections between those two lost, ill-fated female figures. Vladimir Nabokov—with a nimble respelling— makes Annabel Leigh his pedophile narrator's own youthful lost love in the novel *Lolita*.

Who was the source for "Annabel Lee"? Helen Whitman felt certain Poe had written the poem for her. But, then, so did Elmira Shelton. The length of time each woman spent mulling over his marriage proposal while she elicited comments about his character from everyone, including the milkman, showed an almost comical reluctance. What the man himself couldn't inspire, "Annabel Lee" did.

Fanny Osgood—whose relationship with Poe he called an "amour," dramatically over by then—believed that "Annabel Lee" was written for Virginia. No wonder: all the intrigue and ambiguities of his other relationships of this period must have tasted quite sour compared to the deep, simple attachment he had known with the lost Virginia.

Chapter 17

Crime After Crime

Edgar Allan Poe's interest in brainteasers of all sorts—he was a master at cryptography—led naturally to the creation of the first fictional sleuth, C. Auguste Dupin, and that mighty genre, detective fiction. Writing about crime was not merely one more way for Poe to frighten his readers. Poe was responding, too, to cultural influences. He was also testing his readers' ability to think analytically.

Out of the Penny Dreadfuls . . .

. . . came Poe's development of the detective story, although when Poe was writing, in the first half of the nineteenth century, these stories were still called "penny part stories." By mid-century, their target audience expanded to include middle-class adolescent boys, and they looked to the usual boyhood savory subjects of pirates and outlaws to increase their sales. But when Poe was dealing with his own conflict between his passion to shape a national literature and the merciless need to make money and support his family, he paused over the penny part stories—the first "mass market paperbacks" in publishing history.

Roots in England

As early as 1773, the *Newgate Calendar*—or *Malefactors' Bloody Register*—appeared on the scene in England, regaling a fascinated public hankering for a peek into the activities of the criminal classes, with its serialized accounts of true crimes. Here you find everything from the story of famous cave-dwelling cannibal Sawney Beane, to the story of Job Cox, a postal worker nearly executed by an administrative error for stealing a letter containing a ten-pound note, to the story of Kid Wake, sentenced to five years' hard labor for yelling "down with the king," to the story of twenty-one-year old Ann Whale, executed for murdering her husband by putting poison in his hasty pudding.

fact

No surprise that the *Newgate Calendar* was flamboyantly illustrated—for the most part, the graphic sketches underscored the sensational crimes. One sketch, though, called "A devoted parent presenting *The Newgate Calendar* to her child," is particularly interesting. It depicts a stern and extravagantly wigged matron (the "devoted parent") handing little Johnny the book with one hand and pointing fiercely to the scene outside their window, where all you can see is the hangman's gallows.

Because practically every entry in the *Newgate Calendar* gives a sensationalized account of the crime itself and then, in a sentence or two, how the "miserable wretch" was punished, the calendar read like a series of cautionary tales. It was both cheap, popular entertainment and a form of social control. What it lacked, however, was the investigative element that occurs, tantalizingly, between the crime and the punishment—and maybe that's where Edgar Allan Poe saw his opportunity.

Going with the Times

Aside from the rise of interest in true crime in the popular press, a second influence on the penny part stories of Poe's day was the early Gothic novel. An increasingly literate society was frankly enjoying the titillation of swooning heroines, dank castles, supernatural doings, and the occasional "vampyre." These were really the first thrillers, cheap thrills at a penny a week. Despite the workmanlike descriptions of sometimes pretty gruesome deeds, crime was a plain thing in the *Newgate Calendar*; but the taste for Gothic that found its way into the popular press added a dark, sexy, atmospheric side to the penny part stories.

fact

The source for "The Mystery of Marie Roget" was the 1841 murder of Mary Cecilia Rogers in New York City. A beautiful and well-liked young woman, Mary Rogers was raped and strangled, and her body was pulled out of the Hudson River near Weehawken, New Jersey. No one was ever charged in connection with her murder.

It was Poe who found a point of intersection between real-life crime and Gothic fiction, writing his tales of ratiocination, the most famous being the Dupin series—"The Murders in the Rue Morgue," "The Purloined Letter," and "The Mystery of Marie Roget"—where the hero is the analytical crime solver, awash in an atmosphere of dark mystery.

The First Modern Detective Story

"The Murders in the Rue Morgue" was published in *Graham's Magazine* in 1841. The idea beneath the "skin" of the first detective story was, "To observe attentively is to remember distinctly . . ." This was the first in a set of what Poe termed "tales of ratiocination," in which logical reasoning leads to the solution of a mystery or crime. Certainly, his contribution to what has been an extremely popular form of fiction is significant, and "The Murders in the Rue Morgue" deserves special attention because it was his first—an original. Poe came to consider the story one of his best, but that's no surprise when you take into account how interested he had always been in the mind. There had been times, though, when he scoffed at the tales of ratiocination, saying, "Where is the ingenuity of unraveling a web which you yourself . . . have woven for the express purpose of unraveling?"

Poe the Pioneer

For a man who began his writing life as a poet, he was determined to earn his living (and support his family) as a professional writer, which meant trying to figure out the tastes of the reading public and to satisfy them. He was still living in Philadelphia and working as an editor at the former Burton's, when he began to turn over in his mind the possibilities for stories coming out of some of his cultural observations. Both crime and the public interest in it were on the rise, and law enforcement agencies were in their bumbling infancies. What an opportunity for crime solving on the page. It didn't take Poe long to respond, and "The Murders in the Rue Morgue" was not only the first modern detective story, it became a lasting model for one of the most popular genres. Interrogation of suspects, analysis of evidence, final theatrical revelation of the solution—all here, all first. How it differed from its lame forerunners, where the crime itself and just a kind of lucky guesswork were the focus, was in making the character of the detective and his methods central to the story.

fact

Talk about a spoiler! The 1904 Funk & Wagnalls edition of *The Works of Edgar Allan Poe* contains a frontispiece by "The Father of Modern Illustration," Spanish artist Daniel Vierge. Unfortunately for anyone reading Poe's detective stories for the first time, the illustration depicts the bizarre solution to "The Murders in the Rue Morgue."

In this passage from the story, the narrator and his analytical friend come across a news item in the local paper:

"EXTRAORDINARY MURDERS—*This morning, about three o'clock, the inhabitants of the Quartier St. Roch were aroused from sleep by a succession of terrific shrieks, issuing, apparently, from the fourth story of a house in the Rue Morgue, known to be in the sole occupancy of one Madame L'Espanaye, and her daughter, Mademoiselle Camille L'Espanaye. After some delay, occasioned by a fruitless attempt to procure admission in the usual manner, the gateway was broken in with a crowbar, and eight or ten of the neighbors entered, accompanied by two gendarmes. By this time the cries had ceased; but, as the party rushed up the first flight of stairs, two or more rough voices, in angry contention, were distinguished, and seemed to proceed from the upper part of the house. As the second landing was reached, these sounds, also, had ceased, and everything remained perfectly quiet. The party spread themselves, and hurried from room to room. Upon arriving at a large back chamber in the fourth story, (the door of which, being found locked, with the key inside, was forced open,) a spectacle presented itself which struck every one present not less with horror than with astonishment.*

"*The apartment was in the wildest disorder—the furniture broken and thrown about in all directions. There was only one bedstead; and from this the bed had been removed, and thrown into the middle of the floor. On a chair lay a razor, besmeared with blood. On the hearth were two or three long and thick tresses of*

201

grey human hair, also dabbled in blood, and seeming to have been pulled out by the roots. Upon the floor were found four Napoleons, an ear-ring of topaz, three large silver spoons, three smaller of métal d'Alger, and two bags, containing nearly four thousand francs in gold. The drawers of a bureau, which stood in one corner, were open, and had been, apparently, rifled, although many articles still remained in them. A small iron safe was discovered under the bed (not under the bedstead). It was open, with the key still in the door. It had no contents beyond a few old letters, and other papers of little consequence.

"Of Madame L'Espanaye no traces were here seen; but an unusual quantity of soot being observed in the fire-place, a search was made in the chimney, and (horrible to relate!) the corpse of the daughter, head downward, was dragged therefrom; it having been thus forced up the narrow aperture for a considerable distance. The body was quite warm. Upon examining it, many excoriations were perceived, no doubt occasioned by the violence with which it had been thrust up and disengaged. Upon the face were many severe scratches, and, upon the throat, dark bruises, and deep indentations of finger nails, as if the deceased had been throttled to death.

"After a thorough investigation of every portion of the house, without farther discovery, the party made its way into a small paved yard in the rear of the building, where lay the corpse of the old lady, with her throat so entirely cut that, upon an attempt to raise her, the head fell off. The body, as well as the head, was fearfully mutilated—the former so much so as scarcely to retain any semblance of humanity.

"To this horrible mystery there is not as yet, we believe, the slightest clew."

Beginning of an Era

And so with the publication of this "horrible mystery" concerning the violent deaths of Madame L'Espanaye and her daughter, Poe ushered in not only Dupin's first criminal investigation, but the entire genre of detective fiction.

In "Murders," Poe presents a Parisian locked-room puzzle, drawing on his characteristically atmospheric house for the setting, a Gothic fillip that increases the exotic feel of the piece. Dupin investigates the double murder of Mme L'Espanaye and her daughter. To a great extent, the detective's mind is the story. Cerebral eccentrics like Poe's Dupin, Sherlock Holmes, and Hercule Poirot satisfy the reader's need to be the plodding confidantes of their dazzling brilliance. Forever Watson, that's us. In some ways, isn't Auguste Dupin, that premier amateur sleuth in every sense of the word, not just an evolution of the Byronic hero Poe so admired? Aren't Holmes, Poirot, Wimsey, Dalgliesh the brainy, moody loners extolled by the aching romantics of the early 1800s?

fact

Although Poe placed "The Murders in the Rue Morgue" among his best stories, he believed "The Purloined Letter" was the best of the Dupin tales. Critics agree. Not only is it structurally the tightest of the Dupin stories, it delves deepest into the character both of the detective and the criminal he seeks to implicate.

The Very Dark Cautionary Tale

It was Edgar Allan Poe who moved stories about criminal activities into stories about the detection of crime. In his hands, the detective becomes the hero, and his mental gymnastics and startling deductions are the kind of heroics that leave you thrilled and awed. The dragons the detective-hero slays are everything from scofflaws to killers, destroyers of the social order. Detective fiction, when you scratch a little below its appearance of entertainment, clever plotting, flawed characters, is moral at its core. It's crime and punishment. Sometimes it veers into the dense psychopathology of noir fiction, but mostly it's workmanlike, even when it's dazzling. Poe's Dupin was not all that far from the Transcendentalists Poe spurned, because Dupin became a paragon of Man Thinking—Emerson's ideal scholar. Dupin was all analysis, using his intuition and other faculties to push through to knowledge. He brought along his cheering section—the fictional stand-in for the reader—in the person of a goggling sidekick, awed by his clever companion's deductions.

---

fact

Poe was the creator of the "locked room" mystery. Since the 1841 debut of "Murders," there have been many refinements, but this kind of mystery requires a murder committed in a room where there's no apparent way in or out. Dupin, investigating the crime scene with a friend, comments: ". . . neither of us believe in praeternatural events. . . . The doers of the deed were material, and escaped materially." Poe comes out strongly on the side of rational explanations for what to lesser, Watson-like minds appear inexplicable.

But the stories of crime and detection—with or without the great Dupin—are not the only way Poe explored the kind of aberrant behavior that intrigued him. What if he put you in the hands of faceless and omnipotent torturers? What if he put you in the way of a boastful murderer? Because detective stories are cautionary tales directed at fictional disrupters of the social order, you can stand shoulder to shoulder with the Dupins, who you're confident will solve the crime and bring the criminal to justice. But in other kinds of crime fiction, you are snatched from the complacency of your armchair and hurled into an entirely different place. In tales like "The Tell-Tale Heart" and "The Pit and the Pendulum," the "caution" Poe cries out is directed right at his readers.

When Society Is the Criminal

Is there a simple way to discuss the difference on the page between horror and terror? Horror appalls; terror repels. Horror plays with your head; terror, with everything else. Horror moves into your head and re-decorates the space. Terror makes your imagination the last thing on your mind. These terms—*horror* and *terror*—are used inter-changeably about the most famous of Poe's tales. "Masterpieces of terror," you'll hear, or "tales of horror." But did Poe really write either?

When Poe first collected his stories he called the volume *Tales of the Grotesque and Arabesque*. (The "arabesques" were more mainstream, shot through, he believed, with beauty.) So, by his own definition, what he was writing were "grotesques," stories filled with frightening distortion and abnormality.

---

fact

H. P. Lovecraft, the horror/fantasy writer, called Poe "my God of Fiction." Lovecraft, a Providence, Rhode Island, native whose father was a travel-ing salesman, was in many ways a second generation Poe. From Poe he developed a taste for horror and the macabre, but from there he used his background in mythology to create his own "weird fiction," which included a bestiary—and a New England landscape certainly darker than any Emerson or Thoreau would recognize (although Hawthorne might find himself at home).

Do they get all the way to horror—or terror? Possibly, depend-ing on who's doing the reading. Horror and "masterpieces of ter-ror" really refer to the effect of the story on the one taking them in. Two tales that might be considered for the most horrifying/terrify-ing are "The Pit and the Pendulum" and "The Tell-Tale Heart." Both have strange power, but because they are so different from each other, it's better to look at them together in order to decide which gives you "the shivers." Both stories are reprinted in their entirety in Appendix A, and to appreciate the difference a narrator makes—not to mention the full reach of what Poe is saying about the differ-ence between "mere" madness and state-sanctioned insanity—you might want to read them through.

"It was hope—the hope that triumphs on the rack—that whispers to the death-condemned even in the dungeons of the Inquisition,"

Poe wrote in "The Pit and the Pendulum" in 1843. This story is narrated by a man who describes his torture at the hands of the Spanish Inquisition.

> ## fact
> Established in 1478 by Ferdinand and Isabella of Spain, before they funded Christopher Columbus's voyage, the Spanish Inquisition refers to the 350-year period of institutionalized torture, trials, and punishment of Jews, Protestants, miscellaneous heretics, bigamists, homosexuals, blasphemers, witches, Freemasons, and pretty much anyone else considered a threat to the state religion. The Inquisition referred to itself as the Holy Office.

Despite brief appearances of other, almost disembodied characters at the very beginning and end (which lends a creepy impersonality to the events), the story is an interrupted account of one man's attempts to evade the Inquisition's death-dealing designs.

The power of the story lies in the "against all odds" efforts of the engaging narrator/victim to save his own life. He keeps the lid on his own despair by approaching each problem methodically. Because he is an intelligent Everyman—and an underdog, trapped in a dungeon, with only his wits to save him—you can identify with him. No sooner does he outwit one manner of execution, though, than he's confronted with the next. Poe ratchets up the suspense by showing the horrifying futility of the narrator's success.

Whispering Dark Deeds

"TRUE!—nervous—very, very dreadfully nervous I had been and am; but why *will* you say that I am mad?" Poe begins "The Tell-Tale Heart," his 1843 thriller, published in *The Pioneer*.

This story provides shivers of a very different sort from "The Pit and the Pendulum." If "Pit" has a narrator who is a normal individual endangered by a world gone mad, "Tell-Tale" has a narrator who is mad. Poe's great storytelling instincts instructed him to maximize his narrator's madness so there's no buffer between narrator and reader. Where Poe failed with *Politian*, his inert, unfinished play, he succeeds with "The Tell-Tale Heart," which is as close to a demented soliloquy as you're likely to find anywhere.

The narrator addresses you directly, and in his riveting, highly dramatic monologue in which he confesses to the murder of an old man, it's as if he whispers his dark deeds into your ear. You become his confessor—practically his accomplice—very powerful stuff. Unlike "Pit," in which you're scared on that bedeviled narrator's behalf, "Tell-Tale" is frightening because the mad narrator corners you, seeking both your understanding for why he killed the old man, and your admiration for his "cleverness." In him Poe gives you the stark egotism of the criminally insane. Here you get someone who finds release from his own discomfort at the inoffensive old man's rheumy "vulture eye" not by simply leaving but by murdering and seeing in his criminal act some kind of crazy justification because he carried it out so perfectly. He's not a killer, he's a superman who avenges his own irrational vexation—or so he thinks. And your good opinion of him matters. Whose is the tell-tale heart, finally? His victim's—or his own?

fact

The short-lived periodical *The Pioneer* was the brainchild of James Russell Lowell, who—much like Poe with his hopes for *The Stylus*—wanted to elevate the level of popular reading tastes and offer American readers something better than what they could find in the commercial magazines of the day. But *The Pioneer* folded after three issues, and Poe never received the thirteen dollars he was promised for "The Tell-Tale Heart."

Both of these stories succeed because Poe had such a keen understanding of what makes man tick under the pressures of extreme circumstances—either under the threat of death ("The Pit and the Pendulum") or under the spell of a simple provocation that leads to homicide ("The Tell-Tale Heart"). In "Tell-Tale" you get a story about crime and the punishment of conscience. In "Pit" you get a story about the crime *of* punishment. Are they horror stories? Are they "masterpieces of terror"? In some ways, *The Narrative of Arthur Gordon Pym* is a better example of both because the effects of horror and terror are spun out, elaborated, and heightened over the course of a long tale. But there's no denying that in terms of suspense, you can't beat tight, intense tales like "The Pit and the Pendulum" and "The Tell-Tale Heart," where you can see a real master at work.

> "The cunning of the maniac—a cunning which baffles that of the wisest man of sound mind—the amazing self-possession with which at times, he assumes the demeanor, and preserves the appearance, of perfect sanity, have long been matters of comment with those who have made the subject of mania their study."

Suspense à la Edgar

How does he do it? Where are the colorful silks up the sleeve of his black greatcoat? The element of suspense in a story keeps you reading, getting used to that half-sick discomfort of wanting to find out and wanting to slam the book shut forever. But how does it work? It doesn't just happen: it's the result of the kind of careful execution that Poe championed in the development of the national literature. He himself was a master of careful artistic execution. One of his frequently anthologized stories, "The Cask of Amontillado" (*Godey's Lady's Book, 1846*), makes a good specimen for an anatomy of The Shivers.

Drawing the Reader In

Not simply a tale of revenge, "The Cask of Amontillado" is a tale of revenge as supreme private joke between the narrator and the reader. In the very first line of the story, Montresor, the narrator, declares his intention to avenge himself on Fortunato, for some unnamed "insult."

> "The thousand injuries of Fortunato I had borne as I best could; but when he ventured upon insult, I vowed revenge. You, who so well know the nature of my soul, will not suppose, however, that I gave utterance to a threat. At length I would be avenged; this was a point definitively settled—but the very definitiveness with which it was resolved, precluded the idea of risk. I must not only punish, but punish with impunity. A wrong is unredressed when retribution overtakes its redresser. It is equally unredressed when the avenger fails to make himself felt as such to him who has done the wrong.
>
> "It must be understood, that neither by word nor deed had I given Fortunato cause to doubt my good will. I continued, as was my wont, to smile in his face, and he did not perceive that my smile now was at the thought of his immolation.
>
> "He had a weak point—this Fortunato—although in other regards he was a man to be respected and even feared. He prided himself on his connoisseurship in wine. Few Italians have the true virtuoso spirit. For the most part their enthusiasm is adopted to suit the time and opportunity—to practise imposture upon the British and Austrian millionaires. In painting and gemmary, Fortunato, like his countrymen, was a quack—but in the matter of old wines he was sincere. In this respect I did not differ from him materially: I was skilful in the Italian vintages myself, and bought largely whenever I could.
>
> "It was about dusk, one evening during the supreme madness of the carnival season, that I encountered my friend. He accosted me with excessive warmth, for he had been drinking much. The man wore motley. He had on a tight-fitting parti-striped dress, and his head was surmounted by the conical cap and bells. I was so pleased to see him, that I thought I should never have done wringing his hand.

"I said to him—'My dear Fortunato, you are luckily met. How remarkably well you are looking to-day! But I have received a pipe of what passes for Amontillado, and I have my doubts.'

'How?' said he. 'Amontillado? A pipe? Impossible! And in the middle of the carnival!'

'I have my doubts,' I replied; 'and I was silly enough to pay the full Amontillado price without consulting you in the matter. You were not to be found, and I was fearful of losing a bargain.'

'Amontillado!'

'I have my doubts.'

'Amontillado!'"

There you have it, the whole direction of the tale—not the least of which is Montresor's masterful manipulation of his quarry. This raises questions, of course, about this revenge. How gruesome will it be? How final? Is it justified? Will you care? Will it succeed? Again, will you care? Your senses are put on alert. Because you expect an assault of some kind against Fortunato, you interpret everything you read thereafter—clues—as somehow contributing to it. A clue appears, disclosing a piece of information that begins to inspire your suspense.

Master of Suspense

But despite what any clue gives you, it withholds just about as much at the same time. It throws in your face all that you still don't know. For instance, never once after the narrator announces revenge as his goal, does Poe disclose the bold plan. He does not, in other words, short-circuit the tension. At the outset, the narrator outlines some preliminaries about his feigned goodwill toward the unsuspecting Fortunato, who fancies himself a wine connoisseur. Playing murderously on his victim's pride, Montresor lures the other man to his wine cellar to show off a rare sherry. Will Fortunato come? He does. Will he turn back? He does not. Montresor entraps him. Will he relent? Every little action and detail leads to larger, darker questions that create a pattern of growing suspense. The farther along you go in Montresor's catacombs, the more utterly inevitable the ending feels. The fascinating horror of that inevitability induces "the shivers." Like his avenging narrator, Poe has carefully laid brick on brick—and enclosed his readers behind a wall of pure suspense.

fact

Mystery Writers of America annually presents the Edgar Awards® for excellence in crime writing. The coveted "Edgar," which bears a strong likeness to Poe's Ultima Thule picture, honors Bests in Novel, First Novel, Paperback Original, Critical/Biographical, Fact Crime, Short Story, Young Adult, Juvenile, Play, TV Episode Teleplay, and Motion Picture Screenplay.

"The Cask of Amontillado" is also a good example of Poe's brand of black comedy: you share Montresor's inside jokes as he lures Fortunato to the place of execution. Poe leavens this murder-in-the-making with a heap of drollness and irony. And, finally, that irony is all yours: if you laugh, are you immoral?

Chapter 18

Out of Place in the Literary Schoolyard

The first half of the nineteenth century saw self-conscious attempts at forging an American literature. Edgar Allan Poe was at the forefront—but he wasn't alone. The gentleman poet, critic, and a storyteller and his writing colleagues to the north butted heads a great deal, but they were occasionally capable of rising above their differences to recognize each other's worth.

Transcendental, Baby

What must have felt to Poe like the cheesy optimism of the New England Transcendentalists flew in the face of his own personal experience with reality: mothers die, mentors die, fathers desert, fathers withhold, friends recede, professionals cheat. But the Transcendentalists were more than just armchair philosophers swirling their brandies and trying to move worn-out American thought into the new century. They wanted more than the practical personal improvements of Benjamin Franklin: they wanted people to think about the thrilling connections between nature, God, and the human soul. Ralph Waldo Emerson wrote the American version of the philosophy, and then Henry David Thoreau took it out to the woods. The idyll at Walden, had he even known about it, would have seemed self-indulgent to Poe, who by one biographer's calculations, never earned more than $6,200 from all of his writing—which was his stubborn livelihood—over a period of seventeen years. Had he known that Thoreau routinely left the great pond experiment to stroll down to the Emersons' for Sunday dinner, Poe would have been especially galled. Poe's austerity was a fact of life, not a choice.

Poe referred to his writing peers in the greater Boston area as ". . . that magnanimous cabal which has so long controlled the destinies of American Letters . . ." There's no doubt that the Transcendentalists invigorated the American literature of the early 1800s. The movement had its supporters, but it also nurtured some pretty impressive dissenters, even in the North—Hawthorne and Melville, for instance, who found it didn't address the spectral problems of evil and an indifferent universe. This dissenting position was a better fit for Poe, but his intense identification with his own region, the South, still kept him apart from these philosophical kindred spirits. His mission was to establish a true national literature, and to do that he had to disengage it from what he saw as the provincial stranglehold of New England. But at that point in the literary history of a new nation, what did it mean to work toward a national literature?

Was a national literature even possible? Is it even possible in the twenty-first century? There is a strong irony at work here: Poe was enough of a Southerner to resent what he believed was the literary clubbishness of his New England peers. He wasn't quite the diplomat to pull together regional interests into a single, national literature. Although he identified strongly with his Southern roots, his own work is peculiarly devoid of rich Southern materials—there is a timeless, placeless quality to his work that floats it above the narrow confines of the antebellum South.

"The Jingle Man"

"Every real man must be a nonconformist," said that great Transcendentalist guru, The Sage of Concord, Ralph Waldo Emerson. Yankee through and through, and a Harvard graduate who paid his own way and (like Poe at Virginia) studied languages, Emerson practiced what he literally preached as minister of the Old Second Church of Boston when he stopped administering Communion, explaining rather offhandedly to an aghast public that he "was not interested" in the rite. Through years of introspection and pursuit of contemplative solitude, he developed a sure hand on the tiller of his little boat. First know what you feel, then let it be known. His genial, steady nature that had a Northern way of steering clear of attitude disarmed plenty of people, which of course enabled him to get on with his work. And that work, it became increasingly clear, consisted of breathing new life into what looked like inert American institutions. He was primarily an essayist, an orator, an awakener of folks who didn't even know they were sleeping.

Emerson was the front man for the Transcendentalist movement. Thoreau was the field tester, but it was Emerson who brought the ideas indoors to lyceum audiences and the printed page. In a nutshell, he believed souls are divine and eternal, and all souls are identical; God is the Over-Soul to which every other soul belongs and speaks; and Nature, another side of that Over-Soul, has moral properties embedded.

For Emerson, it comes down to the introspection—and enlargement—of the individual, and in that sense, you can see how his philosophy evolved from its contemporary, Romanticism. Transcendentalism was also a challenge to the complacencies of the day—feminists and abolitionists found a haven in the spiritual "home" Emerson built, where nonconformists were enthusiastically welcomed. Others, like Hawthorne and Melville, distanced themselves. After all, they were the greats-in-the-making who believed human beings were more complex and more flawed than Emerson allowed. Drawing on his own life experiences, Melville once said on the subject of Transcendentalism, "To one who has weathered Cape Horn as a common sailor, what stuff all this is."

question

Who were the members of the "Transcendental Club"?

Certainly not Edgar Allan Poe. The most famous members were Emerson, Margaret Fuller, the bluestocking Peabody sisters (Sophia became the wife of Nathaniel Hawthorne), and Bronson Alcott—father of novelist Louisa May Alcott—who was an educator and abolitionist labeled indecent for attempting to integrate sex education into his school curriculum.

They had things in common, Emerson and Poe, but really no opportunities to discover them—that "divide," again, between Northerner and Southerner. Some distances seemed too great to travel, even then, especially when you were either caught up in the whirl of lectures and writing or earning a living. Good writing mattered keenly to both of them. The shape and contours and content of the human soul mattered to them, too. So it was rather a funny dismissal coming from the enveloping Emerson when he was asked what he thought about Poe: "Oh, you mean the jingle man." Hard to imagine Emerson choosing just the right words to offend, so he probably didn't mean to. Still, it begs the question which of Poe's poems jumped to mind just before he said, "Oh." Jingles are at least memorable because there's music in them. Emerson's comment is so reductive it's comical. Poe was after music, all right, and he used all the rhythms and rhymes he could muster, but always in original ways—and never with the feel-good content of jingles. Ironically, it was Emerson who used to come up with snappy little sayings such as "Hitch your wagon to a star." You have to wonder if someone had asked Poe what he thought of Emerson whether he would have said, "Oh, you mean the bumper sticker man."

The View from Bean Town

James Russell Lowell scouted for talented writers from his hereditary position deep within the Boston Brahmin thicket. He was a true Bostonian through and through. Even the famous ditty about patrician New England mentions his family: "And this is good old Boston / The home of the bean and the cod, / Where the Lowells talk to the Cabots, / And the Cabots talk only to God." With Lowell, for some reason, Poe was able to overlook the man's home, education, pedigree, political views, security, and plain good fortune—all of which may have had more to do, finally, with Lowell than with Poe. Lowell was almost alone among all other famous contemporary American writers to recognize greatness in the testy, scrambling Poe.

they said...

"*Now* I ought by this time to have finished the article to accompany your head in Graham, but I have been unable to write anything . . . owing to a Constitutional indolence which was not counteracted . . . in my childhood. You may be sure I am not one of those who follow a fashion which is hardly yet extinct, & call upon the good, easy world to accept my faults in proof of my genius."—James Russell Lowell to Poe, 1844

Lowell's real admiration was responsible for some wonderful passages of frank insights in Poe's letters that no one else seemed able to elicit. As editors, they published each other's work. The

217

compassionate, well-connected Lowell put in a good word for Poe with the publisher of the New York *Broadway Journal*, who hired Poe as an editor. Both men had dreams of their own national literary magazine: Poe had *The Penn/The Stylus*, and Lowell had *The Pioneer*. Unlike Poe, though, who could never get enough financial backing for the project despite years of trying, Lowell's magazine was launched. However, even Lowell's money and cachet couldn't keep such an ambitious magazine afloat for long, and *The Pioneer* pulled up stakes after just a few months.

fact

The Pioneer had a short life of three issues in the winter of 1843, but it published some significant work—notably, Hawthorne's story "The Birthmark," and Poe's "The Tell-Tale Heart." Like Poe, Lowell hoped a literary magazine would entice American readers away from the "fluffy" women's magazines of the day. *The Pioneer* failed partly because Lowell's actual vision deteriorated—as his eyesight worsened, he had to entrust editorial duties to a less competent successor.

On the surface, Lowell and Poe had common interests and goals, and they were compatible enough otherwise—as long as they carried on their paper friendship. In letters, they worked.

The problem started when they actually met.

For some reason, Poe felt very put off by Lowell's appearance—especially perplexing, considering how handsome Lowell was. Poe later told a (Southern) friend he had expected someone nobler. What that image could have been that Poe had entertained over the course of the Poe-Lowell correspondence, who can say? You would think Poe would be intrigued to find a man as noble as he felt Lowell was, sight unseen, to turn out to be a man in jacket and britches like anyone else—although maybe a slightly better than average specimen. On the other hand, despite what he told his Southern friend about Lowell, maybe that meeting in May 1845 brought up too much close and personal information for someone like Poe.

Suddenly, there it all was, embodied in the person of Lowell: every irritant to Poe's bristly, injured nature.

Lowell's good looks, his patrician family, his ease, his advanced education (Harvard undergraduate and law schools)—it was all there. Lowell had stepped far outside any New England reticence or patrician-family Olympian disdain for social issues—he was an early and staunch abolitionist. In an age when bandwagons rolled by with neatly packaged pop philosophies, Lowell was a true free thinker, which edged him outside the comfortable, safe old traditions of Lowells and Cabots, who talked only to God. He recognized—early—the coming greatness of Abraham Lincoln. Lowell wrote antiwar pieces. He considered Thoreau a crank. He satirized the figure of the Yankee. He found power, originality, and eminence in Poe. What a shame, then, that Poe—that son of actors—couldn't pull off his surprise at the sight of Lowell, who picked up on the other man's strange disappointment. From there, everything headed right for the kind of vortex Poe wrote about. Lowell, for his part, found Poe a little tipsy, with kind of a ghastly complexion and fake fastidiousness. These two were in some ways dealing with the kind of shock to the system of a really bad blind date.

> "I received your poem, which you undervalue, and which I think truly beautiful—as, in fact, I do all you have ever written—but, alas! my Magazine scheme has exploded. Should you ever pay a visit to Philadelphia, you will remember that there is no one in America whom I would rather hold by the hand than yourself."—Poe to Lowell, 1843

Poe couldn't leave it at that. He needed to do then to Lowell what he had been doing to so many others in print—skewer and scour. It was a really self-defeating quirk of his nature that he sometimes couldn't help but repay kindness with injury, because kindness from someone else made his own need unbearable. This was the case with Lowell, who had really been a friend. By then, too, Poe had unwisely declared war on Longfellow. All this—Poe's attacks on Longfellow and himself—proved too much for even the good-natured Lowell. In his romp, "A Fable for Critics," in which he pokes fun (some pokes are more like saber thrusts) at American writers, here's what he says about Poe: "Here comes Poe with his Raven, like Barnaby Rudge / Three-fifths of him genius, two-fifths sheer fudge."

Superb Little Schooner Yacht

When Poe was reburied in 1875, a dedication ceremony was held. Nearly a quarter of a century had passed since Poe had died and was hastily buried in the Westminster cemetery with only a handful of men—a cousin, a couple of friends—present. The grave went unmarked. It took schoolchildren to spearhead a project to rebury Baltimore's nearly native son and to attach a proper ceremony to the job. He wasn't moved far, just out of his grandfather Poe's plot and into a more prominent place. Poe's cousin Neilson (who all those years ago had tried to take responsibility for Virginia) had funded the cutting and engraving of a stone monument—which, in an odd cosmic twist suitable to a tale by Poe, had been destroyed by a derailed train. Not altogether a bad thing, really, because the Latin inscription meant to be kind, but came off as patronizing, with its strange insistence that now that he's dead, he's happy.

Poe and Whitman

The rededication ceremony—without the shattered monument—boasted the kind of attendance and acknowledgment of literary greatness missing from the original burial. The only literary lion to feel the occasion was important enough to attend was Walt Whitman. He was fifty-six years old, a beloved old greybeard, hobbling from age and the effects of a stroke suffered two years earlier. Among the true greats of nineteenth century American literature, Walt Whitman was nearly alone in his appreciation of Poe. It was not complete, and it was not lifelong. But the vast generosity of spirit present in Walt Whitman's poetry was present in the man as well, and out of the great in-gathering, accepting, compassionate heart was a literary peer who could rise above the feuds and rumors of his day and find something to like in Poe.

fact

Whitman was twenty-six when he and Poe met, around the time Whitman's "Art-Singing and Heart-Singing" was published in Poe's *Broadway Journal*. Forty years later, Walt Whitman recalled the meeting as "a distinct and pleasing remembrance."

They had met in New York City in the mid-forties. Both men circulated in Lower Manhattan. Poe was editing the *Broadway Journal*, and Whitman submitted an essay. Poe published Whitman's piece, "Art-Singing and Heart-Singing" in the November 29, 1845, issue. In it, Whitman calls for a true American literature, something that turns its back finally on bankrupt old European models and discovers its own strength and excellence. The point of view couldn't have been more "Poe."

Respect and Kinship

Many years later, after the rededication ceremony, Whitman found himself in a small circle of people, telling them he had just finished reading a new volume of Poe's collected poems. He had never used to like them, but in middle age found his opinion revised. "I wanted, and still want for poetry," he said, "the clear sun shining, and fresh air blowing—the strength and power of health, not of delirium, even amid the stormiest passions—with always the background of the eternal moralities." This wasn't Poe. Because Whitman found genius in Poe, he set him among the "electric lights of literature . . . dazzling, but with no heat."

There is always a tendency to like what's most like ourselves because it's easy and familiar and requires nothing from us. In terms of temperament, Walt Whitman and Edgar Allan Poe were very much unlike. No surprise, though, that Whitman, the singing,

"We of the nineteenth century need some worker of miracles for our regeneration; but so degraded have we become that the only prophet, or preacher, who could render us much service, would be the St. Francis who converted the beasts."—Poe on the state of mankind

tramping, loafing poet who celebrated man wherever he found him, was unthreatened by the likes of Poe. In a newspaper article that came out around the time of the rededication of Poe's grave, Whitman described a dream he had in which a "superb little schooner yacht" weathered a terrible night storm at sea. It was ". . . now flying uncontroll'd with torn sails and broken spars through the wild sleet and winds and waves of the night. On the deck was a slender, slight, beautiful figure, a dim man, apparently enjoying all the terror, the murk, and the dislocation of which he was the centre and the victim." This man in his dream, Whitman went on to say, was Poe.

Grisly Man

His friends called him Rufe. Some called him Gris. Poe would have called him the devil incarnate, but by the time that became clear, Poe was dead. If there's a single reason to account for Poe's posthumous negative reputation, it's Rufus Griswold.

A Portrait of Griswold

Like New Yorker Evert Duyckinck, Griswold was an anthologist, but he had none of Duyckinck's largesse in collecting and bringing the work of American writers to the public eye. With Rufus Griswold, it was all about ego. If possible, he was even quicker to bruise—and slower to heal—than Poe. It was, in some ways, a uniquely American literary marketplace that gave rise to the likes of Rufus Griswold. It was an age of invention in every way—both Griswold and Poe inflated their personal histories. Where Poe merely fabricated an undergraduate degree (with honors) from the University of Virginia and painted a picturesque sort of vague heroism off fighting for Greek independence, Rufus Griswold was nervier, more ambitious, attaching unearned doctor of divinity and law degrees behind his name. What's the harm? Who's to know? It was a twist on the ideal of the "self-made man." With the American landscape opening up, you could be anybody you wanted to be—simply by saying so (just ask Henri Le Rennert). All the con men in America weren't rafting on the Mississippi.

Executor of Poe's Estate

There are several amazing points about the career of Rufus Griswold. Considering how universally disliked the man was, he somehow managed to keep himself employed, hired by some twenty publishers and editors over time. But in addition to his embroidered resumé, he was enormously persistent, and apparently willing to work for the same low pay as Poe. What made this man tick? He wasn't a poet, or a novelist, or a storywriter, but Rufus Griswold may have had the kind of ego that wanted to be the literary kingmaker of his day. He wanted the power to determine careers. In Poe, he got his wish—at least after Poe died and Rufus Griswold became his literary executor. There's hardly a better example of bad judgment of character than whatever strange obtuseness made Poe consider Griswold his friend, enough to entrust his work and reputation to the man.

> "Who is to write your life for 'Graham?' It is a pity that so many of these biographies were entrusted to ... Griswold. He certainly lacks independence, or judgment, or both."—Poe to James Russell Lowell, asking about a biographical sketch, 1843

Granted, there's some debate about just how clear Poe's wishes had been, but Muddy Clemm—inconsolable over her boy's sad death—seemed to think Edgar had mentioned a Griswold executorship in passing.

Which pretty much only tells you that Muddy, who possessed all of Poe's material, also wasn't the best judge of character. Griswold was a liar, a dissembler, and a manipulator. Bad enough qualities in someone who wishes you no harm, but the man held a grudge against Poe.

Executor of Poe's Reputation

Griswold was also a man whose relationships with women outdid Poe's in terms of everything from ghoulishness to tragedy. When his first wife died in childbirth, he outdid the most macabre twists in any of Poe's stories when he exhumed her body over a month later and kissed her decaying forehead. Three years later he found the charming Fanny Osgood—and she, in turn, maddeningly, found Poe. Between the fact that Fanny showed no interest in Griswold and plenty in Poe, and the mere scandalous possibility that her third daughter could be the proof of that interest, Griswold's deep, deep dislike of Poe was fixed. The two men had exchanged the usual strokes and swipes over the course of their literary careers, but now all bets were off. Only Poe—who had increasingly come to pick at Griswold's work—didn't know it.

Last man standing, Rufus W. Griswold became Poe's literary executor and the "memoirist" whose descriptions of Poe as a demon and a madman colored the perception of Poe in the years to come. If you have a taste for retribution, the end of Griswold makes interesting reading. An attack of epilepsy literally almost sank him when he was taking the Brooklyn Ferry; the reoccurrence of tuberculosis kept him from finishing some pet projects; his daughter nearly died in a train derailment; he was scarred by a gas explosion; and his third wife left him when he was in the final throes of tuberculosis. He finally died in New York in 1857, but the

> "To act honorably with a scoundrel is so completely to mystify him as to paralyze his utmost exertions. . . . Truth is the sixth sense to the man of wiles. He feels that there *may* be such a thing, but he is bewildered in his endeavors to comprehend its use, and succumbs at once to him who robes himself in a garb so mysterious yet so august."—Poe on dealing with scoundrels, 1840

damage he did to Poe was, ironically, his most effective work. With a strange sort of prescience, it was Poe who, in his revised critical opinion of Rufus Griswold, once predicted that Griswold "will sink into oblivion" and be known forever after as "the unfaithful servant who abused his trust."

One final note to the "contributions" of Rufus Griswold to American literary history. Poe always published his work—all of it—under the name Edgar Poe, E. A. Poe, or Edgar A. Poe. He was, however quietly, renouncing the troubled, volatile role of John Allan in his life. It was Rufus Griswold who later added the foster father's name to the mix—in name only creating Edgar Allan Poe.

In the Dark Corners of the Literary Club

If you make your own "literary salon" of early nineteenth-century American writers, just how bad a person was Poe? If you listen to the discredited Rufus Griswold, Poe was a demon and a madman of practically legendary proportions. Griswold's "memoir" did Poe no good, setting him among his own more dangerous narrative creations, but did also deflect attention from other nineteenth-century American literary beacons. Did all the others look pretty good, compared to what Griswold would have you believe was the roving, deranged Poe?

Thoreau, that champion of sturdy individualism, mooched off of the Emersons on and off for years. Hawthorne spent twelve adult years pretty much living off his mother while he worked exclusively on his writing. He also pulled back from the overly passionate Melville, who craved the kind of understanding he found in Hawthorne.

"I love all men who dive," Melville declared, aligning himself with "the whole corps of thought-divers, that have been diving & coming up again with bloodshot eyes since the world began." But even the author of that centerpiece of American literature, *Moby Dick,* was not exempt from tragedy and drama. Melville's oldest son committed suicide at eighteen, and his second son took off for sea and was mostly estranged from the family until he died in San Francisco of tuberculosis at age thirty-five. Could the secure Longfellow and

"*. . . a man without the commonest school education busying himself in attempts to instruct mankind on topics of polite literature. The absurdity . . . does not lie merely in the ignorance displayed by the would-be instructor, but in the transparency of the . . . endeavours to keep this ignorance concealed.*"—Poe on T. D. English, 1850.

Lowell have thrown more help to those strugglers, Poe and Melville? Did the unfettered "free range" Whitman miss the Brooklyn Ferry by not taking on more conventional responsibilities? Did Emerson—dubbed by Melville "this Plato who talks thro' his nose"—fall short by orating too much on intuition and nonconformity and God as Over-Soul and not enough on the important social issues of the day? Could Emily Dickinson have gotten a job?

Poe had dependents and dependencies of all sorts that tightened their grip on his life. Unlike any of the other major writers of the nineteenth century in America Poe had an alcohol problem. He could be a bitter critic and a friend quick to feel injury. He was probably what would now be called neurotic. He had two dependents at home who utterly relied on whatever he could make by writing, and his devotion to them was non-negotiable. He was unable to launch any kind of attack on a woman—considering he had what James Russell Lowell called a "prussic acid" pen, this restraint really went deeper and cut to the heart of his tenderness toward women. His shortcomings were all self-defeating.

In his adulthood, beyond some final desperate appeals for John Allan's love and money, and the occasional "free will offering" of a bit here and there solicited by Muddy on the little family's behalf, Poe never lived off anyone else's largesse. He chose to undertake family responsibilities, and he met them. Barely, but he did. He didn't have much use for what he called the "reformist demigods" of his day. Temperance, abolition—no, Poe had other fish to fry. None of the issues of the day drew his creative energies away from his one passionate goal, the pursuit of excellence in American literature.

Chapter 19

Overthrowing the Conqueror Worm

Edgar Allan Poe died on the brink of literary fame in Europe, where he has been appreciated ever since, thanks to the efforts of one Charles Baudelaire. His posthumous reputation in America was colored by the efforts of an enemy he didn't recognize as such during his lifetime. Rufus Griswold, who Poe counted as a friend, skewered his image. Contemporary society accepted Griswold's false words, and his image has been forever tarnished.

The French Correction

While Poe lived, he had intermittent successes, but none of them shoved open that window of opportunity once and for all. He was up against as immovable a brick wall as the one Montresor merrily built in "The Cask of Amontillado." The general public, whose literary tastes Poe was constantly trying to elevate, were hardly receptive to his efforts. Even when he wrote to sell—which was most of the time—no single "hit" ever secured his writing future. Add to that the personal shortcomings that hindered his success by damaging his professional relationships. Between a resistant readership and a difficult personality, Poe was never in his lifetime a major success, a recognized literary great.

Not in America, that is.

Not long before Poe's death in 1849, a French poet named Charles Baudelaire discovered the American writer. Smitten by everything Poe, who has "more inspiration than anyone else," Baudelaire painstakingly translated all of Poe's works into French—and for that reason is single-handedly responsible for Poe's European reputation.

question

What other French artists were influenced by Poe's work?

Composer Claude Debussy died before completing the operas he was specifically adapting from "The Fall of the House of Usher" and "The Devil in the Belfry." Other French writers who benefited from Baudelaire's translation of Poe's work include poets Stephane Mallarmé and Paul Valéry—and novelist Marcel Proust. Proust believed Poe's greatness lay in his attempts to evoke what was beautiful without injecting "moral motives."

In Poe, Baudelaire found a spiritual model for his own tastes and opinions. The two men, separated by the Atlantic Ocean, were oddly alike. "A frenzied passion for art," said Baudelaire, "is a canker that devours everything else." Both Poe and Baudelaire were aesthetes—defined by art, mastered by art. Only compared to the fast-living Frenchman, Poe seemed downright plodding and provincial.

Where Poe wrote (and lived) on the edges of precipices and vortexes, Baudelaire savored the precipices fully before leaping into them. Poe had a difficult relationship with his rich foster father, who left him nothing. Baudelaire despised his stepfather, but came into a lavish inheritance from another source. Poe had Virginia, his lovely little cousin/Sissy/wifey, followed by gentlemanly courtships of mostly literary women. Baudelaire had a string of prostitutes. Poe struggled with alcohol, and took himself to task for his lapses. Baudelaire drank, smoked hashish, and used opium—all in pursuit of sensation and pleasure. Whatever killed Poe, finally, it wasn't the syphilis that did in Charles Baudelaire.

fact

Like Herman Melville, who settled into semi-obscurity after the American public pretty much found *Moby Dick* unreadable (it sold 500 copies compared to the 15,000 Hawthorne's *The Scarlet Letter* sold), Poe was undervalued in the United States. But not in France, thanks to Charles Baudelaire.

The French poet, whose one collection of poetry is *Les Fleurs du Mal (Flowers of Evil)*, was a kind of death dancer, a contemplative hedonist, always seeking stimulation. In some ways, he was a performance artist, making his life a canvas right under the shocked upward-tilted noses of the French bourgeoisie. Poe, on the other hand, was after the aesthete's Grail of ravishing Beauty. Baudelaire was along for the ride, only it wasn't a Grail in his view. Too much meaning attached. To the man, who in many ways made himself into one of Poe's extravagant narrators, Beauty was its most seductive when it was useless. On that score, his unwitting guru, Poe, would disagree.

Walt Whitman commented after Poe's death that it was too bad it happened when it did, just when Poe was on the brink of widespread European success. Even Whitman couldn't foresee the influence of Poe on the work of Proust, Dostoevsky, and Kafka. All that tardy fame was thanks to Charles Baudelaire, whose 1847 translation of Poe's tales gave European audiences their first access to the American writer's work.

Westward, Poe

What was post-Poe America like? Poe had been dead for a little over twenty-five years when an elocution teacher and some industrious students brought about the rededication of Poe's grave in Baltimore. This event marks the flickering beginning of new appreciation for his contribution to American literature. In France, Baudelaire had done what he could. It is fascinating to consider why Poe has always had a better "rep" abroad than he has at home. What accounts for it? Certainly, by the last quarter of the nineteenth century, Poe's defenders had charged on to the scene, refuting the damaging Griswold memoir. But the effects of Griswold were never quite banished. For some reason, Americans have liked to confuse the man Poe with the narrative "character" Poe. Why?

An Evil Reality

Take a look at the nation after the Civil War, for one thing. The Union was preserved, but it was bloody and ragged. Then came Reconstruction and all the abuses that came out of a twisted, damaged psychic landscape that was once the antebellum South—opportunistic carpetbaggers, Jim Crow laws, the rise of the KKK, lynching. Evil descended, evil emerged. First we'll burn you, then we'll bleed you. Could even Poe have written these horrors? The Romantic era was just a laughable, out-of-touch fairy tale in a world turned inside out. What about the Transcendentalist notions about the value of intuition and the presence of the divine in every soul? Maybe intuition could help you read your neighbor well enough to move on out before he poisons your mule. And where's the divine in the figures backlit by the ghastly light of the burning cross? These encounters with souls stripped down to their savage cores, set out on a thick, miasmic landscape, later becomes the Gothic gone south, and you can see the anguished remnants of Poe's horror stories. But in the post-Civil War era, what emerged as a vocal counterpoint to the ruins in the east?

As the frontier expanded—railroads helped, Native American warfare "helped," Western Union, statehoods, homesteading, missionaries—the "prevailing westerly" winds made themselves felt. A kind of riverboat reality presented the possibilities of new ways of life, a sense of something young. The American future. Enter the likes of Mark Twain, who mixes a strong, colloquial prose style, classic American forms of humor, and the kind of social commentary no American great is every completely without.

> "Its scenic descriptions are vivid, because they are fresh, genuine, unforced. There is nothing of the cant of the tourist for the sake not of nature but of *tourism*. This ability to . . . use the tools of the rabble when necessary without soiling or roughening the hands with their employment, is a rare and unerring test of the natural in contradistinction from the artificial aristocrat."—Poe on Charles Fenno Hoffman's depictions of the American West, 1850

Twain Versus Poe

Huck Finn's "dark night of the soul" comes at the point in the book where he wrestles with what he believes is his moral duty to turn in Jim, the runaway slave. When he decides not to, and decides to take his licks both in this life and the hereafter, he blurts one of the great anthems in all of American literature: "All right, then, I'll go to Hell." In a way, that realist Twain reveals himself as a natural inheritor of the Hawthorne-Poe-Melville line—next stop on the Dark City Express. Despite all their individual variations of the theme of sin and evil, these writers are on the same frequency.

---

they said...

"It is impossible that a genius—at least a literary genius—can ever be discovered by his intimates; they are so close to him that he is out of focus to them and they can't get at his proportions; they can't perceive that there is any considerable difference between his bulk and their own."—Twain on literary genius

---

Which makes Twain's comment on Poe's work interesting. "To me his prose is unreadable—like Jane Austen's. No there is a difference. I could read his prose on salary, but not Jane's." Not for Twain the parlor intrigues of Jane Austen. And maybe post-war America needed the "corrective" of the realists like Twain during this period. Real life, daily life, was what needed to be attended to—and therein salvation lies. But Twain had his con men, like Melville. And Twain had his savageries that must always defy explanation, like Poe. "What a curious thing a 'detective' story is," Twain mused. "And was there ever one that the author needn't be ashamed of, except the 'Murder in the Rue Morgue'?"

All That Glitters Is Not Poe

If Mark Twain claims you'd have to pay him to read Poe, poet Vachel Lindsay is the man you'd have to pay not to read Poe. Twain is the pure spirit of "expansionist" America, confident, gathering in all the influences and impressions of the rollicking American future. He is a writer who puts his imagination to work—kind of like Tom Sawyer—concocting all the schemes and adventures called "story." He would positively shudder at what he finds in the work of Poe, namely the imagination run amok into every dark place imaginable. Once, when Poe recited "The Raven" in a friendly Richmond parlor, a slave overheard the poem and wondered why Mr. Poe didn't just take a broomstick to that old bird and get him out of the house once and for all. Twain would definitely take a broomstick to those dangerous, lurid jaunts into the nasty recesses of the human mind—if they went on too long.

Vachel Lindsay came along seventy years after Poe died, and his own experiences provide a real counterpoint to the immediate post-Poe period. A Midwest native, Lindsay internalized Poe. And then, in some ways, he went on to live a life of walking disintegration. Outwardly, he was the embodiment of fractured America, trying to pull together incompatible strands—crusader for the arts, temperance spokesperson, agrarian revivalist, Whitmanesque vagabond. He was Whitman extolling the same, great "en-masse," only driven to despair by a Poe sensibility. He was a democratic champion but with all the encroaching despair of a Poe character—and Poe himself. It's one thing to be Poe, keeping in frantic play the brilliance, the needs, the belief in a future where health and recognition bring peace. It's another thing altogether to feel all the effects of Poe on the consciousness, trying to "convert" America to a love of poetry while staring into a personal, Poe-induced void.

Vachel Lindsay, a significant American poet of the late 1800s, was a figure heroically trying to reconcile the irreconcilable. His most famous poem, "Abraham Lincoln Walks at Midnight"—he and Lincoln shared the same hometown—came out in 1914, on the eve of World War I. There were phonographs and movies and Model Ts, American industrialist tycoons and not quite a League of Nations. Native Americans were on reservations and the *Titanic* had already sunk. What could the specter of Abraham Lincoln possibly tell us?

> "There is no such thing as spirituality. God is material. All things are material; yet the matter of God has all the qualities which we attribute to spirit: thus the difference is scarcely more than of words. There is a matter without particles—of no atomic composition: this is God. It permeates and impels all things, and thus is all things in itself. Its agitation is the thought of God, and creates."—Poe on spirituality

Lindsay tried to expel the Poe inside him, denouncing his "artificial glitter." But it's the artificial glitter everywhere else, it seems, that took its toll on this poet successor. It's interesting that Lincoln walks at midnight, a Gothic view that corrals the "Great Emancipator" with something even more supernatural than anything in Poe. Lincoln gone zombie. Gone vampire. Are American institutions so decadent that this is what comes out of them, finally? Compared to Mark Twain, who works American material in ways different from Poe, Lindsay cannot separate himself from the effects of Poe's work. Was the artificial glitter the last thing Lindsay saw before he drank the poison that ended his life?

The Game Is Still Afoot

Granted, Sir Arthur Conan Doyle developed a love/hate relationship with his world-famous fictional detective, Sherlock Holmes. Having rid himself of the brilliant, supercilious crime solver by hurling him over the Reichenbach Falls in 1893, Conan Doyle was deafened by the public outcry and found himself in the unpleasant position of having to resurrect his fictionally defunct hero. Still, when asked at the close of the nineteenth century, the writer of that deathless and beloved landmark character in the development of detective fiction puts Poe's detective C. Auguste Dupin ahead of his own Sherlock Holmes. "Dupin," said Conan Doyle, "is unrivalled."

Doyle takes the esteemed Dupin model and, fifty years down the road and a block off London's Harley Street—where his ophthalmology practice was not exactly thriving—rounds out the character of the detective, adding moods, exuberances, tastes, and habits. Holmes is still Man Thinking, only now we've got someone who falls into funks he alleviates by playing his violin and taking cocaine. He has relationships—Watson, the landlady, the Baker Street Irregulars, his brother Mycroft—and formidable enemies, principally the Napoleon of crime, that titan of the London underworld, the brilliant Dr. Moriarty. He has 221B Baker Street, his homey lair as idiosyncratic as Nero Wolfe's on West 35th Street in Manhattan. He has a disturbing non-entanglement with his intellectual peer, Irene Adler. In some ways, in the turn-of-the-century Gilded Age, Doyle's developments (improvements?) are oddly domestic. Even when he goes over the Reichenbach Falls, Conan Doyle sends him locked in a death embrace with Moriarty. Like rival fraternity boys in some ill-conceived hazing. The peculiar fellowship of death.

Unlike Dupin's three appearances in Poe's tales, Sherlock Holmes appears in fifty-six short stories and four novels, inviting you along with his declaration that "The game is afoot!" So what Poe began with his Dupin stories, Doyle amplified with a detective-hero that has become synonymous with literary crime detection. Like his earlier American counterpart Poe, Doyle also had an interest in spiritualism. "When our fairies are admitted," medical man Doyle insisted, "other psychic phenomena will find a more ready acceptance."

fact

Conan Doyle's interest took an embarrassing turn in 1917 when two young girls in Cottingley, England, claimed to prove the existence of fairies by photographing them in their garden. Conan Doyle championed the girls' story, circulating what became world-famous pictures. You have to wonder what his astute, skeptical creation Sherlock Holmes would have had to say when it later came out that the two girls in Cottingley had faked the photographs.

Still, in an age where American writers were either devaluing native son Poe—or internalizing him so much they couldn't reconcile the interior Poe "landscapes" with the realities of scorched earth or boundless frontier, like Vachel Lindsay—Doyle extended a welcome from the land where the boy Edgar had spent five good years. In that, Doyle was definitely not alone. As playwright George Bernard Shaw remarked, "Above all, Poe is great because he is independent of cheap attractions. . ."

Poe Does Hollywood

By 1942, Poe's "raven-ous" reputation had made its way to the West Coast. He had traveled like his own fictional Julius Rodman, tackling those Rockies, winding up in Hollywood, dragging his tattered biography behind him. The studio took him in, scrutinizing the dead writer carefully to see what they could profitably put up on the screen. It was 1942, nearly the centennial of Poe's death in Baltimore, and with all the patriotic movies, not to mention the toothsome tapping of Shirley Temple and zany antics of the Marx Brothers, and movies with heartthrobs Humphrey Bogart, Henry Fonda, and Errol Flynn, well—bring on the dead poet. Poe had made appearances in the silent era, but now he could step out and enthrall a new, moviegoing generation with his tragic life and romantic recitations.

question

How many of Poe's tales were adapted for Hollywood?

Throughout the 1960s, horror filmmaker Roger Corman churned out a cycle of Poe-based movies for American Pictures International. When the first, *The Fall of the House of Usher* (1960), was successful, Corman loosely adapted other Poe stories and poems for a total of thirteen movies, including *The Pit and the Pendulum, The Tomb of Ligeia,* and *The Masque of the Red Death,* that starred horror greats Vincent Price, Peter Lorre, Boris Karloff, and Lon Chaney, Jr.

Poe's Screen Identity

The question was how to make him sexy, a hundred years later. After all, they couldn't screen test the real thing intoning "The Raven." So what Hollywood came up with was *The Loves of Edgar Allan Poe*—Poe as a kind of David Copperfield this side of the Atlantic. It featured an actor named John Sheppard as Poe, and confident starlet Linda Darnell as the shy young Sissy. The storyline inaccurately shows Poe mooning forever over his childhood sweetheart Elmira, proving himself a rudderless disgraceful misfit to his foster family until Virginia comes along. His "Ma," Frances Allan, is portrayed as the strong loving hand behind his creative genius, and his talent is finally sandbagged by drug and alcohol addiction. All that in sixty-seven minutes of screen time.

When it comes to films about Poe, maybe Hollywood will continue to go down the Poe-as-misunderstood-romantic-lead path—or (and this is more likely) the Poe-as-madman-pervert-addict path—because nearly two hundred years after his birth, he's become a kind of American dark folk hero. For whatever reason, he's become what readers need him to be. Maybe Poe does better not as the subject of Hollywood movies but as the influence on them.

The Master Storyteller

Take Alfred Hitchcock, for instance, who credits his first exposure to the work of Poe for his interest in suspense. Hitchcock was sixteen. He went on to have a film career as a director that spanned some fifty years. When you think of a master of cinematic suspense and horror—with generous dollops here and there of wit—you think of Hitchcock.

fact

What Alfred Hitchcock internalized from Poe's tales was the writer's way of laying out what was really an unbelievable tale with such "spellbinding logic" that readers were persuaded they could fall victim to any of those same horrors at any moment. You can see how Hitchcock's admiration for that kind of storytelling translates to the big screen.

He and Edgar Allan Poe, Hitchcock once said, were both prisoners of suspense. Themes of deception and self-deception, confusion of identity, psychological brinkmanship, the laying bare of crime—these run through both Hitchcock's and Poe's work. Hitch used techniques of odd camera angles to suggest moral distortion or an insecure "known" world; Poe achieved the same effect with lurid descriptive passages. Both men unsettled their audiences by pulling out of proportion what they show us. The human mind, in all its proximity to things that go bump at any time of day, is the truly great subject matter. When Hitchcock commented that "fear is an emotion people like to feel when they know they're safe," he seems to be giving you Poe's view as well.

Southern Gothic

You know the painting. 1930, oil on board, "American Gothic." The artist, Iowa native Grant Wood, had his sister Nan and his family dentist pose for the figures of the Midwestern farmer and his older, unmarried daughter. In the background is the trim clapboard white farmhouse with its upper window, zooming into that pointed Gothic style, sporting a sheer curtain. At first, the human figures seem flat, stern, ramrod straight and unyielding in a blank Midwestern landscape that seems weatherless. Everything is trim, shipshape—her apron, his overalls, the red outbuilding in the back, even the gleaming clean pitchfork. A trident. Neptune stripped of his kingdom and his divinity.

Is the painting a parody of unquestioning, boring dutifulness that is peculiarly American? Is it a tribute to the unquestioning, boring dutifulness that is peculiarly American? Look a little closer and things emerge, the way they always do. Is he staring straight ahead, his thin lips set, his eyes unfocused? What's on his mind? She's standing slightly behind him, not looking straight ahead but either at him or just past him—one brow is furrowed and her chin is balled up and tense, the way you get when you're holding something back. Tears? Speech? Rage?

Poe seeps in at the edges of "American Gothic." Grant Wood's painting only at first glance seems to depict the carefully ordered and controlled world of this farmer and his careworn unmarried daughter. It's not too much of a leap to picture his body walled up in the root cellar, or hers cut up and shoved under the floorboards in the parlor of that nice trim white farmhouse. When you think like Poe, rather than seeing Wood's painting as the depiction of changeless life, you see it now as a world on the verge of eruption. The slashing killer of "Rue Morgue" is always just outside the shot, always just off the page in Poe and his literary heirs. Midwesterner Wood paints a Midwestern scene. Add some Spanish moss and turn up the thermostat and you've got the Southern Gothic element in the American literature that developed out of Poe's work.

they said...

"Mr. Poe, clad, as usual, in black, stepped upon the platform, and, gracefully bowing, commenced his lecture ... During the whole lecture he never changed his position or made a gesture even with his hands, but his expression was constantly changing, and it was almost impossible to remove one's eyes from his face."—Susan Archer Talley, describing Poe's last public lecture, which was well attended by old family friends in Richmond, 1904

The greatest writer in the Southern Gothic stream is William Faulkner, whose stifling landscapes in the fictional Yoknapatawpha County, Mississippi, recall the Everyplace tarns of "Usher." Indomitable wills and hereditary obligations and smothering conditions that lead to insanity—these are Poe, these are Faulkner. That great, overmastering character of the South that creeps through the work of Faulkner, Flannery O'Connor, Robert Penn Warren, Thomas Wolfe, and Carson McCullers, just to name a few, is the source of the genesis, "child rearing," and death struggles of the men and women who inhabit the page. And not all the death ends in death.

Poe has shown you that.

Chapter 20

In Search of Eldorado

The twentieth and twenty-first centuries found unique ways to honor Edgar Allan Poe. Tributes to Poe are everywhere, from the cover of a Beatles' album to the name of a football team. Later generations finally recognized his achievements and built monuments to him accordingly. Poe has become a hip icon of the tortured artist. But his literary sensibility has made itself felt in the great American interiors of the embattled mind.

Just Another Goth

With the publication of "The Raven" in 1845, Poe became sexy. Now, nearly two hundred years after he was born, he's become hip. His "Ultima Thule" portrait is especially popular, with a dissipation that seems present-day; it's what you find on bottle caps, logos, and t-shirts. Today's generations are a tough group to scare, plain and simple, because today's world is a scarier place. A pit and a pendulum? You have to do better than that. So bring on the pop cultural images of Ultima Thule—just another Goth at the lunch counter.

But the tales of horror and the hypnotic, emotional bogs of poems like "Ulalume" aren't the whole story about Poe. In his 1849 poem, "Eldorado," he describes in four stanzas a lifelong quest: "Gaily bedight, / A gallant knight, / In sunshine and in shadow, / Had journeyed long, / Singing a song, / In search of Eldorado." He is given seemingly impossible directions by a "pilgrim shadow" along the way, who tells him to go over the mountains of the moon, to go through the valley of the shadow—of death, presumably. The poem is considered Poe's answer to the news about the gold rush out West. But you can also read it as a statement on his life—an absolutely faithful Sir Galahad-like quest, in Poe's case, for Art, for Beauty. To anyone else, those directions sound like nonsense. The artist knows otherwise.

fact

On the album jacket of the Beatles' *Sgt. Pepper's Lonely Hearts Club Band* (1967), Poe is in the crowd. Let your eye scan to the very last row of "assembled" figures, and you will see Poe's face looming at the center.

Poe's success all over Europe didn't seem to perturb his own, unenthusiastic countrymen. Why? What's the essential literary legacy of Poe? Where has his influence been the greatest? How has he made himself felt in music, in movies, and in American culture in general? What efforts have been made to honor him? Can you sum him up? Finally—why would you want to?

And How Does *That* Make You Feel?

Will readers ever let Edgar Allan Poe off the couch? Scholars, critics, fans, psychoanalysts—getting inside Poe's head has become a cottage industry. It hardly matters that the actual patient is absent. Let's base the analysis on the work. After all, the work is the man, right?

> ### they said...
>
> "We always predicted that Mr. Poe would reach a high grade in American literature, but we also thought and still think, that he is too much attached to the gloomy German mysticism, to be a useful and effective writer, without a total divorce from that somber school."—James Heath, editor of the *Southern Literary Messenger* and an early reviewer of Poe's *Tales*

Starting in 1847, after Virginia died, nurse and neighbor Loui Shew consulted a doctor friend about Poe's terribly sad case. From whatever she described, in those days before CT scans and MRIs, this doctor offered up the possibility of a brain lesion, which might explain those periods of feverish activity (mania) balanced by periods of deep melancholy (depressions). A curbside diagnosis may have provided Loui Shew with some understanding of Poe's behavior during this mourning period, but it didn't seem to help Poe. Then came the over-compensated inferiority complex supporters who accounted for Poe's prickliness (in person and in print) by seeing it as a result of being the son of stage performers no matter how many Moldavias and Russell Squares he got to go home to while the Allans had him, coupled with a bitterness provoked by the acclaim he felt went to other—lesser—writers. Back to the old standards of excellence in Poe—did they get stricter, higher, more unattainable for others the more his "inferiority complex" got pinched?

Other, quicker takes on Poe's psyche came along. Oedipus complex. Morbidity due to complete sexlessness. Pre-adolescent mentality. And, say, while you're in there, check out those latent dream-thoughts. A Cambridge professor makes the point that in psychoanalytic criticism a dream and a work of art both serve the purpose in an artist—the gratification of a forbidden, unconscious wish. But that approach doesn't really take into account the contribution of consciousness.

Is a great story really no more than the working out of material dredged up from the unconscious, material you can neither totally recognize or account for or even manage in a deliberate way? Can the black cat in Poe's gruesome story "The Black Cat" really signify displacement of his mother-hatred? Between those two extremes— cat as symbol of displacement of mother-hatred, and cat as cat— there is what the cat means to the narrator, and not to Poe himself, and what can be made of the story about the narrator's cruelty to the cat. This is what Poe the artist consciously does with his material. This is what takes "The Black Cat" out of the realm of mere newspaper report or subject for a psychoanalytic society's session on mother fixation and turns it into art.

they said...

"I care not a straw *what* a man says, if I see that he has *his* grounds for it, & knows thoroughly what he is talking about. You might cut me up as much as you pleased & I should read what you said with respect, & with a great deal more of satisfaction, than most of the praise I get, affords me."—James Russell Lowell to Poe, 1844

Couch time is just another limited way of understanding what makes Poe tick. But you miss a lot in missing the patient himself. All you're left with is your ability to make inferences and draw conclusions. In an early version of his poem "Romance," which he wrote first when he was twenty and published in 1831, Poe writes, "being young and dipt in folly / I fell in love with melancholy, / . . . I could not

love except where Death/Was mingling his with Beauty's breath—"
Poe, it turns out, suppressed this poem—maybe it exposed too
much. Poe on the couch can tell you some things. So can Poe in the
woods. Or Poe in the parlor. Or Poe on the page.

This Way to the Raven Room

For cyber-travelers, the Edgar Allan Poe Society of Baltimore has an
excellent Web site (*www.eapoe.org*) that has something for scholars
and fans alike. The society has painstakingly pulled together a com-
prehensive bibliographic record of everything written by Poe, and it
includes extremely interesting pieces of its own on many aspects of
Poe's life and work.

fact

In the early days, the Edgar Allan Poe Society of Baltimore (founded in
1923) presented public readings, concerts featuring compositions based
on Poe's work, and exhibitions of Poe memorabilia. Moreover, society
members were instrumental in preserving the Baltimore Poe house. In
the past thirty years, their activities have come to include publications,
the annual commemorative lecture, and construction of the Web site as
a resource for Poe fans and scholars.

Richmond, Virginia, has the Poe Museum on East Main Street,
within sight of the Philip Morris factory. Inside the Old Stone House,
which is the oldest building in historic Richmond, you can sign the
guest register and pay an admission fee (there are reduced rates for
seniors and students) for a tour. Then, if you're lucky, your tour guide
is the kind of Virginian whose soft drawl makes "Poe" a charming
two-syllable word. First you pass portraits of Poe and his birth parents, Eliza and David, on your way to a room containing a scale
model of the Richmond from Poe's time—you can see the Allans'
house, "Moldavia," on Fifth Street, Poe's office, and the hotel where
he lectured. The model spans twenty city blocks, ending at St. John's

Church on 25th Street, where in those crackling pre-Revolutionary War days, Patrick Henry roared about liberty and death.

The museum is actually an enclave of five buildings, so when the tour leaves the Old Stone House, it takes you to a neighboring building that houses one of the largest collections of Poe memorabilia in the world. In some ways, what's most striking is how little there is. The secretary desk belonged to John Allan, Poe's foster father, and Poe probably used it. Poe was most likely familiar with the various Allan household furnishings. The small trunk was actually his, and contains all his personal effects at the time of his death in 1849: a walking stick, boot hooks, and the deceased Virginia's trinket box and mirror. These you can be sure he handled, so to touch Virginia's little mirror is to touch Poe's hand.

At the foot of an old staircase is a sign with an arrow pointing upstairs: Raven Room. Up you go. On exhibit in the Raven Room are the forty-three framed illustrations British artist James Carling submitted to Harper and Brothers Publishers for the 1882 edition of "The

The Old Stone House, Richmond, Virginia, 1865. Today it houses the Poe Museum.

Raven." The publisher chose work by Gustave Doré, instead, and a set of those are on display at the Poe House in Baltimore. But in twenty-first century Richmond, you can't climb the stairs to the Raven Room without hoping that it leads to a portal into Poe's dark imagination, a kind of life-sized, raven diorama with yourself as a player—vapors seeping up through the floorboards, a clattering shutter, a whiff of opium—and, of course, a bust of Pallas Athena decked out with a two-foot long, prophetic black bird.

question

Does Richmond have the only Poe site?

There are several other sites dedicated to Edgar Allan Poe that are open to the public. There's the Poe House and Museum at 203 North Amity Street in Baltimore, the Edgar Allan Poe National Historical Site at 532 North Seventh Street in Philadelphia, and the Poe Cottage in Poe Park at Kingsbridge Road and the Grand Concourse in the Bronx.

Pennies for Poe

"80." Identified only by a number on a small block of sandstone. That was Poe's grave for the first twenty-six years after his death. It took ten years—from 1865 until the rededication of his grave in 1875—for a local elocution teacher, Sara Sigourney Rice, to raise the money for a memorial to be designed and inscribed. With the help of enthusiastic high school students, Rice ran a Pennies for Poe campaign and held various other fundraisers—some of which also helped Poe's sister, Rosalie Poe.

Going Skeletal

Just days before the actual dedication ceremony, when the new monument would be unveiled, the gravedigger had to remove the coffin from its original site in the Poe family plot and rebury it in its more prominent location at the northwest corner of the cemetery. The same man, George Spence, who had buried Poe in 1849, was still on hand and oversaw the opening of the grave. The gravedigger, a fellow named Tuder, set about his work pretty vigorously just at sundown, and finally managed to drive his pickaxe through the plank on top of the coffin, tapping the top of the coffin itself. An inexcusably slow American public had come knocking.

---

fact

If you want to check out more than books, the Enoch Pratt Free Library, at 400 Cathedral Street in Baltimore, houses the Amelia F. Poe collection of Poe-related letters and documents. In addition, the library has a fragment of Poe's original coffin and a lock of his hair.

As the coffin was raised out of the grave, it became clear that either the pickaxe or natural decay had damaged the lid, pieces of which fell out and exposed the remains. This had been no premature burial, like you find in a few of his tales. There were no frantic bloody scratchings on the inside of the casket. And what the onlookers saw was all that was left of Poe, the skeleton. All flesh and fabric had decayed into dust, but otherwise the skeleton was in good condition—except for the ribs, which had settled out to the sides, and the upper teeth, which were scattered. The lower teeth were right where Poe had last used them, and were still very white. On his skull some of his dark curling hair remained.

Dead and (Re)Buried

George Spence moved the bones to another wooden box, and as night approached, the remains were reburied. On the one hand, the story of this coffin-lifting seems to fit with Poe's macabre tales, but on the other hand, there is something oddly peaceful about knowing that the earthly remains are inconsequential, really, compared to the lasting beauty of written work.

Three cemetery workers sat around discussing dead bodies and enjoying peaches direct from the trees nearby. Three days later, the ceremony was a proud event, and the monument to Poe was unveiled. Only the elderly Whitman attended, but letters from other notables who couldn't come were read to commemorate the occasion. All praised Poe—Longfellow, Whittier, Tennyson, Mallarmé—all except William Cullen Bryant, who said in his letter that he declined to come based on what he had heard about Poe's character.

"Fame! glory!—they are life-giving breath, and living blood. No man lives, unless he is famous! How bitterly I belied my nature, and my aspirations, when I said I did not desire fame, and that I despised it."—Poe on fame

Roses, Cognac—and Did You Catch the Score?

Every year since 1949 a mysterious cloaked figure pays a visit to Poe's grave after midnight on January 19, Poe's birthday. (The January 20 birthdate on the memorial stone is wrong.) His face is obscured by a scarf—sometimes black, sometimes white—and he carries a silver-tipped cane and wears a black fedora. His mission is appropriately Poe-like: motivated by a personal fidelity that goes unexplained.

Poe's original resting place is marked today with a headstone.

A large monument marks Poe's current burial site.

The solitary figure, called the Poe Toaster, leaves three red roses and a half-full bottle of cognac.

Interpreters believe the roses refer to the little domestic unit that are still housed together, Eddie, Sissy, and Muddy. The cognac is available for the "toast." Half full? Maybe a tip of the hat to the habit of "Southern conviviality" that Poe enjoyed—and struggled with—suggesting other mysterious evenings of shared pleasures. The Poe Toaster leaves, and despite the respectful witnesses who have gathered over the years, generally there's no attempt to interfere with a ritual that provides just about as many "shivers" as the tales themselves. Unlike Auguste Dupin, some mysteries are better left unsolved.

> "I love fame—I dote on it—I idolize it—I would drink to the very dregs the glorious intoxication. I would have incense ascend in my honour from every hill and hamlet, from every town and city on this earth."—Poe on fame

Changing of the Guard

But the annual Poe toasting birthday ritual experienced some seismic activity in 1993, when a note left behind said, "The torch will be passed." Very alarming. Was the toaster sick? Or sick of the tradition? Wasn't there even a little bit of a sense that Poe was somehow alive only as long as the Toaster was, too? The torch passing was pretty much uneventful, as it turns out, and not until 1999, when witnesses noted that the Poe Toaster's hair (seen somehow from under that fedora) had gone from white to black. But fame becomes a character of its own, finally. Poe's grave has been "optimized" by the Toaster, who every so often leaves notes that make him appear like some kind of Tiresias in a fedora, predicting (inaccurately) a Ravens loss in the 2001 Super Bowl. (In an NFL tip of the helmet to a Baltimore "adopted son," the three mascots of the Baltimore Ravens football team are named Edgar, Allan, and Poe.)

In 2004, the Toaster's note swatted at the French (interpreters see a correlation with France's refusal to join the coalition of the willing), suggesting he would rather leave something other than cognac, but hey, that's the tradition.

To—

. . . all who are open to new ways of thinking about Edgar Allan Poe. It's altogether a good thing that a life and work can't be wrestled into submission. Where is the joy in pinning a thing out flat, like a poor butterfly, only to keep returning to it and finding no new information? The wrestlers and pinners will always miss something, because a great life or great talent never yields up all its truths.

A man can write a monster and yet not be a monster. A man can live a more satisfying life on the page than in the parlor. A man can fail a little bit everywhere he turns over the course of his life—and succeed everywhere he can no longer see after he dies. The lingering mysteries about Poe are not much different, really, than those you find in plenty of other lives. For all his hoaxes and horrors and fingers drawing you into the miasma of felt life, Poe was an authentic voice. When he was twenty, he wrote a poem, "To—," which was long in the way of youthful things. At the end of his life—only twenty years later—he returned to that poem and brought it down to a single stanza, eight lines. And in its plainspoken address to readers 150 years later, it's one of his very best.

> "I disagree with you in what you say of man's advance towards perfection. Man is now only more active, not wiser, nor more happy, than he was 6000 years ago."—Poe on human progress

> To—
> I heed not that my earthly lot
> Hath—little of Earth in it—
> That years of love have been forgot
> In the hatred of a minute:—
> I mourn not that the desolate
> Are happier, sweet, than I,
> But that you sorrow for my fate
> Who am a passerby.

Appendix A

Serving Up the Shivers

Horror? Terror? Or a double helping of both? Here are two of Edgar Allan Poe's most popular stories—"The Tell-Tale Heart" and "The Pit and the Pendulum"—that make interesting companion pieces. In one, a murderous narrator grabs you by the collar and confesses his terrible crime; in the other, a political prisoner describes his relentless torture at the hands of the Inquisition. Which gives *you* the shivers?

"The Tell-Tale Heart"

TRUE!—nervous—very, very dreadfully nervous I had been and am; but why *will* you say that I am mad? The disease had sharpened my senses—not destroyed—not dulled them. Above all was the sense of hearing acute. I heard all things in the heaven and in the earth. I heard many things in hell. How, then, am I mad? Hearken! and observe how healthily—how calmly I can tell you the whole story.

It is impossible to say how first the idea entered my brain; but once conceived, it haunted me day and night. Object there was none. Passion there was none. I loved the old man. He had never wronged me. He had never given me insult. For his gold I had no desire. I think it was his eye! yes, it was this! One of his eyes resembled that of a vulture—a pale blue eye, with a film over it. Whenever it fell upon me, my blood ran cold; and so by degrees—very gradually—I made up my mind to take the life of the old man, and thus rid myself of the eye forever.

Now this is the point. You fancy me mad. Madmen know nothing. But you should have seen *me*. You should have seen how wisely I proceeded—with what caution—with what foresight—with what dissimulation I went to work! I was never kinder to the old man than during the whole week before I killed him. And every night, about midnight, I turned the latch of his door and opened it—oh, so gently! And then, when I had made an opening sufficient for my head, I put in a dark lantern, all closed, closed, so that no light shone out, and then I thrust in my head. Oh, you would have laughed to see how cunningly I thrust it in! I moved it slowly—very, very slowly, so that I might not disturb the old man's sleep. It took me an hour to place my whole head within the opening so far that I could see him as he lay upon his bed. Ha!—would a madman have been so wise as this? And then, when my head was well in the room, I undid the lantern cautiously—oh, so cautiously—cautiously (for the hinges creaked)—I undid it just so much that a single thin ray fell upon the vulture eye. And this I did for seven long nights—every night just at midnight—but I found the eye always closed; and so it was impossible to do the work; for it was not the old man who vexed me, but his Evil Eye. And every morning, when the day broke, I went boldly into the chamber, and spoke courageously to him, calling him by name in a hearty tone, and inquiring how he had passed the night. So you see he would have been a very profound old man, indeed, to suspect that every night, just at twelve, I looked in upon him while he slept.

Upon the eighth night I was more than usually cautious in opening the door. A watch's minute hand moves more quickly than did mine. Never before that night had I *felt* the extent of my own powers—of my sagacity. I could scarcely contain my feelings of triumph. To think that there I was, opening the door, little by little, and he not even to dream of my secret deeds or thoughts. I fairly chuckled at the idea; and perhaps he heard me; for he moved on the bed suddenly, as if startled. Now you may think that I drew back—but no. His room was as black as pitch with the thick darkness, (for the shutters were close fastened, through fear of robbers,) and so I knew that he could not see the opening of the door, and I kept pushing it on steadily, steadily.

I had my head in, and was about to open the lantern, when my thumb slipped upon the tin fastening, and the old man sprang up in the bed, crying out—"Who's there?"

I kept quite still and said nothing. For a whole hour I did not move a muscle, and in the meantime I did not hear him lie down. He was still sitting up in the bed listening;—just as I have done, night after night, hearkening to the death watches in the wall.

Presently I heard a slight groan, and I knew it was the groan of mortal terror. It was not a groan of pain or of grief—oh, no!—it was the low stifled sound that arises from the bottom of the soul when overcharged with awe. I knew the sound well. Many a night, just at midnight, when all the world slept, it has welled up from my own bosom, deepening, with its dreadful echo, the terrors that distracted me. I say I knew it well. I knew what the old man felt, and pitied him, although I chuckled at heart. I knew that he had been lying awake ever since the first slight noise, when he had turned in the bed. His fears had been ever since growing upon him. He had been trying to fancy them causeless, but could not. He had been saying to himself—"It is nothing but the wind in the chimney—it is only a mouse crossing the floor," or "it is merely a cricket which has made a single chirp." Yes, he has been trying to comfort himself with these suppositions: but he had found all in vain. *All in vain;* because Death, in approaching him had stalked with his black shadow before him, and enveloped the victim. And it was the mournful influence of the unperceived shadow that caused him to feel—although he neither saw nor heard—to *feel* the presence of my head within the room.

When I had waited a long time, very patiently, without hearing him lie down, I resolved to open a little—a very, very little crevice in the lantern. So I opened it—you cannot imagine how stealthily, stealthily—until, at length a single dim ray, like the thread of the spider, shot from out the crevice and fell upon the vulture eye.

It was open—wide, wide open—and I grew furious as I gazed upon it. I saw it with perfect distinctness—all a dull blue, with a hideous veil over it that chilled the very marrow in my bones; but I could see nothing else of the old man's face or person: for I had directed the ray as if by instinct, precisely upon the damned spot.

And now have I not told you that what you mistake for madness is but over acuteness of the senses?—now, I say, there came to my ears a low, dull, quick sound, such as a watch makes when enveloped in cotton. I knew *that* sound well, too. It was the beating of the old man's heart. It increased my fury, as the beating of a drum stimulates the soldier into courage.

But even yet I refrained and kept still. I scarcely breathed. I held the lantern motionless. I tried how steadily I could maintain the ray upon the eye. Meantime the hellish tattoo of the heart increased. It grew quicker and quicker, and louder and louder every instant. The old man's terror *must* have been extreme! It grew louder, I say, louder every moment!—do you mark me well? I have told you that I am nervous: so I am. And now at the dead hour of the night, amid the dreadful silence of that old house, so strange a noise as this excited me to uncontrollable terror. Yet, for some minutes longer I refrained and stood still. But the beating grew louder, louder! I thought the heart must burst. And now a new anxiety seized me—the sound would be heard by a neighbor! The old man's hour had come! With a loud yell, I threw open the lantern and leaped into the room. He shrieked once—once only. In an instant I dragged him to the floor, and pulled the heavy bed over him. I then smiled gaily, to find the deed so far done. But, for many minutes, the heart beat on with a muffled sound. This, however, did not vex me; it would not be heard through the wall. At length it ceased. The old man was dead. I removed the bed and examined the corpse. Yes, he was stone, stone dead. I placed my hand upon the heart and held it there many minutes. There was no pulsation. He was stone dead. His eye would trouble me no more.

If still you think me mad, you will think so no longer when I describe the wise precautions I took for the concealment of the body. The night waned, and I worked hastily, but in silence. First of all I dismembered the corpse. I cut off the head and the arms and the legs.

I then took up three planks from the flooring of the chamber, and deposited all between the scantlings. I then replaced the boards so cleverly, so cunningly, that no human eye—not even *his*—could have detected any thing wrong. There was nothing to wash out—no stain of any kind—no blood-spot whatever. I had been too wary for that. A tub had caught all—ha! ha!

When I had made an end of these labors, it was four o'clock—still dark as midnight. As the bell sounded the hour, there came a knocking at the street door. I went down to open it with a light heart,—for what had I *now* to fear? There entered three men, who introduced themselves, with perfect suavity, as officers of the police. A shriek had been heard by a neighbor during the night; suspicion of foul play had been aroused; information had been lodged at the police office, and they (the officers) had been deputed to search the premises.

I smiled,—for *what* had I to fear? I bade the gentlemen welcome. The shriek, I said, was my own in a dream. The old man, I mentioned, was absent in the country. I took my visitors all over the house. I bade them search—search *well*. I led them, at length, to *his* chamber. I showed them his treasures, secure, undisturbed. In the enthusiasm of my confidence, I brought chairs into the room, and desired them *here* to rest from their fatigues, while I myself, in the wild audacity of my perfect triumph, placed my own seat upon the very spot beneath which reposed the corpse of the victim.

The officers were satisfied. My manner had convinced them. I was singularly at ease. They sat, and while I answered cheerily, they chatted of familiar things. But, ere long, I felt myself getting pale and wished them gone. My head ached, and I fancied a ringing in my ears: but still they sat and still chatted. The ringing became more distinct:—it continued and became more distinct: I talked more freely to get rid of the feeling: but it continued and gained definitiveness—until, at length, I found that the noise was *not* within my ears.

No doubt I now grew *very* pale;—but I talked more fluently, and with a heightened voice. Yet the sound increased—and what could I do? It was *a low, dull, quick sound—much such a sound as a watch makes when enveloped in cotton.* I gasped for breath—and yet the officers heard it not. I talked more quickly—more vehemently; but the noise steadily increased. I arose and argued about trifles, in a high key and with violent gesticulations; but the noise steadily increased. Why *would* they not be gone? I paced the floor to and fro with heavy strides, as if excited to fury by the observations of the men—but the noise steadily increased. Oh God! what *could* I do? I foamed—I raved—I swore! I swung the chair upon which I had been sitting, and grated it upon the boards, but the noise arose over all and continually increased. It grew louder—louder—*louder!* And still the men chatted pleasantly, and smiled. Was it possible they heard not? Almighty God!—no, no! They heard!—they suspected!—they *knew!*—they were making a mockery of my horror!—this I thought, and this I think. But anything was better than this agony! Anything was more tolerable than this derision! I could bear those hypocritical smiles no longer! I felt that I must scream or die!—and now—again!—hark! louder! louder! louder! *louder!*—

"Villains!" I shrieked, "dissemble no more! I admit the deed!—tear up the planks!—here, here!—it is the beating of his hideous heart!"

"The Pit and the Pendulum"

I WAS sick—sick unto death with that long agony; and when they at length unbound me, and I was permitted to sit, I felt that my senses were leaving me. The sentence—the dread sentence of death—was the last of distinct accentuation which reached my ears. After that, the sound of the inquisitorial voices seemed merged in one dreamy indeterminate hum. It conveyed to my soul the idea of revolution—perhaps from its association in fancy with the burr of a mill wheel. This only for a brief period; for presently I heard no more. Yet, for a while, I saw; but with how terrible an exaggeration! I saw the lips of the black-robed judges. They appeared to me white—whiter than the sheet upon which I trace these words—and thin even to grotesqueness; thin with the intensity of their expression of firmness—of immoveable resolution—of stern contempt of human torture. I saw that the decrees of what to me was Fate, were still issuing from those lips. I saw them writhe with a deadly locution. I saw them fashion the syllables of my name; and I shuddered because no sound succeeded. I saw, too, for a few moments of delirious horror, the soft and nearly imperceptible waving of the sable draperies which enwrapped the walls of the apartment. And then my vision fell upon the seven tall candles upon the table. At first they wore the aspect of charity, and seemed white and slender angels who would save me; but then, all at once, there came a most deadly nausea over my spirit, and I felt every fibre in my frame thrill as if I had touched the wire of a galvanic battery, while the angel forms became meaningless spectres, with heads of flame, and I saw that from them there would be no help. And then there stole into my fancy, like a rich musical note, the thought of what sweet rest there must be in the grave. The thought came gently and stealthily, and it seemed long before it attained full appreciation; but just as my spirit came at length properly to feel and entertain it, the figures of the judges vanished, as if magically, from before me; the tall candles sank into nothingness; their flames went out utterly; the blackness of darkness supervened; all sensations appeared swallowed up in a mad rushing descent as of the soul into Hades. Then silence, and stillness, night were the universe.

I had swooned; but still will not say that all of consciousness was lost. What of it there remained I will not attempt to define, or even to describe; yet all was not lost. In the deepest slumber—no! In delirium—no! In a swoon—no! In death—no! even in the grave all is not lost. Else there is no immortality for man. Arousing from the most profound of slumbers, we break the gossamer web of some dream. Yet in a second afterward, (so frail may that web have been) we remember not that we have dreamed. In the return to life from the swoon there are two stages; first, that of the sense of mental or spiritual; secondly, that of the sense of physical, existence. It seems probable that if, upon reaching the second stage, we could recall the impressions of the first, we should find these impressions eloquent in memories of the gulf beyond. And that gulf is—what? How at least shall we distinguish its shadows from those of the tomb? But if the impressions of what I have termed the first stage, are not, at will, recalled, yet, after long interval, do they not come unbidden, while we marvel whence they come? He who has never swooned, is not he who finds strange palaces and wildly familiar faces in coals that glow; is not he who beholds floating in mid-air the sad visions that the many may not view; is not he who ponders over the perfume of some novel flower—is not he whose brain grows bewildered with the meaning of some musical cadence which has never before arrested his attention.

Amid frequent and thoughtful endeavors to remember; amid earnest struggles to regather some token of the state of seeming nothingness into which my soul had lapsed, there have been moments when I have dreamed of success; there have been brief, very brief periods when I have conjured up remembrances which the lucid reason of a later epoch assures me could have had reference only to that condition of seeming unconsciousness. These shadows of memory tell, indistinctly, of tall figures that lifted and bore me in silence down—down—still down—till a hideous dizziness oppressed me at the mere idea of the interminableness of the descent. They tell also of a vague horror at my heart, on account of that heart's unnatural stillness. Then comes a sense of sudden motionlessness throughout all things; as if those who bore me (a ghastly train!) had outrun, in their descent, the limits of the limitless, and paused from the wearisomeness of their toil. After this I call to mind flatness and dampness; and then all is madness—the madness of a memory which busies itself among forbidden things.

Very suddenly there came back to my soul motion and sound— the tumultuous motion of the heart, and, in my ears, the sound of its beating. Then a pause in which all is blank. Then again sound, and motion, and touch—a tingling sensation pervading my frame. Then the mere consciousness of existence, without thought—a condition which lasted long. Then, very suddenly, thought, and shuddering terror, and earnest endeavor to comprehend my true state. Then a strong desire to lapse into insensibility. Then a rushing revival of soul and a successful effort to move. And now a full memory of the trial, of the judges, of the sable draperies, of the sentence, of the sickness, of the swoon. Then entire forgetfulness of all that followed; of all that a later day and much earnestness of endeavor have enabled me vaguely to recall.

So far, I had not opened my eyes. I felt that I lay upon my back, unbound. I reached out my hand, and it fell heavily upon something damp and hard. There I suffered it to remain for many minutes, while I strove to imagine where and what I could be. I longed, yet dared not to employ my vision. I dreaded the first glance at objects around me. It was not that I feared to look upon things horrible, but that I grew aghast lest there should be nothing to see. At length, with a wild desperation at heart, I quickly unclosed my eyes. My worst thoughts, then, were confirmed. The blackness of eternal night encompassed me. I struggled for breath. The intensity of the darkness seemed to oppress and stifle me. The atmosphere was intolerably close. I still lay quietly, and made effort to exercise my reason. I brought to mind the inquisitorial proceedings, and attempted from that point to deduce my real condition. The sentence had passed; and it appeared to me that a very long interval of time had since elapsed. Yet not for a moment did I suppose myself actually dead. Such a supposition, notwithstanding what we read in fiction, is altogether inconsistent with real existence;—but where and in what state was I? The condemned to death, I knew, perished usually at the autos-da-fe, and one of these had been held on the very night of the day of my trial. Had I been remanded to my dungeon, to await the next sacrifice, which would not take place for many months? This I at once saw could not be. Victims had been in immediate demand. Moreover, my dungeon, as well as all the condemned cells at Toledo, had stone floors, and light was not altogether excluded.

A fearful idea now suddenly drove the blood in torrents upon my heart, and for a brief period, I once more relapsed into insensibility. Upon recovering, I at once started to my feet, trembling convulsively in every fibre. I thrust my arms wildly above and around me in all directions. I felt nothing; yet dreaded to move a step, lest I should be impeded by the walls of a tomb. Perspiration burst from every pore, and stood in cold big beads upon my forehead. The agony of suspense grew at length intolerable, and I cautiously moved forward, with my arms extended, and my eyes straining from their sockets, in the hope of catching some faint ray of light. I proceeded for many paces; but still all was blackness and vacancy. I breathed more freely. It seemed evident that mine was not, at least, the most hideous of fates.

And now, as I still continued to step cautiously onward, there came thronging upon my recollection a thousand vague rumors of the horrors of Toledo. Of the dungeons there had been strange things narrated—fables I had always deemed them—but yet strange, and too ghastly to repeat, save in a whisper. Was I left to perish of starvation in this subterranean world of darkness; or what fate, perhaps even more fearful, awaited me? That the result would be death, and a death of more than customary bitterness, I knew too well the character of my judges to doubt. The mode and the hour were all that occupied or distracted me.

My outstretched hands at length encountered some solid obstruction. It was a wall, seemingly of stone masonry—very smooth, slimy, and cold. I followed it up; stepping with all the careful distrust with which certain antique narratives had inspired me. This process, however, afforded me no means of ascertaining the dimensions of my dungeon; as I might make its circuit, and return to the point whence I set out, without being aware of the fact; so perfectly uniform seemed the wall. I therefore sought the knife which had been in my pocket, when led into the inquisitorial chamber; but it was gone; my clothes had been exchanged for a wrapper of coarse serge. I had thought of forcing the blade in some minute crevice of the masonry, so as to identify my point of departure. The difficulty, nevertheless, was but trivial; although, in the disorder of my fancy, it seemed at first insuperable. I tore a part of the hem from the robe and placed the fragment at full length, and at right angles to the wall. In groping my way around the prison, I could not fail to encounter this rag upon completing the circuit. So, at least I thought: but I had not counted upon the extent of the dungeon, or upon my own weakness. The ground was moist and slippery. I staggered onward for some time, when I stumbled and fell. My excessive fatigue induced me to remain prostrate; and sleep soon overtook me as I lay.

Upon awaking, and stretching forth an arm, I found beside me a loaf and a pitcher with water. I was too much exhausted to reflect upon this circumstance, but ate and drank with avidity. Shortly afterward, I resumed my tour around the prison, and with much toil came at last upon the fragment of the serge. Up to the period when I fell I had counted fifty-two paces, and upon resuming my walk, I had counted forty-eight more;—when I arrived at the rag. There were in all, then, a hundred paces; and, admitting two paces to the yard, I presumed the dungeon to be fifty yards in circuit. I had met, however, with many angles in the wall, and thus I could form no guess at the shape of the vault; for vault I could not help supposing it to be.

I had little object—certainly no hope these researches; but a vague curiosity prompted me to continue them. Quitting the wall, I resolved to cross the area of the enclosure. At first I proceeded with extreme caution, for the floor, although seemingly of solid material, was treacherous with slime. At length, however, I took courage, and did not hesitate to step firmly; endeavoring to cross in as direct a line as possible. I had advanced some ten or twelve paces in this manner, when the remnant of the torn hem of my robe became entangled between my legs. I stepped on it, and fell violently on my face.

In the confusion attending my fall, I did not immediately apprehend a somewhat startling circumstance, which yet, in a few seconds afterward, and while I still lay prostrate, arrested my attention. It was this—my chin rested upon the floor of the prison, but my lips and the upper portion of my head, although seemingly at a less elevation than the chin, touched nothing. At the same time my forehead seemed bathed in a clammy vapor, and the peculiar smell of decayed fungus arose to my nostrils. I put forward my arm, and shuddered to find that I had fallen at the very brink of a circular pit, whose extent, of course, I had no means of ascertaining at the moment. Groping about the masonry just below the margin, I succeeded in dislodging a small fragment, and let it fall into the abyss. For many seconds I hearkened to its reverberations as it dashed against the sides of the chasm in its descent; at length there was a sullen plunge into water, succeeded by loud echoes. At the same moment there came a sound resembling the quick opening, and as rapid closing of a door overhead, while a faint gleam of light flashed suddenly through the gloom, and as suddenly faded away.

I saw clearly the doom which had been prepared for me, and congratulated myself upon the timely accident by which I had escaped. Another step before my fall, and the world had seen me no more. And the death just avoided, was of that very character which I had regarded as fabulous and frivolous in the tales respecting the Inquisition. To the victims of its tyranny, there was the choice of death with its direst physical agonies, or death with its most hideous moral horrors. I had been reserved for the latter. By long suffering my nerves had been unstrung, until I trembled at the sound of my own voice, and had become in every respect a fitting subject for the species of torture which awaited me.

Shaking in every limb, I groped my way back to the wall; resolving there to perish rather than risk the terrors of the wells, of which my imagination now pictured many in various positions about the dungeon. In other conditions of mind I might have had courage to end my misery at once by a plunge into one of these abysses; but now I was the veriest of cowards. Neither could I forget what I had read of these pits—that the sudden extinction of life formed no part of their most horrible plan.

Agitation of spirit kept me awake for many long hours; but at length I again slumbered. Upon arousing, I found by my side, as before, a loaf and a pitcher of water. A burning thirst consumed me, and I emptied the vessel at a draught. It must have been drugged; for scarcely had I drunk, before I became irresistibly drowsy. A deep sleep fell upon me—a sleep like that of death. How long it lasted of course, I know not; but when, once again, I unclosed my eyes, the objects around me were visible. By a wild sulphurous lustre, the origin of which I could not at first determine, I was enabled to see the extent and aspect of the prison.

In its size I had been greatly mistaken. The whole circuit of its walls did not exceed twenty-five yards. For some minutes this fact occasioned me a world of vain trouble; vain indeed! for what could be of less importance, under the terrible circumstances which environed me, then the mere dimensions of my dungeon? But my soul took a wild interest in trifles, and I busied myself in endeavors to account for the error I had committed in my measurement. The truth at length flashed upon me. In my first attempt at exploration I had counted fifty-two paces, up to the period when I fell; I must then have been within a pace or two of the fragment of serge; in fact, I had nearly performed the circuit of the vault. I then slept, and upon awaking, I must have returned upon my steps—thus supposing the circuit nearly double what it actually was. My confusion of mind prevented me from observing that I began my tour with the wall to the left, and ended it with the wall to the right.

I had been deceived, too, in respect to the shape of the enclosure. In feeling my way I had found many angles, and thus deduced an idea of great irregularity; so potent is the effect of total darkness upon one arousing from lethargy or sleep! The angles were simply those of a few slight depressions, or niches, at odd intervals. The general shape of the prison was square. What I had taken for masonry seemed now to be iron, or some other metal, in huge plates, whose sutures or joints occasioned the depression. The entire surface of this metallic enclosure was rudely daubed in all the hideous and repulsive devices to which the charnel superstition of the monks has given rise. The figures of fiends in aspects of menace, with skeleton forms, and other more really fearful images, overspread and disfigured the walls. I observed that the outlines of these monstrosities were sufficiently distinct, but that the colors seemed faded and blurred, as if from the effects of a damp atmosphere. I now noticed the floor, too, which was of stone. In the centre yawned the circular pit from whose jaws I had escaped; but it was the only one in the dungeon.

All this I saw indistinctly and by much effort: for my personal condition had been greatly changed during slumber. I now lay upon my back, and at full length, on a species of low framework of wood. To this I was securely bound by a long strap resembling a surcingle. It passed in many convolutions about my limbs and body, leaving at liberty only my head, and my left arm to such extent that I could, by dint of much exertion, supply myself with food from an earthen dish which lay by my side on the floor. I saw, to my horror, that the pitcher had been removed. I say to my horror; for I was consumed with intolerable thirst. This thirst it appeared to be the design of my persecutors to stimulate: for the food in the dish was meat pungently seasoned.

Looking upward, I surveyed the ceiling of my prison. It was some thirty or forty feet overhead, and constructed much as the side walls. In one of its panels a very singular figure riveted my whole attention. It was the painted figure of Time as he is commonly represented, save that, in lieu of a scythe, he held what, at a casual glance, I supposed to be the pictured image of a huge pendulum such as we see on antique clocks. There was something, however, in the appearance of this machine which caused me to regard it more attentively. While I gazed directly upward at it (for its position was immediately over my own) I fancied that I saw it in motion. In an instant afterward the fancy was confirmed. Its sweep was brief, and of course slow. I watched it for some minutes, somewhat in fear, but more in wonder. Wearied at length with observing its dull movement, I turned my eyes upon the other objects in the cell.

A slight noise attracted my notice, and, looking to the floor, I saw several enormous rats traversing it. They had issued from the well, which lay just within view to my right. Even then, while I gazed, they came up in troops, hurriedly, with ravenous eyes, allured by the scent of the meat. From this it required much effort and attention to scare them away.

It might have been half an hour, perhaps even an hour, (for in cast my I could take but imperfect note of time) before I again cast my eyes upward. What I then saw confounded and amazed me. The sweep of the pendulum had increased in extent by nearly a yard. As a natural consequence, its velocity was also much greater. But what mainly disturbed me was the idea that had perceptibly descended. I now observed—with what horror it is needless to say—that its nether extremity was formed of a crescent of glittering steel, about a foot in length from horn to horn; the horns upward, and the under edge evidently as keen as that of a razor. Like a razor also, it seemed massy and heavy, tapering from the edge into a solid and broad structure above. It was appended to a weighty rod of brass, and the whole hissed as it swung through the air.

I could no longer doubt the doom prepared for me by monkish ingenuity in torture. My cognizance of the pit had become known to the inquisitorial agents—the pit whose horrors had been destined for so bold a recusant as myself—the pit, typical of hell, and regarded by rumor as the Ultima Thule of all their punishments. The plunge into this pit I had avoided by the merest of accidents, I knew that surprise, or entrapment into torment, formed an important portion of all the grotesquerie of these dungeon deaths. Having failed to fall, it was no part of the demon plan to hurl me into the abyss; and thus (there being no alternative) a different and a milder destruction awaited me. Milder! I half smiled in my agony as I thought of such application of such a term.

What boots it to tell of the long, long hours of horror more than mortal, during which I counted the rushing vibrations of the steel! Inch by inch—line by line—with a descent only appreciable at intervals that seemed ages—down and still down it came! Days passed—it might have been that many days passed—ere it swept so closely over me as to fan me with its acrid breath. The odor of the sharp steel forced itself into my nostrils. I prayed—I wearied heaven with my prayer for its more speedy descent. I grew frantically mad, and struggled to force myself upward against the sweep of the fearful scimitar. And then I fell suddenly calm, and lay smiling at the glittering death, as a child at some rare bauble.

There was another interval of utter insensibility; it was brief; for, upon again lapsing into life there had been no perceptible descent in the pendulum. But it might have been long; for I knew there were demons who took note of my swoon, and who could have arrested the vibration at pleasure. Upon my recovery, too, I felt very—oh, inexpressibly sick and weak, as if through long inanition. Even amid the agonies of that period, the human nature craved food. With painful effort I outstretched my left arm as far as my bonds permitted, and took possession of the small remnant which had been spared me by the rats. As I put a portion of it within my lips, there rushed to my mind a half formed thought of joy—of hope. Yet what business had I with hope? It was, as I say, a half formed thought—man has many such which are never completed. I felt that it was of joy—of hope; but felt also that it had perished in its formation. In vain I struggled to perfect—to regain it. Long suffering had nearly annihilated all my ordinary powers of mind. I was an imbecile—an idiot.

The vibration of the pendulum was at right angles to my length. I saw that the crescent was designed to cross the region of the heart. It would fray the serge of my robe—it would return and repeat its operations—again—and again. Notwithstanding terrifically wide sweep (some thirty feet or more) and the its hissing vigor of its descent, sufficient to sunder these very walls of iron, still the fraying of my robe would be all that, for several minutes, it would accomplish. And at this thought I paused. I dared not go farther than this reflection. I dwelt upon it with a pertinacity of attention—as if, in so dwelling, I could arrest here the descent of the steel. I forced myself to ponder upon the sound of the crescent as it should pass across the garment—upon the peculiar thrilling sensation which the friction of cloth produces on the nerves. I pondered upon all this frivolity until my teeth were on edge.

Down—steadily down it crept. I took a frenzied pleasure in contrasting its downward with its lateral velocity. To the right—to the left—far and wide—with the shriek of a damned spirit; to my heart with the stealthy pace of the tiger! I alternately laughed and howled as the one or the other idea grew predominant.

Down—certainly, relentlessly down! It vibrated within three inches of my bosom! I struggled violently, furiously, to free my left arm. This was free only from the elbow to the hand. I could reach the latter, from the platter beside me, to my mouth, with great effort, but no farther. Could I have broken the fastenings above the elbow, I would have seized and attempted to arrest the pendulum. I might as well have attempted to arrest an avalanche!

Down—still unceasingly—still inevitably down! I gasped and struggled at each vibration. I shrunk convulsively at its every sweep. My eyes followed its outward or upward whirls with the eagerness of the most unmeaning despair; they closed themselves spasmodically at the descent, although death would have been a relief, oh! how unspeakable! Still I quivered in every nerve to think how slight a sinking of the machinery would precipitate that keen, glistening axe upon my bosom. It was hope that prompted the nerve to quiver—the frame to shrink. It was hope—the hope that triumphs on the rack—that whispers to the death-condemned even in the dungeons of the Inquisition.

I saw that some ten or twelve vibrations would bring the steel in actual contact with my robe, and with this observation there suddenly came over my spirit all the keen, collected calmness of despair. For the first time during many hours—or perhaps days—I thought. It now occurred to me that the bandage, or surcingle, which enveloped me, was unique. I was tied by no separate cord. The first stroke of the razorlike crescent athwart any portion of the band, would so detach it that it might be unwound from my person by means of my left hand. But how fearful, in that case, the proximity of the steel! The result of the slightest struggle how deadly! Was it likely, moreover, that the minions of the torturer had not foreseen and provided for this possibility! Was it probable that the bandage crossed my bosom in the track of the pendulum? Dreading to find my faint, and, as it seemed, in last hope frustrated, I so far elevated my head as to obtain a distinct view of my breast. The surcingle enveloped my limbs and body close in all directions—save in the path of the destroying crescent.

Scarcely had I dropped my head back into its original position, when there flashed upon my mind what I cannot better describe than as the unformed half of that idea of deliverance to which I have previously alluded, and of which a moiety only floated indeterminately through my brain when I raised food to my burning lips. The whole thought was now present—feeble, scarcely sane, scarcely definite,—but still entire. I proceeded at once, with the nervous energy of despair, to attempt its execution.

For many hours the immediate vicinity of the low framework upon which I lay, had been literally swarming with rats. They were wild, bold, ravenous; their red eyes glaring upon me as if they waited but for motionlessness on my part to make me their prey. "To what food," I thought, "have they been accustomed in the well?"

They had devoured, in spite of all my efforts to prevent them, all but a small remnant of the contents of the dish. I had fallen into an habitual see-saw, or wave of the hand about the platter: and, at length, the unconscious uniformity of the movement deprived it of effect. In their voracity the vermin frequently fastened their sharp fangs in my fingers. With the particles of the oily and spicy viand which now remained, I thoroughly rubbed the bandage wherever I could reach it; then, raising my hand from the floor, I lay breathlessly still.

At first the ravenous animals were startled and terrified at the change—at the cessation of movement. They shrank alarmedly back; many sought the well. But this was only for a moment. I had not counted in vain upon their voracity. Observing that I remained without motion, one or two of the boldest leaped upon the frame-work, and smelt at the surcingle. This seemed the signal for a general rush. Forth from the well they hurried in fresh troops. They clung to the wood—they overran it, and leaped in hundreds upon my person. The measured movement of the pendulum disturbed them not at all. Avoiding its strokes they busied themselves with the anointed bandage. They pressed—they swarmed upon me in ever accumulating heaps. They writhed upon my throat; their cold lips sought my own; I was half stifled by their thronging pressure; disgust, for which the world has no name, swelled my bosom, and chilled, with a heavy clamminess, my heart. Yet one minute, and I felt that the struggle would be over. Plainly I perceived the loosening of the bandage. I knew that in more than one place it must be already severed. With a more than human resolution I lay still.

Nor had I erred in my calculations—nor had I endured in vain. I at length felt that I was free. The surcingle hung in ribands from my body. But the stroke of the pendulum already pressed upon my bosom. It had divided the serge of the robe. It had cut through the linen beneath. Twice again it swung, and a sharp sense of pain shot through every nerve. But the moment of escape had arrived. At a wave of my hand my deliverers hurried tumultuously away. With a steady movement—cautious, sidelong, shrinking, and slow—I slid from the embrace of the bandage and beyond the reach of the scimitar. For the moment, at least, I was free.

Free!—and in the grasp of the Inquisition! I had scarcely stepped from my wooden bed of horror upon the stone floor of the prison, when the motion of the hellish machine ceased and I beheld it drawn up, by some invisible force, through the ceiling. This was a lesson which I took desperately to heart. My every motion was undoubtedly watched. Free!—I had but escaped death in one form of agony, to be delivered unto worse than death in some other. With that thought I rolled my eyes nervously around on the barriers of iron that hemmed me in. Something unusual—some change which, at first, I could not appreciate distinctly—it was obvious, had taken place in the apartment. For many minutes of a dreamy and trembling abstraction, I busied myself in vain, unconnected conjecture. During this period, I became aware, for the first time, of the origin of the sulphurous light which illumined the cell. It proceeded from a fissure, about half an inch in width, extending entirely around the prison at the base of the walls, which thus appeared, and were, completely separated from the floor. I endeavored, but of course in vain, to look through the aperture.

As I arose from the attempt, the mystery of the alteration in the chamber broke at once upon my understanding. I have observed that, although the outlines of the figures upon the walls were sufficiently distinct, yet the colors seemed blurred and indefinite. These colors had now assumed, and were momentarily assuming, a startling and most intense brilliancy, that gave to the spectral and fiendish portraitures an aspect that might have thrilled even firmer nerves than my own. Demon eyes, of a wild and ghastly vivacity, glared upon me in a thousand directions, where none had been visible before, and gleamed with the lurid lustre of a fire that I could not force my imagination to regard as unreal.

Unreal!—Even while I breathed there came to my nostrils the breath of the vapour of heated iron! A suffocating odour pervaded the prison! A deeper glow settled each moment in the eyes that glared at my agonies! A richer tint of crimson diffused itself over the pictured horrors of blood. I panted! I gasped for breath! There could be no doubt of the design of my tormentors—oh! most unrelenting! oh! most demoniac of men! I shrank from the glowing metal to the centre of the cell. Amid the thought of the fiery destruction that impended, the idea of the coolness of the well came over my soul like balm. I rushed to its deadly brink. I threw my straining vision below. The glare from the enkindled roof illumined its inmost recesses. Yet, for a wild moment, did my spirit refuse to comprehend the meaning of what I saw. At length it forced—it wrestled its way into my soul—it burned itself in upon my shuddering reason.—Oh! for a voice to speak!—oh! horror!—oh! any horror but this! With a shriek, I rushed from the margin, and buried my face in my hands—weeping bitterly.

The heat rapidly increased, and once again I looked up, shuddering as with a fit of the ague. There had been a second change in the cell—and now the change was obviously in the form. As before, it was in vain that I, at first, endeavoured to appreciate or understand what was taking place. But not long was I left in doubt. The Inquisitorial vengeance had been hurried by my two-fold escape, and there was to be no more dallying with the King of Terrors. The room had been square. I saw that two of its iron angles were now acute—two, consequently, obtuse. The fearful difference quickly increased with a low rumbling or moaning sound. In an instant the apartment had shifted its form into that of a lozenge. But the alteration stopped not here-I neither hoped nor desired it to stop. I could have clasped the red walls to my bosom as a garment of eternal peace. "Death," I said, "any death but that of the pit!" Fool! might I have not known that into the pit it was the object of the burning iron to urge me? Could I resist its glow? or, if even that, could I withstand its pressure[?] And now, flatter and flatter grew the lozenge, with a rapidity that left me no time for contemplation. Its centre, and of course, its greatest width, came just over the yawning gulf. I shrank back—but the closing walls pressed me resistlessly onward. At length for my seared and writhing body there was no longer an inch of foothold on the firm floor of the prison. I struggled no more, but the agony of my soul found vent in one loud, long, and final scream of despair. I felt that I tottered upon the brink—I averted my eyes—

There was a discordant hum of human voices! There was a loud blast as of many trumpets! There was a harsh grating as of a thousand thunders! The fiery walls rushed back! An outstretched arm caught my own as I fell, fainting, into the abyss. It was that of General Lasalle. The French army had entered Toledo. The Inquisition was in the hands of its enemies.

Appendix B

Timeline of Edgar Allan Poe's Life

1787	Eliza Arnold born in England
1784	David Poe, Jr. born in Baltimore
1796	Eliza Arnold and family arrive in the United States
1806	Eliza and David Poe wed
1809	Edgar Poe born in Boston
1810	David Poe deserts his family
1811	Eliza and David Poe die within a brief time of each other. John and Frances Allan take Poe into their Richmond, Virginia, home
1815	Poe and the Allan family relocate to Great Britain
1820	Poe and the Allan family return to Richmond, Virginia
1826	Poe attends the University of Virginia, leaving within a year
1827	Poe joins the United States Army
1827	*Tamerlane and Other Poems* published
1829	Frances Allan dies
1829	Poe leaves the Army and applies to West Point
1829	*Al Aaraaf, Tamerlane and Minor Poems* published
1830	Poe enrolls in West Point
1831	West Point expels Poe, who moves to Baltimore and lives with his Poe relatives
1833	Poe wins first prize for "MS. Found in a Bottle"

1834	John Allan dies, leaving Poe nothing
1835	Poe moves to Richmond, Virginia
1835	Poe and Virginia marry in a secret ceremony
1836	Poe begins work as an editor for the *Southern Literary Messenger*
1836	Poe and Virginia marry in a public ceremony
1837	Poe moves to New York
1838	Poe moves to Philadelphia
1838	*The Narrative of Arthur Gordon Pym* published
1838	"Ligeia" published
1839	"The Fall of the House of Usher" published
1842	Virginia begins to show symptoms of tuberculosis
1843	Poe wins a $100 prize for "The Gold Bug"
1843	"The Pit and the Pendulum" published
1843	"The Tell-Tale Heart" published
1844	Poe moves to New York
1845	"The Raven" published
1847	Virginia dies
1848	*Eureka* published
1849	Poe dies

Appendix C

Bibliography

Benton, Richard P. "Friends and Enemies: Women in the Life of Edgar Allan Poe." *Myths and Reality.* Baltimore: The Edgar Allan Poe Society of Baltimore, 1987.

Bledsoe, Thomas, and Mabbott, Thomas. "Poe and Armistead Gordon" in *Phylon* (1940-1956), Vol. 7, No. 4 (4th Qtr., 1946).

Bloom, Harold, (Ed.) *The Tales of Poe.* New York: Chelsea House Publishers, 1987.

Brooks, Van Wyck. *The Times of Melville and Whitman.* New York: E.P. Dutton, 1947.

Carlson, Eric W., (Ed.) *Critical Essays on Edgar Allan Poe.* Boston: G.K. Hall & Co., 1987.

Herzberg, Max J. *The Reader's Encyclopedia of American Literature.* New York: Thomas Y. Crowell, 1962.

Hutchisson, James M. *Poe.* Jackson: University Press of Mississippi, 2005.

Kenin, R. and Wintle, J., (Eds.) *The Dictionary of Biographical Quotation of British and American Subjects.* New York: Knopf, 1978.

Linton, Calvin D., (Ed.) *The Bicentennial Almanac.* Nashville: T. Nelson, 1975.

Mabbott, T.O., (Ed.) *Selected Poetry and Prose of Edgar Allan Poe.* New York: The Modern Library, 1951.

On the Expediency of Fitting Out Vessels of the Navy for an Exploration of the Pacific Ocean and South Seas," 25 March 1828, *American State Papers*: Naval Affairs Vol. 3, pp. 189-197.

Ostrom, John Ward, (Ed.) *The Letters of Edgar Allan Poe.* New York: Gordian Press, 1966.

Poe, Edgar Allan. *The Complete Tales and Poems.* New York: Vintage Books, 1975.

Poe, Edgar Allan. *The Narrative of Arthur Gordon Pym of Nantucket.* London: Penguin Books, 1986.

Poe, Edgar Allan. *Poetry, Tales, and Selected Essays.* U.S.A.: Library of America, 1996.

Quinn, Arthur Hobson. *Edgar Allan Poe: A Critical Biography.* Baltimore: Johns Hopkins University Press, 1998.

Thomas, Dwight and Jackson David K. . *The Poe Log: a Documentary Life of Edgar Allan Poe,* 1809 - 1849. Boston: G.K. Hall & Co., 1987.

Walker, I.M. (Ed.) *Edgar Allan Poe: The Critical Heritage.* London and New York: Routledge & Kegan Paul, 1986.

Wright, Elizabeth. "Modern Psychoanalytic Theory." *Modern Literary Theory.* Jefferson, A. and Robey, D. (Eds.) U.S.A.: Barnes & Noble Books-Imports, 1982.

www.eapoe.org
www.lva.lib.va.us
www.pbs.org
www.wikipedia.org

Index